The Golly in the Cupboard

By

Phil Frampton

Our Past is a Present

For Ellie, Sidonie and Gail

First published May 2004

This revised edition, July 2004

ISBN 0-9547649-0-0

Published by Tamic Publications

Tamic Publications Ltd, PO Box 182, Manchester M21 7XY

www.tamic.co.uk

Book and Cover Design: Lendon Lewis and Roan Farley,
Stretch (UK) Ltd

Sub Editor: Ben Carlish and Matt Sinha

With special thanks to: Margaret, David and Tim Ellis, Elf and Frances Jackson, John and Vicki Seddon, Andy Walsh, Maureen Sinha, Joanne Marr, Delma Hughes, Andrea Enisuoh, Wendy Bunn, the late Roger Houghton, Philip Gwyn Jones, Jane Kinninmonth, Sandra Wheeler, Perminder Banger, Paul Redgrave, Debbie Pickvance, Jo Lee, Gail Frampton, Kenneth Frampton, John Hunt, Lydia Callaway and Ann-Marie Hastings.

British Library Cataloguing in Publication Data. This publication is being catalogued by and will be available at the British Library.

Printed by: Creative Print & Design Group

Foreword

The Golly in the Cupboard is a very powerful and moving love story about what happens when a child is denied love. It tells us how one young person overcame that deprivation and emerged as a caring and successful adult, capable of showing to others the love he never had.

Phil Frampton, who never knew his parents, is the son of a Nigerian man and an English woman. His father returned to Nigeria when she was pregnant. She sent Phil to Barnardo's Homes where he lived until he grew up, often lonely and unhappy, apart from one short period when he was with foster parents.

This book, which is brilliantly written, describes his life, as he remembered it and his determination to trace his own mother and father and learn something about them.

It is in that sense a gripping detective story, showing how strongly motivated he was and how far he got in his search, which was really an expression of his need to convey to them the love they never showed to him.

But it is also the story of how Phil, despite the misery that he experienced and describes, was able to become a mature and capable adult. Indeed, the fact that he has those qualities probably tells us more about his parents than he realises because he must have inherited some of those qualities from them.

This book, which is immensely readable, reminds us of the importance of love for children, the tragedy when it is denied, how life can be rebuilt even without it and still allow love to be re-created in relation to others, permitting this story to have a happy ending after all.

The Rt. Hon. Tony Benn

About the Author

Phil Frampton has written for *Independent on Sunday, Manchester Evening News, The Guardian, Big Issue, Malaysia Star, Pakistan Daily News, Wanderlust* and a range of other newspapers and journals. He is author of three travel books: *Hidden Kerala, the travel guide, Emilia Romagna, Italy's Hidden Gem* and *Hidden Greenwich, the travel guide,* and co-authored the Football Governance Research Centre's publication *Fresh Players, New Tactics: Lessons from Northampton Town Supporters' Trust.* He has also worked in the fields of marketing and research consultancy, training, lecturing and public speaking.

Chapter 1

Putting My Pieces Together

"HE MUST NEVER KNOW THE TRUTH."

Dollars, 1967

"You could have kept in touch. You didn't have much excuse if you were living in Manchester," said David Bryant. He'd been with me as a child in the Barnardo's home 30 miles away in Southport, Lancashire. "You could have looked in the phone book," he added.

True, I could have looked in the phone book. True, I didn't have much of an excuse. When I left the home, I just ran to save myself and hardly gave a look back. But now I was back in the fold. Life had pulled back the prodigal, the fugitive. And how!

Each one of us has our story and some more of a story than others. I had always wanted to put the pieces of my life together, but so much of its beginning was shrouded in mystery and assumption. For many years I couldn't tell friends how? why? where?

I had half stories and conjecture. Just as the world was flat and began with Adam and Eve, so the circumstances of my childhood, for all I knew, were as good as fantasy. I knew very little of what had happened to put me in Barnardo's care. I knew a little about my mother, less of my father and even less as to why they had left me in care from the time of my birth.

A few years ago I happened by chance to see a television documentary concerning Barnardo's and how they were allowing former Barnardo children to access their files. I hadn't even known that Barnardo's had such files. For 40 years they had kept a file on me without me knowing. They also had my medical files. It really was a Big Brother organisation. In early 1998 I decided to get hold of my file and make another effort to find my father. That wasn't so easy. Barnardo's said that I was at the back of a three-year waiting list.

It took a year of anger, MP's letters, several solicitors' notes and a near-fatal illness in November 1998 to force Barnardo's into agreeing to hand over my files. My being in a Manchester hospital and as close I could get to the Almighty finally proved decisive.

A call came from the Barnardo's After-Care worker in the Cumbrian town of Kendal. She would have to meet me and counsel me before giving me the dossier. I would have to sign a form saying that I accepted that what was in the files was confidential and the contents would be revealed to no other person. My childhood was a military secret.

My childhood had to remain a mystery to all but one stranger and myself. Not even my children must know.

I had read the glossy Barnardo's magazines, with their saccharine sweet tales of the beautiful life and the Doctor's one big happy family. I thought: "Have those kids forgotten hearing the screams from the bathroom as they came down the road, being beaten, being caned, being abused, absconding, brother being separated from brother, sister from sister? Being caught, being told you were the nastiest set of children in the world?" I knew that there was another Barnardo story to be told.

I signed the form in bad faith, so please remember that what I will relate to you is told in strictest confidence.

I expected the file to contain maybe 30 to 50 pages with a scant letter here, and a note there, to give me some clues about my mother and father.

"It's a big file," she said, "733 pages."

733 pages! A grand novel about a little boy! So important! I was happy. Wanted or unwanted as a child, you might think that I was lucky to have so much information on my childhood. Many people are left with only vague memories of their early years and a few childhood stories offered by relatives and close friends. I thought I was lucky too.

Then I became apprehensive. I had thought I could be dispassionate about my enquiries. My childhood story mostly concerned people long since out of my life and their human frailties. I was compassionate enough to handle that. So I had thought. Instead, I was facing a trip into a labyrinth of undiscovered emotions. It was my emotions that concerned me. What angst stalked in those recesses? What anger, sadness and despair?

I was 45 years old and facing a journey through the dark. It was a journey I had to take to fill those gaps, to answer why and how.

In April 1999, I took the 09.14 train from Manchester to Kendal for my rendezvous with the unfortunate Barnardo's After-Care worker. I say "unfortunate" because I was angry with Barnardo's. To my mind I had a lot to be angry about. Barnardo's had made me fight for a year to secure my files and seek information about my father. Barnardo's had, to my knowledge, come between my mother and me. Most of all, by then I had become aware of the horrors inflicted, with Barnardo's connivance, on my childhood friends.

The train pulled into Kendal station on a crisp, sunny spring morning. There to meet me was a woman in her fifties wearing a navy blue, cotton skirt and a jacket to match. Her boyish, short, grey hair emphasised her kindly face and the wrinkles of her misfortunes. At first her manner was brusque, as was mine. I had power-dressed for the occasion, putting on my best suit, shirt and tie. I didn't want her counsel but to pick up my files and then take the earliest possible train back home. On the other hand, she had already informed me that I had to read through all my files in her presence, there and then, before I would be allowed to take them away with me.

The After-Care worker drove me to the town centre where she had hired a small meeting room in one of those buildings with rooms occupied by a multiplicity of voluntary organisations. The poor woman had reason to be apprehensive. She knew that I was angry with Barnardo's. She had also read my files and had some idea of what I might have to go through. She also knew that she could have few answers to my questions. Like me, she would only have been a child in the fifties and knew no more than myself concerning the circumstances of the time.

We entered the room. Apart from a table and half a dozen wooden chairs, it was bare. On the table was a cardboard box containing a stack of A4 sheets - my childhood. I began to rummage through my mother's life whilst the After-Care worker organised tea and sandwiches for our expedition. I knew that I couldn't read through 733 pages in one day but I didn't want a confrontation. I quickly scanned the pages, stopping only for shocks and surprises. There were enough. At times I had to leave the room and drag hard on a cigarette.

I survived the meeting and secured my file. In the late afternoon, I left the After-Care worker at the train station. I decided that she was a compassionate woman after all. Months later she sent me a letter. She had read my story in *The Guardian* and cried.

I headed back to Manchester with my 733-page file, my past life, contained in a Booth & Co. Grocers' plastic carrier bag. I was drained. There were still questions, such as what had happened to my father, that remained to be answered, but that would be another quest for another time.

I was glad to have filled in many of the gaps in My Life I Never Knew. I no longer had a story with no beginning, with half tales and conjecture. It was not the type of shock I had expected. Instead I felt anger. Then came numbness and a sadness for all concerned. I'd crammed 18 years of birth, rejection, love, loneliness, guilt and death into four hours. There it was in a plastic bag with a photo of a little boy, with a big smile and bright eyes, brushing his teeth.

On the train I was able to reflect on my past. I thanked providence that I had survived my brush with death in 1998. Had I died in that Manchester hospital, I would have expired without ever knowing so many truths about my mother and father. I would have left my two daughters with a mystery. I would have left so many things unsaid to those that I have loved. Aren't there so many things that in hindsight we wish we had said to those we cared for, so many words that we wish we had heard?

No two of us see the past through the same prism. Our stories vary as to where we came from and where we thought we were going. I have tried to piece together my childhood story for many years. Now I have most of it. Access to my files also presented me with the opportunity to question my mother's old friends in more detail than ever before. I was able to assemble the jigsaw of my arrival in the world.

My task was to weigh up their many tales against my files, letters I had held on to for 30 years, and my own experiences. I set to work to weave them all together and create my tapestry of the forces and events that had dictated my childhood journey.

I had so many threads of truths to work on. Truth is powerful but it is strange. Even as you hold it in your hand, truth can change from being painful to being inspiring, from a source of joy to a cause of despair.

For my truths I was beaten. I was sent to bed early. I was threatened and derided. You may know how it feels to grow up being disbelieved. Even now I blush with a sense of guilt whenever questions are raised in my company of responsibility for something going wrong or going missing. It is that assumption brought of my childhood - that the accuser can determine my guilt and override my total innocence.

In this case I had to try to extract the truth and apply my imagination. Nothing I tell you is told for sensational advantage. I had to apply myself not to distort the truth, but to assist you (as I assisted myself) to understand my tale, minimise speculation and entertain you along my twisting and turning odyssey.

In this story I have changed many people's names and a few of their details in order to protect them. Otherwise, what is written here is as it was related to me or as it was documented. It is a tale of a child grappling with abandonment, rejection, love, prejudice and courage but it is also a story of an unwanted child and his unwanted childhood friends – the other Barnardo story.

Chapter 2

"Missconduct"

I was born as a thought, a white child-thought. The year was 1948. As a thought, I was very much part of the marital bliss that my mother dreamed of. In that sense, I was part of a normal dream for a young, white, middle class woman and those other women in Cheltenham, training like my mother, to become teachers.

I was in no way out of place with the thoughts of her college friends who, like Mavis, saw teaching as a respectable means of making a living. Entering the teaching profession would allow them to save up for that most glorious day that would follow their most brilliant hour – the hour of their marriage.

Her, dressed in white, stood next to a tall handsome man in black pin stripes; a fine and generous catch who would offer and pay for the convertible gleaming silver Bentley that would carry the couple off beneath a shower of sun and confetti to that honeymoon on a West Indian paradise island.

As a thought, I had a comfortable existence. I was the shining star of my mother during contemplation time. Standing out was rather easy, for my companions were a ragtag bunch of insecurities, fears and hurtful memories.

I do admit to a sense of apprehension. Were it not for the few memories of happy days with her father, and nights drinking tea and laughing with her college friends, I would have been alone in being a pleasing thought. So I developed as a special thought. No matter whether I was abstraction or unwanted real distraction, that sense of being special never left me.

How jealous of me the other thoughts were! For it was I who was cherished and embraced on those lonely nights when the rest had overwhelmed her with tears.

And I was normal. Not all the thoughts of Mavis Frampton were. How she longed to be rid of them. I called them "The Dreads." When her friends were round The Dreads were banished by that casual chatter of the young middle classes, drowned by gossip, giggles and the beckoning future. And so they had to be, for The Dreads were too shameful to be paraded around in company.

Then the friends were gone. The chatter lingered on. But soon The Dreads returned. Personally, I laid the blame for The Dreads being so influential on Mavis at the door of her mother, Mrs Church. Not that mothers should bear all the blame for all Dreads or that Mavis's mother acted alone in creating The Dreads.

When you know Mavis's story, hopefully you will understand the reasons why I reached those conclusions and why I was loathed by those very Dreads.

Born in Tottenham a few months after the great Wall Street Crash of 1929, Mavis was brought up as an only child in wartime London and Swindon during the Depression years. In 1922, her mother, Mrs Church (née Winifred Gladys Cook), the daughter of a Swindon cemetery superintendent, had married Clyde Frampton, 10 years her senior but the son of a London building contractor. Clyde Frampton was considered to be a fine catch – a man whose career would take him to an elevated position in the Post Office.

The couple saved up for seven years before Mavis Ann was born, by which time Clyde was already a Higher Clerical Officer in the Post Office. But Mavis Ann was born into a very unhappy house, which resounded with slammed doors, clipped manners and eerie silences. Mavis, who suffered an attack of poliomyelitis resulting in paralysis in her early years, grew up to be quite unhappy and nervous of her hectoring mother. Mrs Church, then Mrs Frampton, also grew unhappy and perhaps that explained the reason why the 40-year-old mother had affairs with the American servicemen stationed nearby.

It was one Empire Day in May when all the schoolchildren were given the day off that Mavis had first caught her mother at home with another man. Mavis had been packed off to school that morning insisting that she wasn't well. At the school she heard the address of the headmaster in the school hall. The head used a long stick to point to all the pink areas of the large map of the world hanging from the ceiling. He pointed to pink Canada, pink Australia, pink Africa and pink India and the pink West Indies.

"Romulus and Remus may have built Rome but through the efforts of our great British ancestors, " he informed the children, "we have helped to civilise two thirds of the world."

Mavis joined her school friends in singing the glories of the Empire as they were marched out for the annual procession through that part of London. Thousands of people cheered: "God save the King!" They waved Union Jack flags, as soldiers, sailors and local worthies marched by. Mavis always enjoyed this day but today she felt sick and was allowed to go home early. There she found her mother with her dressing gown thrown over the black negligee she usually only wore on

Saturdays. Saturdays were the days when Mr Frampton kissed his daughter and said: "Now do be asleep when I get home."

Her mother was rapidly combing her unkempt hair. A young American soldier in uniform was stood in the living room, sporting a crew cut and smoking a cigarette. In the years to come she would meet several more young men – and always when her father was away from the house.

Of course, when news of Winifred Frampton's affairs reached Clyde's ears, the cuckold put a decisive end to the stormy marriage with successful divorce proceedings.

Mavis learned that her mother's men friends were more than just friends. She learnt in court. She was called as a witness to testify as to the number of men she had seen in her parents' home when her father was absent.

Winifred was left to bring up Mavis Ann on her own. She returned to Swindon to raise her child with her grandparents' assistance. Clyde remarried and so eventually did Winifred, which is how she got the surname Church and provided Mavis Ann with a stepfather. But Mavis Ann couldn't stop loving her father and this, it seems, only excited Winifred to unreasonable rants against the man who had divorced her, leaving the child without a father. That was Winifred's view, but her daughter, Mavis Ann, saw the situation differently. Mavis never considered that she had lost her father. Rather that he had been driven away by her mother's unremitting bullying, bickering and unfaithfulness. Mavis loved her father even more.

Did Winifred suffer the torture of an unfaithful woman's guilt at separating her child from her father? Did she suffer the torture of her child's undiminished affections for the cuckold? Did Winifred's frustration at this affection battle with her guilt and unbalance her love for her child? Or did her daughter's testifying against her in the divorce courts turn Mavis's mother? Nobody is alive to answer.

Once divorced, Winifred Church tried as she could to bring her daughter up to be a suitable catch but the relationship between mother and child was torture for Mavis. To Mavis entering her early teens, it seemed that, whatever she did, she would be the target for her mother's spite, sarcasm and ridicule.

"It's no wonder your father left you. Just look at the state of you. Oh that I had a child that wasn't so sickly and spindly! Can't you stop that foot from hanging lame when you walk? Do you really need to wear those awful glasses? I don't know if I'll ever get you married off!

Hold your head up and stop bursting into tears every time I speak to you."

Mavis slept with her head on a wet pillow next to her teddy bear and Golliwog. She dreamt that she was Wendy and that her secret brother would appear at the window. Like Peter Pan, he would take hold of her hand and fly her off to the motherless, wondrous Dread-free world of Neverland.

Mavis Ann was not the source of happiness that her mother had hoped for. The more spiteful her mother became, the more Mavis saw in her father the source of an inspiring tranquillity. Hence the more frustrated again became Winifred Church. To add to Winifred's unhappiness, her becoming Mrs Winifred Church was also a failure and Mr Church also walked out on her.

Mavis Ann learned to live with The Dreads – her looks, her clumsiness, her manner, her mother's hectoring, her parents arguing, her horrid stepfather, her crying, her never going to be married, her growing up alone to grow old alone. Then circumstance came to Winifred's assistance in multiplying her daughter's Dreads.

Everybody said that Mavis was very musically talented and at least sending the girl to a music tutor would mean that the awkward, spindly child with the dipping left foot might make her way in the world as a musician.

Mavis had taken to playing on her mother's piano from an early age. As a little girl she spent her Saturdays playing tunes that she had made up herself or listening to records given to her by her father. When her father gave her a book with several scores of music, Mavis took to playing *Peter and the Wolf* and it became her favourite tune. She played it so often that Mrs Church decided Mavis must have music lessons, otherwise the tune would drive both of them insane.

From the age of seven, Mavis would visit her music tutor every week. Now she spent her Saturdays practising her scales and arpeggios. It wasn't as much fun as making up your own tunes but she was happy that it pleased her father. Sometimes her mother would come to sit in at the tutor's house and listen to her play. The old woman, who tutored Mavis, had studied at the Royal Academy of Music in London and when she gave the slightest praise to her young pupil it delighted Mavis's mother. When the tutor passed words of criticism, Mavis winced because, if her mother was there, she would not hear the end of the matter for weeks.

"I am paying for you to take these Grades. So don't you slacken." her mother would say, "What have you been doing in that room? Sleeping?"

Mavis was not totally happy in her music. She had hoped that her achievements would win her mother's praise. Sadly, the praise that came was faint but the criticisms were repeated over and over again. Mavis would take herself through daily waves of self-criticism, winding herself up until she could feel the knots of anxiety in her stomach. Mavis lost her music tutor just before she took her Grade 8 music exam. The elderly woman suffered a stroke and decided to retire.

Winifred Church then sent her daughter to a man with a fine reputation as a music tutor who lived in the next town. The tutor, recognising his new pupil's potential, pushed Mavis through her Grade 8 exams and started Mavis playing at music festivals and in competitions. Travelling to see the tutor was tiring but Mavis didn't mind. In her head she was preparing to one day play at the Albert Hall in London or Carnegie Hall in New York. She was reading the glowing reviews of her performances in *The Times*.

Sometimes she would stay for weekends at the house of the tutor and his wife. There, Mavis and the tutor would spend the time alone while she practised the pieces he set her to play and the tutor tested her on her sight-reading and aural work. Her life was almost controlled by her tutor. He would feed her, tell her how to dress, what to say and who to talk to. In that sense it was an intimate relationship, the kind that can come about between tutor and the keenest of pupils.

Mavis went along with everything the music tutor wanted. He was the route to her mother's praise and her own ambition to spend her life playing the music she loved. If the man told Mavis that she had to practise on her pedal work on each visit then she accepted the order without questioning. That practising her pedal work meant the tutor kneeling and holding Mavis's feet, then her calves, then her thighs, was him making her perfect. Him telling her how to sit and holding her sides and running his hand down her spine, was all to make her perfect. Him asking her to knit him a condom out of wool, was not. But then it was too late. He had taught her that what was wrong was right.

Mavis started to return home from visits to the tutor in a sullen silence. She became increasingly reluctant to attend. Mrs Church scolded her daughter for wishing to throw away all the hard-earned money that had been spent on her music lessons.

"It's the only way you'll ever get a job."

The visits ended up in court with the child, Mavis, at Mrs Church's insistence, testifying against the tutor who had sexually abused her. Mavis was left with more Dreads to carry. But such revelations of the sullying of her spindly, bespectacled child with the limp left foot did not increase Mrs Church's affections. Even then, I could only wonder as to whether it was Mrs Church who poured onto Mavis a sense of guilt rather than highlighting the music tutor's shame.

"What did you do to make him think he could behave like that with you?"

Her mother bemoaned how the trial had become public knowledge and how everyone must know that it was her child in court and how people would gossip and snigger about her and her daughter:

"How can I ever get you married off now? Darling, you'll have to become a nun or, better still, a missionary in Africa where no one can see you."

Mavis was left alone to deal with The Dreads of unwarranted guilt and the uncertainty of how men would see her in the future. Whether or not Mavis was sullied in her essence, she felt defiled and even more deserving of her mother's lack of affection.

At the same time, the teenager craved for more affection; for someone to consider her the star in their sky. But her father hardly ever came to see her and The Dreads grew. Her relationship so deteriorated with her mother that when the teenager passed her General Certificate and was offered the chance to go away to college and abandon her attempts to become a professional musician, Mavis leapt at the opportunity. She had resigned herself to the thought that she would never be good enough for her mother. In her mind, her bags were already packed. She opted for a teacher training college in Cheltenham, where she would study to become a music teacher.

When her bags were finally packed, Mavis sat on her bed, waiting for her grandfather to arrive in his car to take her down to the bus station. There she would take the Black & White coach to Cheltenham and restart her life. She jumped up and gazed at her reflection in the wardrobe mirror.

Her long, pointed nose and plastic spectacles dominated her face. Her forehead, she thought, was too large. Her Uncle Reg said that meant she had brains but Mavis believed that her forehead was too large to make her pretty. Her softly permed hair had been shaped to fall just below her ears and gave her long face an even more elongated appearance. She pulled up her hair but the unusual length of her face remained. She took off her spectacles and smiled. "Now, you look pretty," Mavis told herself.

She made out she was meeting a young man at her new college and lowered her chin and put on those flirting eyes she had used to keep the regard of the music tutor who had promised to "make her perfect." Then she cursed her eyesight for being so poor that she even had to wear her spectacles in the bedroom.

She turned her face to the right and gave it a side-glance. That nose was too long. That chin jutted out. The "woman in the moon", one of her classmates had called her. She peered down at the rest of her frame. "Far too thin." And those damned ankles that always went on the school Sports' Day. She brought her hands to her face. Long hands, slender hands, the hands that could have taken her to the Albert Hall.

"THE MOTHER IS STATED TO BE A REFINED AND CULTURED WOMAN. SHE IS AN ONLY CHILD, AND WAS BORN IN LONDON, AND LATER EDUCATED IN SWINDON, AND AT CHELTENHAM COLLEGE. THE GRANDPARENTS DID NOT LIVE HAPPILY TOGETHER, AND EVENTUALLY WERE DIVORCED. BOTH HAVE REMARRIED, BUT THE GRANDMOTHER IS SEPARATED FROM HER SECOND HUSBAND."

Barnardo's Report, 1953

"HER STEPFATHER SEEMS TO HAVE BEEN A MOST UNSAVOURY CHARACTER."

Dollars, 1953

I suppose that it was at St Mary's College in Cheltenham that I first really emerged as a thought. Getting to the Regency town on the coach seemed to take forever. The journey across the undulating, green hills of the Cotswolds with their yellow and green patchworks of fields was pleasant enough. However, it being market day, the coach was often halted by streams of cattle and sheep blocking the roads.

Mavis hauled her bags down the drive to the college hall. The long lawn, the lake and the rows of poplars and beech trees were as pretty a sight as she had imagined. But Mavis was more intent on inspecting her fellow women students walking down the drive with her or sat around on the lawn. This was post-war Britain – the Britain of grim, rubble-ridden cities, of ration books and radios, gramophones and *Pathé News*, when the first modern computer had yet to be invented.

The impact of the war was evident in women's fashions. These were the years when women's blouses, shirts and blazers had padded shoulders. A cameo brooch was worn, like the knot of a necktie, at the heart of the blouse and waists were pulled in with Waspy belts. The overall effect recreated the military style. They were women still in uniform, still embracing the increased status and freedom that they had snatched to the sound of wailing sirens and crashing bombs.

Many of the young men who survived the fighting still donned their uniforms when they wished to impress. Those who had been too young to fight would wear their uniforms too, since now they were being conscripted into the regiments to do their National Service and defend the pink world from the new menace of red communism.

But it was a world of hope, especially for those middle class young men and women whose parents could afford to pay for them to be educated at St Mary's College. The war had been horror without end but their generation would learn from it. They would teach their children never to go to war again and, now that Britain and the United States ruled the world, there would be no more war.

At the college, Mavis's musical talents shone through. Her initial encounter with another student, however, was somewhat humbling. You know that feeling when you arrive at a new college, all full of confidence, then some know-all spouts off and you start worrying that you will be totally out of your depth? On her first day, Mavis's roommate had asked her what she thought of Beethoven's *Opus 110* as compared to *Opus 57*. Mavis was at a loss to hide her ignorance. It was several weeks before she learned that using such technical musical language was par for the chatter of the students she studied with for her teaching diploma.

Mavis excelled in her work, particularly in the aural and harmony tests. When she was asked to play Mendelssohn's *Variations Serieuses*, the beautiful but hauntingly sad tune so fitted into Mavis accommodating her Dreads, that she played it to perfection. The tutors were delighted. They asked her to play the Variations time and time again. Finally, they requested that she perform the piece in public.

Mavis revelled in the praise from her tutors and her classmates. Their plaudits gave her a growing sense of self-worth. She came to believe that she was playing her music for herself and not for her mother. For the first time since that time when she had learned Peter and the Wolf, Mavis was truly happy with her music.

"PERSONALLY SHE IS A SINCERE, GENUINE AND PLEASANT PERSON."

Dollars, 1953

Mavis joined the college's Chapel Choir, where the women were also joined by the men from St Paul's, the all-male, teacher training college. For Mavis, being in the choir was very successful. Not only did the choir win prizes at Cheltenham's annual choral competition but also the choir was considered good enough to perform with the conductor, Benjamin Britten. Membership in the choir also reintroduced the young woman to the company of men. When she went off to the college hops, she was often seen being escorted by a boyfriend. There she would waltz and dance the quickstep. Mavis sat out the tango on account of her weak ankles but she always had a partner for the last waltz.

Mavis made good friends with some of her classmates. Amongst them was Martha Watson, a woman who would eventually play a small but quite influential part in my life as a child. The two of them would sit in their rooms after the ten o'clock curfew and giggle as they peered through the window looking out on the spacious grounds and the lake beside the college. The cause of their titters was Miss Jones; the college principal whom they would watch as, armed with a torch and her dog, she avidly searched the grounds for canoodling couples breaking the curfew.

It wasn't all plain sailing for Mavis. When the young women talked about boyfriends, she was uncomfortably aware that she knew much more than her friends about those matters.

Take the time when Mavis and her friends returned from manning jamboree stalls at the college Open Day fête. Mavis, Martha and their friends, Barbara and Muriel, were sat in Muriel's room. Knowing that the men from the male college would be attending the fete, the four students had all dressed up for the day. Mavis was wearing a dark green, fronted blouse top with padded shoulders and a cream back. Her top matched her cream, calf-length, flared skirt. Her clothes and her white sandals emphasised the fragility of her whole frame.

Her friend, Martha, whose hair was short enough to display the nape of her neck, had opted for a tight perm that curled around her rotund face. She was wearing a maroon and yellow hooped dress with a shirt-type collar that had a cameo brooch fixed at its centre. Barbara wore her great-grandmother's double string of pearls over a white blouse. Her green and yellow, striped blazer was draped over the back of the chair on which she was seated. Muriel had opted to wear a blouse with padded shoulders too. Her tight, black, Waspy belt and tartan, flared skirt made her the most fashionable of the four.

It being their second year, the students were much more relaxed and confident than when they had first arrived. As they sat around dangling their legs in Muriel's room, they drank tea and they began to relate stories of their encounters with boys and boyfriends. In those days a woman was not expected to allow a boy to kiss her until she had been out with him three or four times. She would be considered disgraceful were she to engage in any heavy petting until they were betrothed to one another.

Muriel confessed to her past innocence and ignorance: "You know, in my first year I went out with that boy, Bill, a few times. Well, he put his hand up the back of my jumper and felt my bra strap. I thought he had done something awful. But it seemed to feel right. I phoned my mother to tell her and all she would say was: "Thanks for telling me, darling."

"I never told her about the boy from home that I went off blackberry picking with. He was returning after relieving himself in a field. He bent down. His buttons popped open and there was his thing. I was terrified. I thought that if one soul got to know about it, then I would have to marry him!"

The students laughed. Mavis felt her face tingle and brought her hands up to cover the reddening. She really did know too much.

After two years at Cheltenham, Mavis had qualified with distinction for her Certificate of Education, awarded by the University of Bristol. She became a trainee teacher at a school in Birmingham and began her studies to gain her diploma to become a Licentiate of the Royal Academy of Music. Being an LRAM would mean that she was a recognised practitioner in the art of playing and teaching the piano.

Mavis's college friend, Martha Watson, went off to London but not before the two of them had sworn to stay in touch with each other "forever and a day." Mavis took the train to the industrial grime of Birmingham. She was happy in the knowledge that some of her "Old Chelt" friends would also be working in the Midlands city. Once settled in, the "Old Chelts" began to frequent a venue owned by the International Students' Club. Mavis joined them. The club provided a chance to meet interesting men and women from all corners of the world - parts of the world that Mavis had only read about in books or heard mention of on the radio.

The self-selected young men and women who attended the International Club were not restricted by the wooden etiquette of white middle class society. After all, here were people of all colours, defying national and racial prejudices. Rather like today's e-mails, these new experiences in post-war Britain had no rules. These particular young Britons found it hard to look down their noses at their international visitors from the Dark Continents.

Instead, the Britons were dazzled by the contrast between the animal-like racial stereotypes that had underpinned their education and the brilliance of the young colonial minds they met.

As the students sat discussing the world and its future, the H-bomb, the Chinese Revolution, the new National Health Service, Jazz, Sartre and the Universe, the meetings of minds and fusion of shared dreams germinated many thoughts in those days of hope. It was on some of these days that I began to turn from being a white to a brown, even black, child-thought.

It did not happen on the first day that she met Isaac Ene, the intelligent, black Nigerian student who stood over six feet tall. Mavis, however, was certainly impressed at his princely bearing, which would one day go with the title he was destined to assume. Isaac, being 29 years old, was somewhat older than Mavis. A talented mining engineer, he had been sent by his British-owned company to study research methods at Aston Mining College (now Aston University).

Mavis began to admire the tall handsome black man with his big smile and deep, booming laugh. But she was well aware that such relationships were taboo. This was a time when Britain was steeped in racism. The governments still operated apartheid in the colonies. Students would tell of how, in their corners of the Empire, they had to walk in the street whenever they came across whites strolling the pavements. They would relate stories of terrible punishments meted out to their friends for insulting whites or indulging in political activity.

When Mavis and her white friends chatted in the privacy of their homes, how they wished that the black man was not taboo as their thoughts drifted off into private fantasies of life with their young princes in faraway mysterious lands.

The reality of apartheid, of racial separateness never entered their heads – save for it meaning that those beastly laws would leave their fantasies caged.

Only now and then would the fantasies break out amongst their peers. Then rumours were whispered concerning the fate of those who crossed the taboo line.

"Look what happened when Seretse Kharma from Bechuanaland married Ruth Johnson, that typist from London! And what about when Sir Stafford Cripps's daughter, Peggy, married that Joe Appiah from Ghana? It was front page news and everyone was howling with anguish."

"Disgusting," some of them said. Even the most enlightened of parents shrivelled before the fear of social disapproval. "It's alright for someone else but not our daughter!"

"What if your mother found out you were seeing a coloured man?

"She would go through the roof."

"It's all so beastly!"

So even as a black child-thought I had a precarious nurturing. Isaac was intent on completing his research and returning to Nigeria where he would be married and assume his princely role in his Ibo tribe. He admired in Mavis her sensitivity and her love of music.

Mavis in turn sensed that his little kindnesses towards her and stolen glances offered her respect and warmth. In those heady days, the world was wrong and the young were right and anything that stopped the impetuous youth from indulging their desires was ghastly.

Those meetings with her foreign friends laid the embryo of myself as a black child-thought. But I would not be safely out of the womb, as a fully formed thought, for some time yet.

Mavis wondered why Isaac was not married: "After all, wouldn't he be a fine catch back home? He had a good job and good prospects and, so handsome!" The more she marvelled, the more fantasy rattled at its social chains. He might be black and from a foreign land but didn't he and she share an interest in music? She wondered as to where he had learned so much about the classical composers.

The two shared a common humour. Mavis laughed a lot and Isaac found her joy endearing. For doesn't laughter heal the soul? Laughter came easy for a young woman written off by her mother. Freedom from the taunts of her mother was a joy in itself. Thanks largely to her mother; Mavis could identify with all those tales of misfortune that make up humour. The Dreads remained but laughter drowned them out as Mavis bathed in her increasing confidence.

My egg, as black child-thought, was first fertilised by that comfort Mavis found in Isaac's company, and her sudden awareness of that sensation. The sensation came when the couple found themselves sat alone in the club. Aside from her father and grandfather, it was the first time that Mavis had felt truly at ease with any man. The music tutor had made sure that she would mistrust both men and herself.

Once fertilised, as embryo to the black child-thought, I grew quickly, feeding off Mavis's sense of well-being. In those weeks the trainee teacher eagerly looked forward to her visits to the International Club, dreaming her way through her days spent teaching at her school. The black child-thought embryo needed Isaac's presence to sustain it. To reach the mature stage the embryonic thought required a decisive gesture by Isaac.

It came on a November day. Mavis was sat at the club's piano playing one of Chopin's *Polonaises*. It was a week since Mavis had volunteered to her friends at the club that she was born under the sign of Sagittarius.

"I am a Sagittarius too," piped up one of her girlfriends. Which makes us both flirtatious and playful socialisers, adventurous and rather inclined to excess."

The gaggle of friends laughed. Mavis felt a big, smarting red blush coming on and hid her face.

"My birthday is on November 28th. When is yours, Emma?"

"November 30th, if any of you men wish to know. Of course, I'm not flirting." Emma replied to more laughter.

Mavis glanced over at Isaac who was enjoying the merriment.

"But we are also trustworthy and charming, if inclined to put our foot in it sometimes, like when I…" said Emma.

"They say we are broadminded and very knowledgeable too," added Mavis.

"But also optimistic to the point of carelessness. Rather inclined to trust people too much," added her friend, "and, if you're the same age as me, then according to the Chinese, we were both born in the year of the Earth Snake, which makes us altruistic, intuitive to the point of our heart ruling our head and always ready to fall in love with love itself."

"I had better concentrate on being knowledgeable then," concluded the blushing Mavis with a laugh.

One week later, the frosty autumnal day of November 28th arrived. Mavis eyed her mail wondering whether she might receive any cards from her club friends. Isaac sending her a card would be a special sign. Then he would really be flirting. There were none. She did receive a card from her father and her grandparents and Uncle Reg but was almost relieved not to have her birthday acknowledged by her mother.

In the evening, Mavis combed her hair in front of the mirror and speculated as to whether Isaac would appear at the club that night. She had her hair in the same soft perm and cut mid-length, the way she had worn it in her college days. This occasion, she hoped, would be a special occasion. She decided to dress up in her best outfit.

Mavis put on her scarlet satin blouse with its padded shoulders and Peter Pan collar. At the heart of the collar she placed her cameo brooch. Over the blouse, she wore a close-fitting, white cardigan, which, with the aid of her black Waspy belt, emphasised her narrow waist and her hips. A flared tartan skirt ran down to halfway between her knees and ankles. She sat on the bed and put on a pair of flat, ballerina-type shoes and jumped up to inspect the overall result in her wardrobe mirror. Altogether, one could say, Mavis looked quite demure, quite respectable. She practised a few flirting poses, grabbed her coat and keys then skipped off down the stairs.

Mavis entered the club to a chorus of Happy Birthdays followed by singing, which closed with "*For She's a Jolly Good Fellow*." Cards were duly presented to her. They included one from Isaac. That made Mavis blush.

"Come on, girl," shouted one of the men, "play us Chopin's *Ballade 3*. You know you play it so well."

So Mavis sat at the piano but played just part of the piece. Stopping abruptly, she declared: "I'll play the rest privately another time to all those who wish to hear it." Her friends, who had been standing around the piano, laughed and applauded and their little party began. Mavis's place at the piano was taken by her friend Emma. "Now, sing along everybody!" cried Emma and she began to play the number one hit of the time, *How Much is that Doggie in the Window?*

After a few more of Emma's melodies, the young men and women sat down to gossip and discuss the world and his uncle, as her father would say. They concluded on the merits and demerits of television. Suddenly, the night was over. The friends had buses to catch, work to prepare and studies to complete. As the group broke up and Mavis rose to leave, Isaac followed her.

"I have two tickets for a performance of Mendelssohn's piano music, featuring his Variations Serieuses at the Theatre Royal. I was wondering if you would like to have them," asked Isaac, stooping down.

Mavis's heart took a leap and she blushed: "How very kind of you, Isaac. It's marvellous. How did you know that I adore the Variations?"

Isaac said he had had no idea but he, himself, considered the piece to be the finest of the composer's works. Mavis strongly suspected that one of her friends had let her musical preferences be known to Isaac.

Then she set her gentle trap, declaring: "I really do want to go but I don't know anyone in particular who I could go with."

The implied offer was what Isaac had been waiting for.

"Then let's go together," he replied with a grin, "Arm in arm down the aisles."

They laughed and Mavis hoped that he could not see her slender chest heaving or hear her heart thumping. As a matter of decorum she added: "Still, we should see if anyone else wants to go and then we can go as a party."

Of course, neither expected that they would make much effort to bring anyone else along. The couple had a date and her heart thumped away. Those thumps were the first kicks of the black child-thought embryo.

Mavis went off home in a happy mood but not before stealing a look into Isaac's eyes as she bid him goodnight.

"Down the aisle!" Three words took her all the way back home in a gleaming convertible silver Bentley. The Dreads clung to the undercarriage.

At this time Mavis was residing in lodgings in a small terraced house in Erdington. Her landlady, Mrs Stokes, had lost her husband and two sons. Mr Stokes was crushed to death by falling masonry during the Blitz. Her sons were both machine-gunned down in the D-Day landings.

Mrs Stokes was that sort of landlady who quietly took a note of every movement of her tenants and hardly ever failed to notice any variation in the daily movements of life on the quiet street. Her hair never seemed to emerge from beneath the crimson cloth wrapped around her head and tied at the forehead with a bow that gave the stout woman her extra antennae. Mavis would find occasion to remark that the woman was forever outside the front of the house, dressed in her scarlet, cotton women's overalls and polishing the doorstep or gossiping with the other landladies in the street.

Each week, Mavis spent a few hours at the home of Pixie Johnston in Etwall Road, on the edge of the Solihull district. Miss Johnston taught at the school where Mavis was training. She had long had the nickname of Pixie on account of her short stature and slight build. Pixie shared her home with her father, whom she called Pa, and a close friend, Miss Catherine Dolby.

Dollars, as Catherine Dolby was affectionately called, was a headmistress at another school in Birmingham and a few years older than Pixie. Pixie and Dollars both wore the simple cotton, sometimes silk, shapeless dresses that were more fashionable amongst women older than they were. The two women were very close. Whether by design or otherwise, neither of them would ever marry and they only parted company when death overtook their friendship.

Mavis's friendship with Pixie began quite mundanely with the senior teacher helping out her much more junior colleague. Pixie found Mavis quite charming but: "a rather dainty creature who requires some protection and nurturing." In her first days in the staff room, Mavis had appeared nervous and quite shy. But with Pixie as mentor and with her willingness to learn, Mavis soon settled in at the school. Pixie commented on how her colleagues would often steal a moment to delight in the trainee's little indulgences on the piano and this gave Mavis all the esteem she required for the staff room.

Very quickly, Pixie had invited the young woman to dine at her home, joking: "You can sing for your supper. Pa would be so pleased to here you play."

And Pa was overjoyed, from then on always ensuring that Mavis did not leave the house before she had sat down at the piano.

After some months, the two teachers were talking about mothers. Mavis let one of her Dreads slip off her tongue.

"Mother is always worrying and never lets a letter go by without scolding me."

"Isn't that what mothers are for?" replied Pixie, "Where would the poor things be without anxieties for their children? They spend 20 years worrying about their little babies and the rest of their life feeling that they should still be worried."

When Mavis failed to raise a smile at her comments, Pixie understood that this particular mother might be no source of comfort for her daughter. In time, Pixie became a confidante. She grew used to seeing Mavis's eyes dim with the mention of motherhood and families. She knew when Mavis had received a letter from her mother because Mavis always appeared dispirited.

She came to understand why her friend went home to see her mother so infrequently. Mavis once cried: "She says I'm wicked, ghastly, ungrateful! What can I do!" All this was confirmed when Pixie was shown one of Mrs Church's screeds.

"THE GRANDMOTHER WROTE ABUSIVE AND VINDICTIVE LETTERS TO THE MOTHER'S FORMER ADDRESS IN BIRMINGHAM."

Barnardo's report, 1953

So, in the days after Mavis and Isaac's visit to the Theatre Royal when Mavis sat down in Pixie's kitchen and rattled away about the family she wished to have, Pixie knew that something was afoot. The sparkle in her friend's eyes gave the existence of my thought-embryo away. Pixie was pleased for Mavis and sought to tease out the cause of the young woman's joy.

Mavis revealed her secret but Pixie's victory brought on the worst scenario that she could have hoped for. Pixie tried to conceal the extent of her despair at her friend's naivety.

"Courting a coloured! You must not believe that anything will come of it, dear."

Her very words triggered the violent birth pangs that would issue me into life as black-child thought. Pixie of course meant well. Her objections and warnings came fast and direct. They were aimed at soothing away Mavis's alarming fantasy. But for the young teacher the words struck as hurtfully as any that had ever shot off her mother's lips.

"You must know that so many things would go against you. Look at how they treated Miss…and Mrs… And those coloured men get such bad treatment here. Didn't you tell us of how Isaac passed through Handsworth and men, women and children shouted: "Golliwog" and, "On your way, Nigger."?

"Besides, think how upset your father would be. Your mother would be furious. It could get you both into trouble at work.

"Isaac is a lovely man but he is better waiting till he gets home before having a relationship. Even there, they say that when whites and blacks marry they are frowned on both by our people and by theirs. Life would be awful.

"If you were to build up his hopes, it would be cruel. Then you would both end up being very hurt. Think of your futures. You must not lead him on, dear."

"WE HAVE TRIED TO DISSUADE HER FROM THIS FRIENDSHIP AND MARRIAGE."

Dollars, 1953

Acid streaked across the womb from which I, the black child-thought, would emerge.

When Mavis returned to her lodgings, The Dreads had a gala night. "Am I just a stupid, unattractive woman aching for love to the point of being prepared to ruin two lives?" she asked herself, "Was that what Pixie was trying to say? Was Isaac the music tutor in a black skin? If he is really capable of loving me and I turned him away, will I ever experience such joyful feelings again? Will I lose the respect of father?"

The Dreads circled above as she lay on her bed. Sometimes she found them spinning rapidly, sometimes dipping to catch her eyes and drain them of tears. Mavis tried, in vain, to confront them. At times, they appeared to spin so fast that a void appeared in the middle, a vortex that would carry her to lifelong humiliation and unhappiness.

The Dreads were suffocating me, the black child-thought, to the point of expiry. They wanted to crush me before I had even got halfway out of the womb.

The most terrifying prospect for Mavis was that of losing her father's respect. Then, save for her grandparents, she would be left totally alone in the world. The threat circled around for the umpteenth time. She attempted to confront the issue. As The Dreads came round again, Mavis resolved that The Dreads were being unfair to her father: "Isn't he a reasonable man? Doesn't he scoff at those social taboos that have turned mama into a monster? Hasn't he always tried to understand me and pushed away mama's prejudices and taunts? He will understand."

The admiration she felt for her father and the comfort she found in his presence won out. At that point came the burgeoning rebellion inspired by love; that point in romance where the rest of the world is shut out; where romance blurs all obstacles.

The Dreads disappeared swiftly into the night to be replaced by a sweet yearning to be at Isaac's side.

Mavis expected to see him the following evening at the club and with this comforting thought the young woman fell asleep. The black-child thought was born.

Isaac did not appear at the club, confounding Mavis's expectations. Friends noticed her distraction and while Mavis tried to hide her disappointment, The Dreads returned to threaten the newly born thought.

"Perhaps," she told herself, "Isaac, like Pixie and Dollars, has concluded that continuing our relationship would be dangerous and irresponsible. Perhaps friends too had warned him off. Perhaps he was off seeing some other woman."

Mavis went home early and, Mrs Stokes being out, took advantage of the landlady's invitation to use the piano in the sitting room whenever she wished. There she sat down and played her favourite piece by Mendelssohn. At least, the Variations Serieuses was her favourite when she was feeling low. In those times she would allow the melancholy tune to soothe away The Dreads.

As powerful as The Dreads were, sweet yearning pushed them back and Mavis slept as peacefully as she might have expected.

After one week of not hearing Isaac's voice, The Dreads had gained the upper hand again. Weaning of the infant child-thought had been brought to a halt and the thought would be left to die. Mavis concluded that Isaac's non-appearance was an intentional sign from him that they both should be careful not to breach the racial barriers. Mavis even resolved to stay away from the club for a while.

"Wasn't Pixie right to insist that my career was the most important matter to concentrate on?" Mavis pondered, "Wasn't I foolish to think that I was attractive enough to inspire a man to possibly sacrifice all for me? I've made rather a fool of myself and I'm not going to do that again."

So, feeling uncertain of how she might react should she set eyes on Isaac again, Mavis thought that safety dictated that she should cease her visits to the club. "Besides," she concluded, "I have been spending so much time there that I have neglected my music practice."

Mavis gave Pixie the excuse of having too much piano practice to catch up on to avoid her expected weekly visit to Pixie's house. She wished to avoid another grilling and the embarrassment at having to admit that she had been foolish. But her resolution not to visit the club soon found an excuse to ebb away.

Emma insisted that Mavis's non-attendance at one of their mutual friend's birthday party would be "utterly bad form." Mavis convinced herself that she would have to be strong, "And, anyway, perhaps..."

Had Emma known of Mavis's predicament and fate, perhaps she would have been less insistent. Mavis arrived at the club. She almost went faint as she struggled to breathe beneath a tidal wave of emotion brought on by the sight of Isaac. Attempting to disguise her awkwardness, she hid herself in her friend's merriment. But it was Emma who, dragging Isaac by the arm, brought him into her presence. They were laughing and Mavis made as if to laugh with him, she, acknowledging to herself that he was just as charming and handsome as she had previously concluded.

"He's acting as if nothing has changed between us." Mavis thought, "I wish that I could put up such a front. What on earth should I say to him? I'll try to keep the conversation going but I don't know if I can."

Emma's frivolity occupied Isaac's attention for a short time, though long enough for Mavis to suspect that he had spent the previous week's nights with her undoubtedly much more attractive friend. But, after a volley of preparatory glances at Mavis to prepare his approach, Isaac wheeled to face her.

"How are we, Mavis?"

"As well as can be expected," replied Mavis with a hint of jealousy.

"I am so glad to be back here," said Isaac, "I was forced to spend the last week in bed with a heavy cold. It knocked me sideways, as you say. I cannot see what your people see in this country. It is cold. It is damp and I've seen more grey smog than green grass in my time here."

Mavis, aghast with her foolishness, smiled with relief. That his heavy cold might be an excuse for his absence to flirt with Emma did enter Mavis's mind for a moment, but Isaac's constant retreat to his well-used handkerchief convinced her that she had jumped to a rather silly conclusion.

"That really is too awful. We must take you to our verdant countryside so that you can catch a cold there."

Isaac saw the joke and laughed: "No more colds for me, thank you very much. Let me take you to my country where we have lots of much more exotic illnesses that you could catch in the sunshine."

"Besides," he added, "It's my birthday soon and I expect that you will do me the honour of inviting me to the next concert you deem worthy enough of your attendance."

Isaac's mind was set on reaching out for the forbidden white fruit. Here was excitement. Here was a wall to be scaled into the secret garden from which all his fellow countrymen were banned. In that Birmingham world, where all women were white, where a flirtation could only be with a white woman, he succumbed to male bravado. He plunged into the deep.

The invitation came from Mavis and she and Isaac once more visited the Theatre Royal together. In a Chopin sonata, love took a firm hold of the young woman. It was followed by strolls in the countryside and picnics in the parks. The infant black child-thought had survived.

Mavis meanwhile continued to avoid seeing Pixie outside school hours. But the effort of declining Pixie's offers soon made Mavis feel so awkward that Mavis concluded that she would have to pay her and Dollars a visit. It prompted one more incident that imperilled my black infant-thought existence. The effect of the clash was as violent as those previous ones.

Dollars and Pixie had agreed to refrain from mentioning Mavis's intentions regarding the coloured man while their friend was in their house. Pixie considered that the right timing had to be chosen for those moments of frankness and that if Mavis persisted that there was little the two of them could achieve by pressurising the woman. Pixie and Dollars's pact of silence worked, at least on the first occasion.

However, the following week, when Mavis mentioned how happy she was in her teaching and how much she was enjoying her music and attending concerts, Dollars, seated in her comfy chair, could not help herself from offering the most frank of advice.

Dollars suddenly took on a stern countenance. She leant her head and shoulders forward: "My dear, you are a trainee teacher; on probation, so to speak. From what Pixie has told me, you have a very bright future. But you must consider that, should the powers-that-be hear about you having a relationship with a coloured man, they will not want a teacher with a reputation for irresponsible behaviour."

Her words came like a thunderbolt and blew me, the scandalous black-child thought almost into oblivion. No career. Disgrace. Humiliation. Was love worth this?

What does love know about its worth?

Love's shield brought Mavis to repel Dollars's brutal comments just as emphatically.

"Dollars has no man in her life. How can she know what a woman will risk for this extraordinary feeling inside of me?" thought Mavis, "Besides, we can go to Africa."

My existence as thought was secure. It was as if I had been through a rebirth. Now I was no longer weak and insipid but powerful and robust. So, having been born as thought and forcefully premature, underweight and threatened continually by The Dreads, Mavis's growing love for Isaac kept me alive. Indeed, that very conflict with The Dreads taught me to survive and mature in Mavis's fantasies.

Mavis regretted me not. For, as thought, I was part of the happiest time in her life. The Dreads slept. The world became a haze, which she would shape to become a carpet along which love would amble.

Fantasy had broken out of its cage unaware that Reality stalked, waiting to snare it once more.

The only Dread that Fantasy allowed room for was the thought of Mavis's mother's reaction should she ever learn of her daughter's friendship with Isaac.

Bliss; some of us pay heavily for it. Some of us turn it into a lifetime partnership. Some of us crave for it, then toss it away like a toffee paper wrapping when we see the first point of difficulty. Whichever way, it is a supreme moment, or collection of moments, in our lives. Implicit in every moment is its death. Bliss passes.

We do not choose Bliss. It secretly enters through our eyes, ears and pores, then buries itself in our minds and launches a struggle to capture our whole being. When Bliss disappears, sometimes violently, sometimes stealing away in the night, we are left trying to recall the immensity of its power. Each attempt to summon Bliss back sees it hanging in the wind, a few feet away, teasing, impish, defiant.

When Bliss has gone we are left to carry its offspring. Hurt, Remorse, Marriage, Children, Death, Devastation, Shame - who knows which child we will bear? But one cannot deny that Bliss is the most supreme and mysterious of moments.

So would you blame the awkward, spindly, bespectacled mother-hen-pecked young teacher from grasping at her moments?

During this time Mavis visited Pixie in Etwall Road less often. Nevertheless, she did go. She was keen to keep their friendship and was prepared to listen to the strictures of her two friends. But she listened with a mirror in her ears. She dismissed their warnings as revealing more about themselves than her.

Mavis cut herself off from the criticisms and warnings, preferring to drift headlong into the affair. She told Isaac about Pixie and Dollars's fears. Isaac, as much taken up by Fantasy, would respond by pulling Mavis close to him, saying: "Is it a crime for two people to love one another? Let us be judged in God's eyes."

Isaac was of the Christian Ibo group of tribes in Nigeria and his reply would soothe Mavis who feared that he would be angry with her friends. Isaac, however, considered the two spinsters well-meaning but lacking authority to interrupt Bliss. He felt that they resented Mavis's Bliss and the fact that she had found it with a black man.

His suspicions were confirmed on the only occasion that the couple met the two teachers. Mavis and Isaac were seated at a ballet performance in the Theatre Royal when Pixie and Dollars appeared, moving to sit a few rows behind them. Mavis beckoned her friends over. She felt that a meeting was due. All they had to do was to meet her lover and they would surely grow to like him and he to like them. Polite conversation ensued.

During the interval of the performance, the foursome met up and passed the time proclaiming on the excellence of the individual performances. Mavis seemed so happy that Isaac decided to try and break the ice further.

"Can I venture to suggest that we dine together after the final curtain? There is a fine new restaurant on the high street."

Dollars and Pixie declined: "That's awfully kind of you but we have a long way to go to reach home and it will be too late."

"Perhaps we can do it another time then," said Isaac.

The two women nodded their heads and gestured that the performance was about to restart. When the final curtain fell and the audience shuffled along the rows, Pixie and Dollars waved to Mavis.

"Well goodbye then," they said in unison and in unison missing the opportunity to show willingness by trying to arrange a future dinner appointment.

Mavis smiled nervously and Isaac said a polite: "Farewell."

Isaac's offer was merely a diplomatic withdrawal. He took Mavis's friends' reticence as a sign of disapproval and their night's conversation as mere politeness. He would never contemplate repeating the invite.

"Are your friends racially prejudiced?" Isaac asked Mavis.

Mavis blushed: "I don't think so but I did tell you that they think that nothing good will come of us being together because of this society we live in."

Isaac replied in anger: "Who do these people think they are! The British government is travelling the world to bring black people to this country to work on their buses and in the hospitals. Black people are arriving from the West Indies in boats paid for by the British government. Do the British expect that they will work in their factories and never speak to their women, never fall in love? I have heard that in Liverpool and in Cardiff there are black men married to white women. Then why can we not love each other?"

"PIXIE AND I MET HIM ONLY WHEN WE WENT TO THE BALLET AT THE THEATRE ROYAL. I THOUGHT HE WAS A VERY PLEASANT PERSON."

Dollars, 1968

"HE WAS A VERY GOOD LOOKING MAN AND VERY TALL, WELL OVER SIX FEET I SHOULD SAY."

Martha Watson, 1968

Mavis was disappointed. For some days this incident brought The Dreads back to the fore. Mavis was depressed and anxious. Her long-postponed visit to see her mother, Mrs Church, was due and this added to her anxieties. After a few days she telephoned her mother cancelling the visit on the excuse that she was unwell.

On the telephone, Mrs Church had simply responded: "Very well. Very well."

Mavis knew all was not very well and within two days a furious, vitriolic letter arrived in the post.

In it her mother wrote: "How could I have been so cursed to have such an uncaring, irresponsible child! I slaved to bring you into this world and put you where you are. What thanks do I get?"

The words grated but no longer brought Mavis to tears.

"I'm no longer a child," she thought, "and I don't want her to treat me like one."

Once more, I emerged as thought. For whenever Mavis thought of Isaac she could see nothing but a future spent with him, whether in England or in some far away land.

Whether I ever existed as thought with Isaac, it is difficult to say. Don't most men caught up in romance think more of the present than the future? At 29, Isaac was probably not a virgin. In which case, his survival as a childless bachelor would have led him to believe that children would only arrive in the years after marriage.

"FRIENDLY WITH ISAAC ENE, MINING ENGINEER FROM NIGERIA, FOR TWO YEARS, AND MARRIAGE WAS CONTEMPLATED. MISCONDUCT TOOK PLACE AND MO. (Mavis – PF) BECAME PREGNANT."

Barnardo's Report, 1953

Love-making, or misconduct, as Barnardo's referred to fornication, between the couple probably took place on several occasions. Oh! Glorious Missconduct! The entrée to a thousand legends. Where would the world be without it? The sweet loss of her virginity brought Mavis's Bliss to its height and the illegitimate relationship to its peak.

Outside the law, who dictates what constitutes lawlessness?

"Pixie and Dollars, you do not know what you have been missing!"

The decisive misconduct took place sometime in November 1952. Perhaps it occurred on Mavis's birthday. In any case, sperm met egg and black child-thought became black child-embryo, black love-child embryo.

I had arrived. Not that anyone but Mavis's body and myself knew at that stage.

I had arrived.

But so had Mrs Church.

Chapter 3

Arrivals and Departures

Mrs Church was on the train to Birmingham. Anxious at the failure of Mavis to contact her after she had sent the child that stern letter of rebuke, she had decided to pay her daughter a visit. With her she carried a large box of chocolates intended to be her daughter's birthday present. Mrs Church arrived at Mavis's lodgings by taxi. When she enquired of the landlady as to the whereabouts of her daughter, the landlady replied: "I haven't set eyes upon her since yesterday. She may be visiting the coloured chap who comes here from time to time."

Winifred Church remained expressionless - stunned by the shock. In the brief moment of silence that followed, all manner of thoughts went through her mind:

"Can she really have done this to me? The brazen hussy! Do I deserve further shame! I knew that I shouldn't have let her leave home. So immature! So immature! That father of hers has put a curse on me! Is this his doing?"

But these were thoughts only and she replied to the landlady in her superior voice: "I hope you are not insinuating that my daughter is having a relationship with a coloured."

"It's not for me to say, madam," the landlady said, affecting submission, "I only know that he comes here and he is at the mining college. His name is Isaac and he's always very polite and kind."

Mrs Church's knees shook, whereupon the landlady offered her a chair into which she collapsed:

"The stupid girl! What will become of her! Can a mother ever have had so many problems with her child!"

The landlady, who had witnessed similar, if not quite so dramatic scenes in the ten years that she had let rooms in her house, offered Mrs Church a cup of tea. The visitor returned a distracted nod of her head and was quickly left alone as the landlady disappeared into the kitchen.

In the living room, Mrs Church took the time to compose herself, as was the intention of the landlady. When the landlady reappeared, Mrs Church asked: "Would you mind very much if I remain here till my daughter returns?"

The landlady, wishing to be helpful, but also intrigued as to what would be the outcome of the drama, replied: "No, madam, not at all. But you will pardon me for disappearing for a while. I must go down to the shops on the high street before they close."

"Of course," came the reply. Then after a pause, Mrs Church leaned forward: "Can I ask you one last question? Is this man married?"

"Sorry madam, I don't know. I did notice that he wasn't wearing a wedding ring but do those people wear them?"

Mrs Church pursed her lips and frowned. Married or not, it was a calamity.

So, it turned out that it was 4pm on a sunny, if chilly, late November afternoon that, as embryo, I travelled to the terrible confrontation between Mavis and her mother. Mavis arrived at 4.30pm. She was happy, having spent the day with Isaac in Worcester. They had chosen to visit the pretty town, where none of the staff from her school or his college were likely to be, to begin their Christmas shopping, or window-shopping, as Mavis joked. That passers-by stared at the couple was a source of irritation. Annoyance turned to amusement when one gawking old man walking along the pavement managed to almost knock himself unconscious as he crashed into a lamppost.

As Mavis turned her key and entered the house, her mind was set on catching up on her preparation for the following week's school lessons. She was searching through the mail on the sideboard in the porch when she heard a shout from the living room.

"Is that you Mavis?"

It was Mavis's turn to feel her knees shake. Not that the young woman had any suspicion that her mother knew of Isaac. Mavis had long since ceased to look forward to spending time in her mother's presence. Mrs Church's arrival without invitation was rude enough an intrusion without the harangue, which Mavis expected, would follow.

"Hello, mama," said Mavis with a polite smile as she entered the room, "I hope you haven't been waiting for me for too long. If I had known you were coming I would have returned earlier."

"Please sit down darling." beckoned her mother, "I came all this way because I was worried about you."

The drawing room manners couldn't last for long.

"But I'm very well thank you and very happy here," replied Mavis.

"Yes, I am sure you are but I have been given reason for concern."

Mavis tried to hide her alarm.

"Surely Pixie and Dollars would not have told her about Isaac!" she said to herself.

"What is his name?" said Mrs Church with the smile of a tiger already consuming its prey.

Mavis froze. She saw no way forward and no means of retreat.

"How had she found out? Had she been spying? Had the landlady said something? What if she tells father?"

"Oh darling, do come on. I know more about him than you think," Mrs Church teased.

Mavis felt her cheeks moisten with tears and turned her head away. As thought I totally disappeared. As embryo, I shuddered. The Dreads partied. Mavis knew that her mother would continue with this spiteful torture until she had been told everything. Then there would follow an inestimable fury and – the punishment.

"If I don't obey her she will tell father and my grandparents all sorts of terrible stories. I must try to calm her down and see if I can get to father first. At least he will be more understanding," Mavis decided.

"His name is…"

"Isaac," Mrs Church's interjection was as intimidating as any could be, "Isaac what?" she added.

"Ene," replied Mavis, blurting out, "But he's a fine man from a good background and well-educated!"

"And he's a coloured, a savage in a suit," replied her mother, adding in derision, "He'll have Ene-woman, I suppose." (Ene is pronounced Eneh, similar to 'any')

Mavis broke into a sob attempting a defiant reply: "He is more educated than you will ever be!"

"You will make me and your father laughing stocks. People are talking already. You will be the scandal of the city and you will never ever be allowed to teach children when you show you have the morals of a harridan."

"How can you of all people say that to me! What you did to my father was unforgivable!"

"I didn't flaunt myself before a savage. You will stop seeing him immediately or there will be trouble."

"You can't threaten me. I am a grown adult. I am not your baby anymore, mama!"

"Mark my words. Wait till your father finds out what you have been up to," declared Mrs Church as she rose to leave.

Mavis remained slumped in the chair as she heard the door slam. The sobbing began again and didn't stop even when she had reached her room and collapsed onto her bed. Mrs Church hurried to catch the last train. Mavis's landlady passed her on the way down the street but received barely an acknowledgement. On her living room floor Mrs Stokes discovered a box of chocolates. "My reward," the landlady thought as she untied its pink ribbon.

It was ten o'clock at night when, having cried herself to sleep, Mavis rose to write a letter to her father explaining her "friendship" with Isaac and pleading for his support. "Father will understand what mama is like," she concluded, ruing her failure to head her mother off with a similar argument that there was nothing wrong with a platonic relationship with any good and single man.

Sleep came easily once Mavis had convinced herself that she could prevent her mother from harming her relationship with her father.

On the following day, Mavis went to visit Isaac in his room. She told her lover all that had happened. Isaac was downhearted but tried to raise her spirits: "Maybe we will never be married but who are they to stop us loving each other."

Isaac had killed me off as thought too. As embryo, my future seemed precarious. The couple determined to live for the moment. Love-making became so intense that I feared that I would have to make room for a score of siblings.

However, as embryo, I began increasingly to draw on my mother's body for sustenance. And so I entered Mavis's dreams, more as wish than thought. For some time, these dreams captured the waking thoughts of Mavis. To her they were promises of future bliss, directives as to the path she must take to happiness. Little did she know that they represented not portent but present.

Mrs Church despatched a volley of vitriolic letters but Mavis's father sent a screed so understanding and sympathetic, that Mavis once again dared to contemplate the possibility of marriage to Isaac.

It was on the Saturday exactly two weeks after Mrs Church's visit that Mavis arrived at Isaac's lodgings. Involvement in the end-of-term Christmas festivities at her school had kept the teacher from seeing him for several days. A fellow lodger from India welcomed her into the house.

"Will you please tell Isaac I am here?" requested Mavis.

The student stood and turned to face Mavis: "I am sorry but Isaac is not here. This morning he caught a train for London. From there he will take a boat for Lagos."

I can only guess at the depths of Mavis's despair. The Dreads had a carnival of misery.

"Wh... wh... wh... wh... what happened?"

"I am sorry but I do not know. He only told me that he had to go back to Lagos. He left early this morning."

"Wh... wh... when will he return?"

"I am sorry but he did not say."

"Did he leave a note for me?"

"He left nothing at all. He emptied his room of all his belongings."

Mavis attempted to console herself with the thought that Isaac had probably had a family bereavement and had been forced to hurry back. That would mean he wouldn't return until after Christmas.

"The time without him will be unbearable. But why had he not told me? Was he too upset? Are there some of his feelings that he will not share with me? Some of my friends have said that coloured people were that way, that their parents meant more to them than any lover could ever do, that love in Africa and Asia was a very different thing to that in England. Perhaps they were right."

This pondering only returned Mavis to her Dreads.

"Was it all a fantasy? Did he really love me or was I just an easy target for him? Did I play the part of the lonely woman desperate for love? He said that I was the most important part of his life. Yet he disappeared without so much as a goodbye. When he returns, will our relationship be so precarious?" Then she reminded herself: "That is, of course, if he returns."

"Perhaps he has told his family about me and they have ordered him home to be married. Perhaps the college had failed him for not taking his work seriously."

Whatever the reason, it hurt that Isaac had felt unable to tell her. As she walked home through a dense fog, she grasped at the possibility that she may have just missed him and that he would have dropped a letter off at her lodgings. She began to run through the dimly lit streets, bumping into an old lady shuffling along the pavement, and almost losing her balance as she avoided a stray dog.

By the time Mavis had opened the door of the house, she had built herself up to a throbbing excitement. She glanced at the side table. There was not a letter in sight.

"Perhaps the landlady or one of the other lodgers has put the letter under my door." She ran up the stairs but found nothing beneath the door. She opened the door to see if the letter had been slid beneath it.

Sure enough, there was a letter. Her heart seemed like it would crash out of her body. She ripped the letter open without looking at the handwriting on the front.

"Miss Frampton, can I remind you that you are three weeks behind with your rent."

Tears came. I think you'll agree that they were in order. How we drive ourselves to the extremes of excitement, hoping against hope, until our frenzy of deluded expectation collapses at the failure of fantasy to realise itself.

At school, Mavis taught so poorly in the week that followed that, had it not been the end of term when teachers relax and pupils are distracted, she believed that she would have been called into the head teacher's study for a good ticking off.

Soon Mavis's consternation was added to by the lateness of her period. Irregular as they were, they had caused constant worries since her love-making with Isaac had begun. But they always arrived. It was the last day of term when Mavis realised that she could well be pregnant.

Mavis concluded that if she were pregnant, then her teaching career was over and if Isaac didn't return, her whole life would be finished. The suspicion of my existence so empowered The Dreads that, in the days to come, they were on the point of destroying Mavis, and myself with her.

So it happened that Christmas, that at the very revelation of my existence, of her duality, Mavis felt herself to be totally alone in the world. When she thought of her father, she thought of shame. When she thought of her friends, she thought of shame. When she thought of the school staff room she thought of shame, and when she thought of her mother, Mavis thought of unending vitriol.

Only when she thought of Isaac did Mavis climb out of her shroud of misery, as she held out the hope that her lover would return and they would marry and sail off to live in Nigeria.

For three days Mavis remained in this restless mental state, going through the motions of washing, dressing, checking the sideboard for a letter from Isaac, walking to the library and to the club to see if she might find him there, then returning home, undressing, washing and going to bed for a restless, tearful sleep.

She finally managed to compose herself as she had been invited to spend Christmas Day with Pixie and Dollars. Her non-appearance would have alarmed her two friends. Mavis never mentioned Isaac during the whole day and, though the young woman looked rather "out of sorts," Pixie and Dollars felt relieved. They wrongly concluded that Mavis had heeded their advice and put a stop to her folly.

"Better we not mention it," they whispered to each other over the washing up, "Mavis will be upset enough as it is. It is good enough that she has come to her senses."

The New Year and morning sickness had begun when a letter appeared on the sideboard with Isaac's handwriting on it. Mavis's semi-comatose state was instantly broken as she eagerly tore at the envelope:

"Dear Mavis,

"Please accept my deepest apologies for leaving without informing you. A terrible misfortune has beset me and us both.

"On the Wednesday after we were last together I was called into the office of the college vice-principal. I was told to return home on the agreement of my company and the college. The vice-principal informed me that your mother had complained that I was having a liaison with you. They had also been contacted by the Colonial Office who had told them that the liaison was unwise and against your mother's express wishes. The vice-principal said much more but my mind could take nothing else in, except that he said that he did not consider it likely that I would ever be permitted to return to England. He said I had abused the privilege of being allowed to study in your country.

"Now I return to my company and family in shame. I think that my company will keep me in their employment but my prospects will be poor. As for my mother and father, I will beg their forgiveness. I hope that in time they will understand that my actions were not dictated by sexual desire or the abandonment of my upholding the family honour but by the fact that we both are very much in love.

"What a terrible thing it is that the racism of your nation means that a Christian man and a Christian woman cannot love each other simply because of the colour of their skin. Did Jesus Christ not say that we should love all men?

"As for myself, I still love you with all my heart and always will. I have spent not one minute without thinking of you. I can not write the words to tell you how sad I am and how sorry I am that we can no longer be together. That I could not summon up the words to tell you of my demise before I left for home, please forgive me. Even now as I write I find it hard to avoid my tears staining the page.

With love forever,

Your Isaac."

It is hard to believe that Mavis had any tears left to shed, but cry again she did. She lay on her bed and sobbed for so long that on several occasions she had to pick up the letter again to confirm that he had actually written the words that swirled around her head.

"THE MOTHER BECAME FRIENDLY WITH A NIGERIAN ENGINEER, WHOM SHE MET AT THE INTERNATIONAL CENTRE IN BIRMINGHAM. THEY HAD MUSICAL INTERESTS IN COMMON, AND THEY HOPED TO MARRY. THE MOTHER BELIEVED THAT IT WAS THROUGH THE GRANDMOTHER HEARING OF THEIR FRIENDSHIP THAT THE PUTATIVE FATHER WAS SUDDENLY ORDERED BACK TO LAGOS IN DECEMBER, 1952."

Barnardo's Report, 1953

That her lover had been snatched from her she was certain. Isaac's sincerity was unquestioned. Had he any alternative in those British Empire days of doing anything but return home? They could have run off together and been followed by a pack of police officers.

"If he had told me then I would have gone back to Nigeria with him on the next boat."

But that she knew was a fantasy.

"What right have I to ruin his career?" she reflected as her own career headed for oblivion. "Do I tell him of my condition, of our child? What a miserable situation we are in!"

At this point in time she felt no anger towards her mother. That was not Mavis. She had disobeyed her mother's wishes and she had been punished for failing to recognise her mother's omnipotence over her life. That spell, by which her mother held her, would only be broken by others.

The new school term began with Mavis in a state of mental turmoil that sunk, at times, into hopeless despair. It was Pixie who first recognised that Mavis was in a distraught condition.

On the first day of term, Pixie had been called into the head's study and questioned about Mavis's friendship with a coloured man.

"We have received a rather vitriolic letter from Miss Frampton's mother declaring that her daughter is having a relationship with a coloured man. She requests that I take action on her behalf," said the head, "Do you know anything about this?"

"THE GRANDMOTHER KNEW OF HER FRIENDSHIP WITH A NIGERIAN MAN AND CONTACTED THE COLONIAL OFFICE, CLUB AND SCHOOLS."

Barnardo's Report, 1953

"Yes, I do. Mavis is friendly with some coloureds at the International Centre but so are many other young teachers. I have seen some of her mother's letters and she is quite inclined to exaggeration. I suggest that you simply ignore the letter," replied Pixie, hoping that she would be forgiven, up above, for her white lie. "Mavis's mother is really quite preposterous," she said to herself, "she will be the ruin of her own daughter."

But, on this day, Pixie determined to keep news of Mrs Church's letter from Mavis. One week later, when they were both alone in the staff room, Pixie chose to seize the moment. She intended to discover what was troubling her friend, but the door to the room opened, issuing in another member of staff, and Pixie retreated.

"Mavis, dear, can we meet after school?"

"Now, is my teaching to be questioned as well?" thought Mavis.

"Yes, that's fine," replied Mavis clearly upset by the request.

That afternoon, Mavis could feel her confidence in her teaching ability slip by the minute. Her fingers missed the piano keys and she was close to shouting at one of the children who couldn't help but sing out of tune.

"I might as well give up teaching now. I am really becoming quite hopeless," she said to herself, wishing the world would allow her to sleep for five years. She could then wake up and start again. But then there was me, embryo.

The end of school arrived and Mavis returned to the staff room half of a mind to offer her resignation to Pixie. But then Pixie was not the head teacher and the head was not in school that day.

"Should I tell her of my situation? She will think me so shameful and so stupid, so pathetic."

Part of Mavis remained opposed to saying anything. Part of her wanted to resign from her post and disappear. To where, she did not know. Another part wanted help, and the latter prevailed because Mavis clung to the hope that there might be, somewhere, a way out of her situation and that she had to talk to somebody. She didn't dare speak to her mother or father or her grandparents. If there were a way of staying in teaching, Pixie and Dollars would help.

If the matter of my abortion ever came to Mavis's mind, she never mentioned it. She was not prepared to give it serious consideration. Abortion was then a quite dangerous affair and, after all, I was to be Isaac's child too.

"When I tell him, we will be married. Even if we have to live in Nigeria and in shame, we will, the three of us, have each other. I can become a music tutor, part-time, if they will not let me teach or look after Isaac's home and raise Isaac's children. We will have a hard life but we will be in love."

In Mavis's mind, I, the embryo, remained a difficult but certain road back into her lover's arms. My embryo existence was assured. Well, that also required Mavis to contemplate her own continued existence, and on many a day she was close to hurling us both into the next world.

Pixie entered the staff room and smiled knowingly at Mavis, not that she had half a mind as to the tale she was about to receive. "Please, just give me a minute to collect my things dear, then I'll be with you?" asked Pixie.

As Pixie busied herself, she spoke without looking at Mavis: "Have you any plans for this evening or would you like to go to that lovely café on Derbyshire Road?"

"The café will be fine," replied Mavis, alarmed at having to sit in judgement before the tribunal of Pixie, Pa and Dollars. She sensed that Pixie's offer was the prelude to what would amount to a reprimand, and added the excuse: "I really do need to get home early and catch up on my preparation."

"Is it regarding my teaching?" she continued.

"What dear?"

"The reason why you wish to see me on my own."

"Oh, no dear!" responded Pixie, "I had simply noticed that you were a little off colour and might need a little support."

"Now let's go!" Pixie declared, donning her navy blue, woollen winter coat and permitting Mavis no time to decline her offer.

As the two teachers walked along the street, Pixie passed the time away by inquiring of Mavis's opinion on the progress of the various children in the classes that Mavis taught. As this conversation flagged, Pixie switched to prompting her friend as to her opinion on a performance of *Orphelia*, which they had both attended the previous autumn.

Only when they were seated in the café and the waiter had taken their order did Pixie feel ready to question her charge.

"Now my dear, what is the matter? Is it Isaac or your mother?"

Mavis didn't sob this time. She was in a public place. Determined as she was to maintain her decorum, the tears nevertheless wandered down their well-trodden paths. They were halted when Mavis became sufficiently collected to extract her handkerchief from her cardigan sleeve.

"It's everything," replied Mavis. You can be assured. It was everything.

"Isaac has been ordered back to Nigeria," announced Mavis, proceeding to stumble her way through the story.

Pixie listened showing no emotion. She wanted to hear the whole of the story before committing herself to expression. When Mavis had concluded the tale of her lover's demise, Pixie's initial thoughts were that Mavis had got off lightly. Pixie attempted to comfort her friend by pointing out that while her mother had behaved badly, both Mavis and Isaac had gone beyond the pale. At least they were both young and intelligent and had a future ahead of them.

"Isaac will get to his feet again and so will you. You really are quite an exceptional musician and an excellent teacher and you will be such a catch. I quite envy you."

"I'm having a child," Mavis declared in a whisper so faint that Pixie misheard her.

"I know you're not a child dear," replied Pixie fearing that Mavis considered her remarks to be patronising.

Mavis lifted up her head: "You don't understand. I am pregnant."

Pixie's mouth opened as she took a deep breath that blew in the total calamity of her friend's situation. With lips pursed and transfixed eyes, Pixie asked: "Isaac?"

Mavis nodded. For Pixie I became a black child-thought – the greatest possible calamity. "Dollars will know what to do," she told herself.

"Let us finish our meal and then you must come with me to see Dollars. She will know what to do."

Pixie finished her food. Mavis was still picking at hers when Pixie ushered the waiter, paid the bill and requested their coats.

As a headmistress, Catherine Dolby was considered by Pixie to be both friend and mentor, very clear-headed and incisive when dealing with obstacles in her path. The warnings Dollars had meted out to Mavis had gone unheeded and, despite the young woman having rejected her previous advice, Dollars would still be prepared to help the poor unfortunate. Dollars liked Mavis. They both did. Pa liked to hear Mavis play on the piano.

But was help possible?

Chapter 4

Romulus

Musing on her friend's condition, Pixie speculated that, were she to face the same predicament, she would take the risk and have an abortion. But abortion was illegal and destroying my embryo risked both the law and Mavis's life (Mavis and I needed each other at that point in time). Besides, Pixie considered abortion such a hazardous route that only Mavis could suggest it. Dollars, she knew, would be of the same opinion.

So it was left to the two spinsters to consider a solution to the problem – me, as embryo and as black love-child.

As it turned out, the conversation between the three teachers in Pixie's house broached no solutions that night. When Pixie and Mavis turned up at the house, Pixie took Dollars in the kitchen, then returned to usher her father up the stairs to his room. Mavis was left seated on the couch while Pixie and Dollars disappeared again. Their counsel was held in a whisper and concluded, whereupon the women made their entry into the living room as delicately as a grand jury could. Proceedings began.

Dollars was systematic but gentle in her questioning of Mavis. The chief witness sat with her head in her hands addressing the hearth in the fireplace with a monotone voice while Dollars picked through all the details of her client's circumstances. As counsel, she gently probed to discover Mavis's most desired and most deliverable options. Isaac, Mrs Church, Mr Frampton, Mavis's grandparents, uncles, friends and career prospects were all carefully examined.

At the point when her client covered her face in her hands and emitted several whimpers, appearing too distracted to hear her questioner, Dollars called an end to the proceedings. The exhausted Mavis allowed herself to be led upstairs to the spare bedroom. She was only half undressed when she lay down on the bed and fell fast asleep.

With Mavis out of the way, the jury began its deliberations. The two spinsters needed no convincing that both Mavis and Isaac were guilty of the utmost folly. They had crossed the racial dividing line and had pre-marital sex, courted scandal and the demise of their careers. To cap it all, Mavis was now pregnant. Both had been impossibly naïve. Isaac, they believed, would never return to England, even if he were permitted to. Nor would he wed Mavis across the colour bar in his country. Both families would be outraged.

Dollars ventured: "If Mavis decides to have the child, then she will have to do so on her own."

"She will have it. I am certain of that," replied Pixie, "She is convinced that Isaac and she will be married. She is prepared to go and live in Nigeria."

"If she has the child, could she continue in teaching?" asked Pixie.

"Why, not at all!" exclaimed Dollars, "With an illegitimate child! And black at that! Not one head would be prepared to consider her. Her teaching career would be at an end."

"And she is such a fine teacher and an even better musician," sighed Pixie, "Perhaps she would be able to make her way in that profession."

"With a child to bring up? I doubt it very much. They say that it's a very precarious life until one reaches the top," answered Dollars, closing off that option.

"Couldn't she go and live with her father?" suggested Pixie.

"I really can't see his new wife accepting the baggage from his past marriage. From what Mavis says, the money he pays to his ex-wife is already draining him. I don't believe he has the sort of fortune that will support mother and child.

"Don't even think about suggesting Mavis's mother. She is a terrible woman and would have her daughter out on the street."

"Any other relatives?" queried Dollars.

"It seems that Mavis has a rather eccentric wealthy uncle in Swindon but, as with the others, Mavis feels that any mention of the child will create such a to-do that she would be totally ostracised."

Dollars paused for a moment before delivering judgement: "She will have to be persuaded to give the child away. She can get it adopted."

"Who will want a black child?" asked Pixie.

"If she can't get it adopted, she will have to put the child in a home. There are children's homes run by the Salvation Army and by Barnardo's. They say the Barnardo's homes are very well run."

Pixie shook her head: "That would be awful for Mavis. Besides, while she holds out the hope of Isaac marrying her, she will not contemplate any such suggestion."

"But if it is in a home, she could still visit it and if she marries, she could take it back when she has made a proper home for it. At least if she continues teaching, she will earn some money and in time will be able to buy a house," argued Dollars.

Pixie replied: "That's if she can continue in teaching. From what she says, she will be eight months pregnant by Whitsuntide and is due to give birth on the last day of term."

"Then, she will have to try and hide her condition," said Dollars, "If she can do that until half-term, she could feign sickness."

"But what of her friends and the school? They might find out."

"We'd have to whisk her away where not a soul might find her."

"Where to?"

"That's what we must find out dear," Dollars concluded. It was her call to action.

The two women were convinced that the plan they had adopted was in their friend's best interests. My fate as child was delivered in the courtroom of 40, Etwall Road. Mavis succumbed. Nevertheless, she remained convinced of Isaac's love. They would be married. She hoped that that day would come sooner rather than later.

"Dearest Beloved Isaac,

"My heart pounds every day when I check my letters hoping for more news of you. Our separation is the cruellest act. That it was my mother who engineered your expulsion, is my shame. I am horrified to think that she could have gone to such lengths.

"I do not know how she found out about us but it terrifies me to think that I am of the womb of that vindictive woman. I swear that I will never speak to her again.

"Still, less of her. I have news too important to spend more words on her. This news you may find to be a source of joy or terror. The doctor has informed me that I am pregnant. Isaac, I am carrying our child. He is the symbol of our love – something that my mother cannot take away from us.

"I hope that you are in agreement that we should be married. Let me know your feelings. I am ready to gather my belongings and take the next boat bound for the Gold Coast.

"We can still have that future of which we once dreamed – our children, Isaac.

"Write soon my darling. Each day I spend without you is a misery.

"Your ever loving Mavis."

The very act of writing these words impelled Mavis into loving me as embryo. In the days that followed she would caress her stomach as if her troublesome foetus was Isaac himself.

Indeed, Mavis did appear to Pixie to be in better spirits. Two weeks later, on a visit to Etwall Road, Mavis gleefully announced that she had received a letter from Isaac. She read it out loud:

"Dearest Mavis, It is with great delight that I heard of our child. How it saddens me that I can not be at your side now. I am trying to establish the circumstances in which we might marry. As you will understand I have to exercise some discretion. Either you can come and live over here or I will return to England and we will be wed.

Eternally Yours,

Isaac."

Mavis finished on a note of triumph that disturbed Dollars.

"Do not raise your hopes, dear." Dollars warned her, "It is a harsh regime out there and I, for one, am not certain that he will be allowed to return."

Nevertheless, Dollars was less certain of her view that Isaac's love for Mavis was mere affectation. "Perhaps this bond is stronger and more courageous than I had believed," she mused, knowing very well that her own experience with men had been all too brief.

For several weeks Mavis occupied her time with visits to libraries to acquaint herself with her new country of residence and its customs. I enjoyed my occasional metamorphoses into black African child-thought. The silver Bentley was replaced by a huge, caparisoned African elephant, by safari trips through the savannah, watched on by lions and antelopes, ostriches and eagles. We travelled on motorboats accompanied by crocodiles, past mangrove swamps and mothers immersed in the river, washing their children. And the people sang. And we were happy.

She wrote to Isaac of what she had learned. She asked her lover so many questions about her newly adopted country and pressed him to speed up his investigation into their marrying in Lagos. A letter arrived from Nigeria putting an end to her trips to the library.

"My Dear Mavis,

"I have enquired as to the circumstances of our marriage and it breaks my heart to inform that all those that I have spoken to advise me to desist from marrying you in my country.

"Apartheid still exists in this country. It is horrible that marriage is not advised between our races. Were we not considered equal enough to be soldiers in your war against Germany? Do we not worship the same God?

"In our country a white man can marry one of our women, or at least take her for his mistress but a black man with a white woman is seen as an outrage. One day our country will be free and then we will do as we please.

"My anger only parallels my sorrow. Please take care of my child. Hopefully one day the world will change and we will be together again. I will try to save up as much as I can and seek permission to return to England. Then we can be married.

"In the meantime, please look after yourself and our child. I will send you what I can to provide for you both.

"Eternally Yours,

"Isaac."

This letter, Mavis did not read out at Etwall Road. The blow to her dreams could have been devastating but while Isaac held out the hope of marriage, she was able to face the world with some courage. For the moment, she knew that she would have to face the world alone.

Not quite alone. In March, the morning sickness began. As embryo, I no longer offered Mavis a quick passage back to Isaac's arms. But I was part of him and the love that the couple had shared. As embryo I remained loved.

Mavis and I grew up together during that spring of 1953. The music teacher felt her breasts grow and her stomach bulge, and became increasingly attached to her child. A craving for green apples began and, while she could store them away in her bag in the school staff room and munch at them in the toilet, she was less careful on those nights when she played piano for the city's Bach Choir.

When her chorister friends teased her as to whether she was pregnant since she was acting so, Mavis blushed and laughed blaming her lack of time to prepare her evening meal, adding: "I should say that if I was pregnant, I expect that I will give birth to a pip."

"And how is Pip?" asked the alto soprano one day.

That day I became Pip, a child of Great Expectations. My pre-christening brought Mavis to her hope that her child would rise above whatever misfortune she might suffer. But who would be my Abel Magwitch? My provider? Why! Uncle Reg! Eccentric and secretive, he would fit the part well. Dollars would be Miss Havisham and Pip would be so handsome that he could find an Estella on his own.

Mavis sent a letter to her mother condemning Mrs Church for what she had done to Isaac. She wrote: "I no longer want anything to do with you. You have ruined your own life and now you seem set on destroying mine."

She said nothing of me as embryo and never would. Mrs Church would never be allowed to possess me, as grandchild-thought or as grandchild.

Meanwhile, Pixie and Dollars prepared Mavis's deception of her school, her mother and her father. Dollars wrote off to agony aunts gracing the problem pages of women's magazines. She requested assistance in finding her friend a place to stay and bring me into life. It had to be a special place where her friend's condition could remain unknown to the world at large, where no one of consequence would possibly discover her.

I was to be borne in secret and born as secret.

To avoid Mavis's landlady discovering her lodger's condition and relaying the news to Mavis's mother, the pregnant woman was moved out of her lodgings and taken to live with her friends in Etwall Road. Mavis left no forwarding address. Mavis was also instructed to write to her father and to her grandparents indicating that any friendship that she had with Isaac Ene had been vastly exaggerated by her mother and that, since his removal in February, the matter was at a close.

Pixie and Dollars advised Mavis of how to hide her pregnancy: "Three corsets dear! Nice and tight! It works a treat!"

Mavis was, in any case, so slight that, after six months, the fact that the young teacher had put some flesh on her face was seen as a sign that she was at last looking after herself properly.

A reply came from one of the agony aunts whom Dollars had contacted. She referred Dollars to the Christian Moral Welfare Society in Cornwall. Dollars wrote off again, this time to the society. She requested permission for her friend to be accepted for the last days of her pregnancy and the six weeks that would follow. She explained that the intention was that the child be placed in care in order that the mother, a young unmarried teacher, could return to her employment.

After some time the society consented to accept the young teacher to stay for the final days of her pregnancy at Rosemundy House, their home in St Agnes. The news was only too welcome for Mavis. What with the summer warmth, the three corsets and me, the teacher had often found herself close to fainting in her lessons. Her colleagues noted her now pallid condition, which became a subject for whispered concern. Pixie seized those moments to suggest that she feared her friend might have tuberculosis.

This talk provided an excellent pretext for the day when Mavis sent a note via Pixie to say that she had been feeling rather poorly and had been advised by her doctor to take rest. The deception was furthered by Mavis seeking sickness benefit and, on the following weekend, Pixie and Dollars made ready to escort their patient, with foetus, to Cornwall.

"So far, so good," sighed Dollars, smiling at Mavis. "If the doctors are right that the baby is due on July 18th, then you will be ready to return to teaching in September."

"But what will happen to Pip?" asked Mavis, "What if I can't bear to leave him?"

Dollars replied: "Dear, we have been over this so many times. What you must keep in mind is that your return to teaching is in the best interests of both you and the child. The society has said that they will help you find a foster placing for it until you are ready to take it back."

"Until Isaac returns," interjected Mavis.

"And should a foster placing not become available," continued Dollars, feigning to ignore Mavis's wishful thinking, "we will find a good home for the child."

"I have spoken to friends of mine and they say Barnardo's homes are very good," said Pixie. "They say that the children are well looked after and the staff are ever so caring."

Mavis travelled on that train journey to the rolling hills and rugged sea cliffs of Cornwall with many emotions. She felt relief at the prospect of emptying herself from her suffocating corsets. She felt joy that she was soon to give birth to her and Isaac's child, but sadness that her lover was kept 4,000 miles away, as well as bitterness at her mother's actions and fear that her father and grandparents might discover her situation.

The trio finally arrived in a sun-drenched St Agnes. Entry into the fresh seaside air all but brought Mavis to collapse. Fortunately, a woman from the society met them. After some brief words to Dollars, their host marched them off through the small town to a local café. There, Pixie accompanied Mavis to the ladies' toilet where the corsets of deception and suffocation were removed. Mavis reappeared in the café in her full bloom and I was able to breathe again.

A taxi then took us to Rosemundy. Pixie and Dollars briefly inspected Mavis's quarters and bid Mavis farewell, explaining to their host that they had a long trip back to Birmingham and would have to travel overnight, if they were to be ready for work on the Monday.

Mavis shed a few tears as she waved goodbye to her friends. I kicked out at my womb, reminding her of why she was facing incarceration in Cornwall. She was resigned to her fate.

Could it all have turned out very differently?

Mavis was, depending on how you look at it, fortunate and unfortunate to be "connected", to be of the middle classes. What would she have done if she had been from a socially less advantaged background, working in a factory, isolated from her parents and still not contemplating an abortion? Could she have struggled on? What Isaac said of blacks and whites living as couples in Liverpool was true but Isaac had been in Britain at the mercy of the Nigerian and British colonial administrations.

It is most likely that Mavis would have been left on her own to ensure our survival.

I am convinced that she could have struggled on and survived with child in those early days of Welfare State Britain.

As a middle class woman, she could also have struggled on. What stopped her from explaining her condition to her relations and appealing to them for support? You should know the point of my speculation. For as much as you might sympathise with her condition, any child abandoned by their parents will one day ask: "Why? Was there no alternative? Was their act of abandonment one of selfishness? Was her act one of motherhood or an attempt to avoid the consequences of motherhood, leaving the child to pick up the consequences? Mother or child? Father or child?

Once Isaac had committed himself to the irresponsibility of Missconduct his fate was not sealed. He resisted the option of toughing it out with his child and lover in Nigeria. But could he have fought the shackles of racism and colonialism? Was my mother equally chained by racism and sexism?

Or were they both simply afraid of Shame?

The scales swing this way and that. What can be said, is that at this stage Mavis was not aware of where her decisions and her friends' prompting were leading.

Nowadays, Rosemundy House is a hotel. Then, it was a home for unmarried mothers-to-be, sinful mothers, fallen angels who were taken in by the society. For the Christian Moral Welfare Society, their assistance to these sorry creatures was not to be gratuitous. Those who stayed had to show their willingness to allow their immoral welfare to be corrected. They had to perform acts of repentance for past sins. Rosemundy House was a home of sadness, a "Magdalene Laundry", as they were dubbed in Ireland.

Pixie and Dollars had been pleased as to what they had seen in the Home of Sadness. The summer sunshine that can make even a council sink estate seem pretty, had lit up the home's gardens and interior. All appeared spotless and bright.

What they overlooked were the faces of the angels. Guilt and Shame and the horror of Eternal Damnation pervaded the Home of Sadness. These loose, irresponsible women in the Home of Sadness may have believed that they could escape the shame of society in this place of refuge. However, the worthy Christians of the Moral Welfare Society had no intention of permitting the mothers-to-be a shield to protect themselves from the Judgement of the Lord. These women had to understand that they were on the edge of Hell.

Every word from her correctors sent Mavis onwards towards the Hell of The Dreads of growing old, alone, in shame, without Isaac, without her Pip. That dream of the gleaming silver Bentley had long since gone. It was replaced by the Dread of the rag-and-bone man's cart.

And, as I thought of my mother's infinite sadness in the Home of Sadness, I thought of songwriter, Joni Mitchell's, words:

"Branded as a jezebel I knew I was not bound for heaven
I'd be cast in shame into the Magdalene laundries.
Most girls come here pregnant some by their own fathers.
Bridget got the belly by her parish priest.
We're trying to get things white as snow,
All of us woe-begotten-daughters,
In the steaming stains of the Magdalene laundries.
Prostitutes and destitutes and temptresses like me-
Fallen women – sentenced to dreamless drudgery.
What do they call this heartless place, Our Lady of Charity?"

The Dreads must have had a field day, as Mavis scrubbed floors, clothes and skin. Not a day went by when she was not made to feel as if she were one of the most wicked women on earth. The joy of being freed from her corsets had been replaced by the suffocation of this house of holy correction.

True, there were some women who seemed strong and impassive here. There were also tears. There were screams, rejected babies and babies who wouldn't be breast-fed and babies that would be dead, that hideously stripped away motherhood and the last threads of pride.

Mavis prayed to the Lord for forgiveness – forgiveness for being born. And as she knelt she heard a whisper from the Taunton girl prostrate beside her, "For what we are about to deliver, may the Lord make us truly thankful." Mavis suppressed a giggle and knew she had found a friend. From then on, they sat down at mealtime to say grace and smiled a cheeky smile at one another.

Only Isaac's letters forwarded on by Pixie and Dollars relieved her gloom. Letters from the pair kept Mavis informed as to their progress regarding a foster place for Pip and, as you can imagine, gave her little pleasure. Mavis held on. Pixie and Dollars sat contentedly in their living room in Etwall Road. Their scheme had gone to plan.

On the sideboard were two unopened envelopes bearing the handwriting of Mavis's mother. Beneath them was another envelope, which Dollars had opened "by mistake". The tone of the letter, which was also addressed to Mavis, they found so vile that they resolved not to send any of Mrs Church's letters on to Cornwall for fear of causing further upset. Besides, Mavis swore that she had ceased replying to her mother's letters. Mavis could receive the open and unopened tyrannous scrolls when she was safely back in Birmingham.

What drove Mrs Church to her next act is hard to say. Perhaps her actions were born of a mother's instincts for her child. Perhaps the mother was driven by despair at losing her child. Perhaps the woman was propelled by that demented desire for self-destruction that seemingly dictated her life.

With no news from her daughter for several months, Mrs Church wrote to Mavis's previous landlady only to be informed that her daughter had departed leaving no forwarding address.

"You could try her school," suggested the landlady, "Her friend from there comes to pick up her letters."

Mrs Church wrote to the school. The head teacher replied that Miss Frampton had been taken sick and, having been ordered to rest, was thought to be in a sanatorium in the countryside. This information, combined with her daughter's failure to respond to her letters, brought on Mrs Church's suspicions that Mavis was deceiving her.

"The little slut is off in Nigeria with that man and they are covering up for her," she thought. A consideration that her daughter might be seriously ill did cross her mind, as did many others including pregnancy. She spoke to Mavis's grandparents in Swindon and wrote to Clyde Frampton. They replied that they were none the wiser, but Mavis had responded to their letters but given no clue as to any problems or illness.

Her suspicions further fuelled, Mrs Church visited Swindon police station.

"I am terribly worried about my daughter's whereabouts and condition. I cannot root out one word from anybody as to her whereabouts. If she really is ill then it is inconceivable that she would not have informed me. I fear that she may have left the country for Nigeria in which case she could come to terrible harm on her own. She is such a sickly thing and it is awful to think that that Nigerian man she was with has dragged her over there. Please do everything in your power to find my child."

The police investigation began. Birmingham police station was contacted and a lone policeman was set on the trail of Miss Frampton, "Missing Believed Abroad".

His enquiries quickly led to 40, Etwall Road.

Dollars invited the policeman in. Her first fears were that Mavis had truly been taken seriously ill, if not worse. She beckoned Pixie, who was knitting in the back garden, and invited the police officer into the living room.

"Please be seated."

"Thank you, madam."

All three were sat down when the police officer began: "I am enquiring as to the whereabouts of Miss Mavis Ann Frampton. I understand that she was staying in your house until recently."

"Has Mavis left the nursing home?" thought the alarmed Pixie.

"If he has come to inform her that someone in her family has died then we are heading for a terrible calamity," thought the equally alarmed Dollars.

"She has been living here, that is true. What is the nature of your enquiry?" responded Dollars, cautious not to give too much away to this man until he had explained himself.

The policeman went on: "The young woman's mother, Mrs Church, has been in touch with us. The mother is very worried that she has had no word from her daughter for six months. Mrs Church said that she has been in contact with the school where her daughter teaches but that they had no word of her whereabouts save that she was ill and resting at a sanatorium in the countryside.

"Mrs Church is of the opinion that this may be true but, while Miss Frampton has been in correspondence with her father and grandparents, they say that she made no mention of any illness. She also believes that her daughter has possibly committed a deception to one and all. She believes that she may have gone to visit a coloured man in Nigeria.

For our part, the station is worried that her daughter may have disappeared altogether."

"Oh dear, Officer!" responded Dollars, "You do not need to be alarmed. Mrs Church really is a troublemaker."

Dollars went on to relate the story of Mavis, her mother and Isaac, finishing with an entreaty to the police officer not to inform Mavis's school or Mrs Church:

"For the good of this young woman and her child, it is better that this information is kept between us and us alone. I think that you can see that, should Mrs Church discover her daughter's situation, no good will come of it. I will inform you of Miss Frampton's whereabouts and you can check it for yourself."

"What shall I say to Mrs Church?" asked the officer.

"It would be most helpful if you simply inform her that her daughter is resting at a sanatorium in the countryside and wants no contact with her mother. We will ensure that Mavis contacts her father and her grandparents to this effect and Miss Johnston will speak to Mavis's head teacher, won't you Pixie?"

Pixie nodded.

"Very well, Miss Dolby, I will make a report to that effect after we have contacted Miss Frampton in Cornwall," replied the police officer, concluding, as he rose to leave, "I don't know what we'll do with all these coloureds coming into the country now."

".... FINALLY PUTTING POLICE TO TRACE MO'S (Mavis – PF) PRESENT WHEREABOUTS. M-GD-MO (Mrs Church - PF) APPEARS TO BE A WOMAN OF VIOLENT PASSIONS AND VINDICTIVE. HER LETTERS TO MO'S ADDRESS IN BIRMINGHAM HAVE NOT YET BEEN PASSED ON TO MO, AS THEY ARRIVED WHEN SHE WAS IN LABOUR; THE LETTERS ARE VERY BITTER AND IT WAS DEEMED PRUDENT TO WITHHOLD THEM FROM MO UNTIL SHE IS ON HER FEET AGAIN. M-GD-MO HAS BEEN SENDING THREATENING LETTERS ABOUT MO TO VARIOUS PEOPLE AND THOUGH POLICE HAVE BEEN TOLD OF MO'S POSITION THEY WILL NOT DIVULGE THE WHOLE FACTS TO M-GD-MO, AS IT WOULD BE FATAL FOR M-GD-MO TO KNOW OF CAND: (Me –PF) OR OF MO'S WHEREABOUTS."

Barnardo's report, 1953

Mavis was duly paid a visit by a policeman from St Agnes police station. The society was quite used to these visits to its fallen angels. A visit would not have been necessary had it not been for the Birmingham police station considering that the scale of deception was so great that the women in Etwall Road might have been sending the police on another trail of fabricated stories. But Mavis was there and the police were satisfied. Mrs Church was informed of her daughter's wishes. That did not stop Mrs Church from declaring that her daughter must be pregnant in the spiteful letters arriving in Birmingham but Mavis and I were saved from any intrusion.

"MAT: GT-GD-PTS (My great grandparents-PF) ARE BOTH OVER 80 AND LIVE IN SWINDON. THEY HAVE BEEN VERY GOOD TO MO AND HAVE BEEN TOLD THAT MO IS STAYING IN THE COUNTRY WITH A BREAKDOWN IN HEALTH."

Barnardo's report, 1953

Mavis was told the details of what the police intended to report to her mother. Of course the very visit stirred The Dreads and, to add to her woes, the society staff put a P against her name, listing her with the most worrisome of their lost flock.

I was to be born Pip. The doctor named July 18th as the day and that day came when Mavis brought me forth. The day of my birth was one of anxiety, confusion and happiness. Mavis was happy that she had finally given birth to her child-thought – and a boy at that. But the scrawny, squawking, wriggling mass in her arms was pink. It wasn't black like Isaac. It wasn't black like the children she had seen in newsreels on Africa. It wasn't black like her black child-thought. The staff looked on with smiles but with pity.

And Mavis knew what they must have been thinking: "Why, he is as white as the seagulls of St Ives!"

She felt at a total loss: "Isaac was the father. He really was. I have made love to no other man in these last five years. What will they think of me! What will Pixie and Dollars think of me!"

Would they ever believe her?

Mavis held me in her arms, then took me to her breast, murmuring: "Oh Pip! Oh Pip!"

"He's so tiny!" remarked one of the nursing staff, "Pip is the right name."

That comment worried Mavis and after a sleep and some pondering, she decided that if her child was to be so small, then people might treat the name Pip with derision. She opted for the closest alternative.

"I will call him Pip, but christen him Phillip, Phillip Roy."

Where she took the second name Roy from and why Phillip had to have two L's, I will never know. But I can guess that Prince Philip had just joined Queen Elizabeth as her consort and too many couples were naming their children after the one-L Prince.

In the washroom, the midwife commented: "These women should call their children Romulus or Remus. They all dump them in the reeds and wait for some wolves to come along and rear them."

"Can you see any of them building Rome?" quipped the doctor.

I would be 21 years old before I would receive my birth certificate from the government records office at Somerset House in London. I read it with some dismay.

"WHEN AND WHERE BORN: EIGHTEENTH JULY 1953, 184 ROSEMUNDY HOUSE, ST AGNES RD, ST AGNES.
NAME, IF ANY: PHILLIP ROY
SEX: BOY
NAME AND SURNAME OF FATHER: -------------------------"

Name and surname of father – Nothing, just a black dash across the page. He was a black line, a nobody, a Father Unknown.

Did Mavis really not know who the father was? Had she slept with others at the time, perhaps a white man? Had her bringing to life a pale skinned scrawny, squawking, wriggling baby, made her wonder whether her great strapping six-foot black giant could be the father?

Some say that she may have withheld Isaac's name from the birth certificate to prevent her mother going to Somerset House and discovering that he was the father. But wouldn't Mavis's situation have been even worse had her mother suspected that Mavis did not even know who the father was?

My guess is that, the doubts of the Moral Welfare staff had led to her being instructed to make her Isaac a dash. The society worthies were happy. To them I was a Romulus.

The society's doubts were to all intents and purposes soon squashed by the summer sunshine. By September, I was a "Half-Caste" child. Who knows what that ever meant? Half-black caste, half-white caste or caste half white and black or not fully caste at all?

"HALF-CASTE WITH BLACK HAIR, SUN-TANNED APPEARANCE. NIGERIAN FEATURES. BORN 5LBS 14½ OZS. BREAST FED. UNTRAINED HABITS."

Barnardo's report, 1953

You might also wonder as to what whoever wrote the report considered to be Nigerian features. I am sure that Mavis insisted that my features were Nigerian and was relieved to see these "facts" written down. Of course, Mavis had little more clue of what most Nigerians looked like than her carers did but these assertions underlined her insistence that her Isaac was the father.

So, I was born a Cornishman, by the sea, a black Cornishman and a black Cornishman in care – in the custody of the Cornish Moral Welfare Society who would probably think no more of my morals now than they did of my mother's.

Mavis informed Isaac who expressed his delight, reading of which gave Mavis great pleasure. His letters and telegrams came in rapid succession. Mavis clung to her dream.

"Dear Dollars,

"The letters, which you have passed on to me from Isaac, have given me so much pleasure. I know you doubt the strength of his feelings, of our feelings, but I can tell you that our correspondence has, since Pip's birth, been so sweet. We are determined to marry after he has saved up enough money to return to this country. He is convinced that, with so many coloured people being taken into employment over here, he will be able to find work and we can build a home for Pip.

"I do still intend to return to teaching and thank you for all that you and Pixie have done. However, I am convinced that Isaac's return will not be long delayed and have no wish for Pip to be adopted or be anywhere where I cannot visit him. Can you help me find a suitable foster placement for him in Birmingham? Otherwise I do not think I will be able to bear being parted from him.

"Pip and I are progressing well and the sooner we can escape from this place of sadness the better. We hope to see you both as soon as you return from your holiday.

Yours truly,
Mavis"

The young mother grew in her affection for her little baby with his tufts of soft curly hair and his skin turning brown, as she always knew it would. After all, he had generous lips like Isaac's lips and a squashed up nose like Isaac's nose. Pity, she thought, that it had her ears, but Isaac would not mind. He would be proud of his son.

"....THEY HOPE TO MARRY WHEN POSSIBLE BUT IT IS FELT THAT THE COLOUR BAR IN NIGERIA WOULD OPERATE HARSHLY AGAINST MO IF SHE WENT THERE. P.FA WAS ON SURVEY COURSE IN MINERAL RESEARCH AND HE WROTE THAT HE WAS EAGERLY AWAITING DETAILS OF CAND: CABLE SENT TO P.FA AND HE WAS VERY THRILLED TO HEAR OF THE ARRIVAL OF CAND: MO HAS BEEN OFFERED TEACHING POST AT A BIRMINGHAM SCHOOL ON 5TH SEPTR, 1953 AND WOULD HAVE TO LIVE IN LODGINGS, SO WOULD BE GLAD IF CAND; COULD BE ADMITTED UNTIL MO AND P.FA CAN BE MARRIED."

Barnardo's Report, 1953

In accordance with Mavis's wishes, the Moral Welfare Society tried to find me a foster home. While I shielded Mavis from the endemic misery of the Home of Sadness, she was unaware of the storm of letters and phone calls that we were generating outside.

The Cornish society soon drew a blank on their search for foster carers in the county. It was impossible, they said, to foster a black child in Cornwall. The good Christians of Cornwall offered not one stable for a coloured child. In the neighbouring county of Devon the doors of the Christian inns were just as strongly bolted.

Dollars turned to plan B, contacting Barnardo's, to whom she wrote a detailed letter requesting that I be found a place in a Barnardo's Home. She felt it important to write the following;

"MISS FRAMPTON HAS NO ONE FROM WHOM SHE CAN EXPECT HELP OR SYMPATHY. SHE HAS KNOWN THE FATHER OF THE BABY FOR SEVERAL YEARS AND IS VERY, VERY ATTACHED TO HIM. SHE HAS ALWAYS TALKED OF THEIR MARRIAGE, IN SPITE OF THE DIFFICULTIES, WITH CERTAINTY.
"I WRITE THIS TO SHOW THAT SHE IS NOT A CASUAL, LOOSE LIVING GIRL WITH NO MORAL SENSE. WE HAVE TRIED TO DISSUADE HER FROM THIS FRIENDSHIP AND MARRIAGE. SHE IS STILL CONVINCED THAT THE BABY'S FATHER WILL KEEP FAITH WITH HER BUT I AM NOT OF THAT OPINION AND FEEL THAT SHE HAS A DIFFICULT TIME AHEAD.
"IF SHE CAN RETURN TO HER WORK AND BE SURE THAT THE BABY IS WELL CARED FOR SHE CAN BECOME A DUTIFUL CITIZEN ONCE MORE."

Dollars, 1953

Dollars was attempting to take my fate out of Mavis's hands. She was convinced that Isaac would not return and stated so. She therefore concluded that I was in for a lengthy stay in care and that Mavis would come around to the idea.

Miss Ackroyd, matron at Rosemundy House for the Cornish Moral Welfare Society had grown fond of the well-spoken music teacher, who had confessed all to her and seemed genuinely repentant and loving of her child. She wrote to Barnardo's in Mavis's favour. A Barnardo's internal memorandum commented on the matron's request:

"THE CANDIDATE WHO IS ILLEGITIMATE IS THE MO'S ONLY DEPENDENT AND I DO NOT THINK WE SHOULD RELIEVE HER OF RESPONSIBILITY. SHE IS A SCHOOLTEACHER AND SHOULD BE ABLE TO SUPPORT THE CHILD WHEN SHE STARTS WORK AGAIN. EFFORTS SHOULD BE MADE TO FIND A FOSTER HOME AND ALTHOUGH I REALISE THAT THIS IS DIFFICULT AS THE BABY IS COLOURED, I DO NOT THINK THAT WE SHOULD MAKE AN EXCEPTION UNLESS OF COURSE ALL EFFORTS TO FIND A FOSTER HOME FAIL."

Barnardo's, 31st July, 1953

A representative for the Barnardo's Chief Executive Officer sent a blunt refusal to Miss Ackroyd at Rosemundy House. However, the letter omitted Barnardo's moral imperatives.

"I HAVE TO INFORM YOU THAT ON THE INFORMATION AT PRESENT BEFORE US, WE CAN FIND NO JUSTIFICATION FOR OFFERING THE CHILD ADMISSION TO THE HOMES. I BELIEVE YOU ARE AWARE THAT IT IS NOT OUR NORMAL PRACTICE TO ADMIT THE ONLY DEPENDENT CHILD OF AN UNMARRIED MOTHER WHO IS CAPABLE OF FOLLOWING EMPLOYMENT, AND THE USUAL FORM OF HELP GIVEN IN SUCH CASES IS BY WAY OF A GRANT TOWARDS THE CANDIDATE'S SUPPORT IN A FOSTER HOME, THE MOTHER PROVIDING THE BALANCE OF THE MONEY REQUIRED OUT OF HER WAGES.

"I REALISE THAT THE MOTHER, BEING A PROFESSIONAL WOMAN IS BOUND TO FEEL HER LAPSE SOMEWHAT HARD, BUT SHE IS OBVIOUSLY FOND OF HER INFANT AND COULD VISIT MORE REGULARLY IF HE WERE FOSTERED.

"MISS FRAMPTON PLANS TO RETURN TO BIRMINGHAM TO WORK, AND IT OCCURS TO ME THAT WHILE YOU HAVE STATED THAT A FOSTER HOME IS NOT KNOWN IN YOUR LOCALITY, YOUR OPPOSITE NUMBER IN BIRMINGHAM COULD POSSIBLY FIND A SUITABLE WOMAN TO HAVE PHILLIP AT A REASONABLE COST."

The representative of the chief executive officer added:

"SINCE HE IS A COLOURED CHILD WE WOULD BE PREPARED TO RECOGNISE A FOSTERING FEE OF £2 PER WEEK INCLUSIVE OF CLOTHING."

Barnardo's, 8th August, 1953

What a misfortune it was to have a black child in those years. Nobody wanted to look after them. Today, some denied, white would-be-fosterers of black children complain that they are being racially discriminated against. In the fifties and early sixties fosterers were paid extra money to entice them to take black children off the hands of the local authorities and charities. Why? Did a black child need more feeding and more clothes? Were the Homes worried that their funds would suffer if there were seen to be too many black faces in the dormitories, black faces that would be difficult to export to the homes in whites-only Australia? It is difficult to say, but the practice of offering more money to fosterers of black children was widespread and racism was no stranger to Barnardo's.

The Barnardo's report form states:

"FULL NAME OF CANDIDATE; ***FRAMPTON, PHILLIP ROY***
GENERAL HEALTH: ***GOOD***
EVER HAD FITS, OR IS SUBJECT TO FITS: ***NO***
HAD MEASLES: ***NO***
SCARLET FEVER: ***NO***
WHOOPING COUGH: ***NO***
DIPTHERIA: ***NO***
IMMUNISED: ***NO***
CHICKEN POX: ***NO***
MUMPS: ***NO***
ANY OTHER PHYSICAL DEFECTS OR MALADIES: ***HALF – CASTE.***

Barnardo's Report, 28th July, 1953

Whether my colour was seen as a physical defect or a malady, I am uncertain. The dictionary defines a malady as: "any unhealthy, morbid or desperate condition."

The Birmingham branch of the Moral Welfare Society was contacted but equally came up with no fostering alternatives. Their search, they said, was restricted because of the mother's expressed concern that the local education authority discover that it was her child, in which case the teacher would lose her job. Barnardo's advised the society to approach the Church of England's Children's Society to see if they would take in the little black baby. The Children's Society also informed them that there was no room at the inn.

On the 31st August, five days before Mavis Ann was due to begin teaching, Colonel Birnie, Secretary of the Children's Society wrote to Barnardo's requesting to know why Barnardo's had refused to entertain my presence.

Mavis grew particularly anxious at the fear that she might lose her job anyway. Dollars crossed her fingers, hoping that Barnardo's would relent. An internal memo written the same day records Barnardo's reluctant capitulation to her wishes:

"URGENT
FRAMPTON
IT SEEMS IMPOSSIBLE TO FIND A FOSTER HOME FOR THE CAND. AND I SHOULD THEREFORE BE WILLING TO MAKE AN EXCEPTION AND ADMIT THE CHILD ALTHOUGH HE IS THE MO'S ONLY DEPENDENT, IN ORDER TO ENABLE HER TO TAKE UP HER TEACHING APPOINTMENT, PROVIDED IT IS NOT NOW TOO LATE. THE RATE OF PAYMENT TO BE FIXED WHEN MO'S SALARY AND EXPENSES ARE KNOWN – ANY PAYMENT FROM THE PUT. FA. TO BE PASSED ON TO US."

Barnardo's Memorandum, 31st August, 1953

The Moral Welfare Society was phoned posthaste and a letter of confirmation was sent to Miss Ackroyd in Cornwall on September 3rd.

"..I AM WRITING NOW TO TELL YOU THAT WE HAVE, ALTHOUGH WITH SOME RELUCTANCE, TO TREAT THE APPLICATION AS SOMEWHAT EXCEPTIONAL AND RECEIVE BABY PHILLIP INTO OUR CARE WHEN WE HAVE A VACANCY TO OFFER. MAY I TELL YOU THAT OUR DECISION TO RECEIVE THE BABY HAS BEEN ARRIVED AT PRIMARILY WITH THE OBJECT OF MAKING IT POSSIBLE FOR MISS FRAMPTON TO TAKE UP HER TEACHING APPOINTMENT."

For the Chief Executive Officer, Barnardo's, 3rd September, 1953

Mavis was informed that she could return to Birmingham and begin her teaching. In the meantime, I was to be kept at Rosemundy House in St Agnes until Barnardo's had secured a place for me in one of their nurseries. Fostering Pip, she was told was impossible. "Unfortunately, he is a coloured child dear."

Dollars's plan had been successful. I wondered when I read her letters why Dollars was so keen on my being placed with Barnardo's when there were other children's homes. An old friend of Mavis's, and one of the few that Mavis trusted with her secret, wrote to me recently:

"AS FOR DR BARNARDO – JUST LIKE YOUR GLOSSY BROCHURES. THE HOMES HAD SUCH A GOOD NAME! 'SHE REALLY IS SO LUCKY TO HAVE HIM IN THERE.' FRIENDS WOULD SAY."

Joanne Marrs, January, 2000

Little did they know or understand.

If I entered the world being unwanted, I was at least "exceptional." Mavis kissed me, thanked Miss Ackroyd for her assistance and left for Birmingham.

Romulus turned and stared at the wolves in their green nylon overalls.

On September 12th, 1953, Mavis signed my life over to the wolves:

"I, MAVIS ANN FRAMPTON....HEREBY AGREE WITH THE ASSOCIATION:
1. TO THE CHILD ENTERING INTO THE CARE OF DR BARNARDO'S HOMES, AND TO THE CHILD BEING BROUGHT UP BY THE ASSOCIATION IN ANY OF ITS BRANCHES, OR IN ANY OF ITS BOARDING HOMES IN THE BRITISH ISLES:
2. TO THE CHILD BEING BROUGHT UP IN THE PROTESTANT FAITH:
3. TO THE ASSOCIATION WITHOUT FURTHER CONSULTATION, TAKING SUCH ACTION IN RESPECT OF THE CHILD AS MAY BE DEEMED NECESSARY IN THE CHILD'S INTERESTS:
4. TO THE ASSOCIATION PLACING THE CHILD WHEN IT DEEMS IT PROPER IN THAT OCCUPATION WHICH IT CONSIDERS BEST FOR THE CHILD:
5. TO ABIDE BY THE RULES OF THE ASSOCIATION, AND TO CO-OPERATE WITH ITS OFFICERS IN THEIR EFFORTS ON THE CHILD'S BEHALF:
6. TO RECEIVE BACK THE CHILD INTO MY CARE IF AT ANY TIME REQUESTED TO DO SO."

Barnardo's form 300624, September 12th, 1953

The witnesses who signed the statement were Pixie and Dollars.

Isaac began to send small amounts of money for my upkeep and his letters continued as frequently as ever. Mavis felt contented, though never ceased to look forward to her next trip to see her Pip. She informed her grandparents and father that she had returned, quite recovered from her illness. She was back in Birmingham and had begun teaching again.

They were pleased for the young woman who had been the cause of so much concern. Mrs Church's fears and ranting had proved groundless, they mused. She had told them that her daughter was pregnant to the African man and that shame would be heaped on the whole family. Little wonder, they said to one another, that Mavis wanted nothing to do with her.

As for my transfer to a Barnardo's home, that was to take some time. Barnardo's accepted me into their care in October. Miss Frampton was ordered to pay them 30 shillings each week for her son's upkeep. But there was still no room in the Barnardo's inn. Hence, in the meantime, they paid for me to be taken in by a nursery in the sleepy village of Instow that sits at the mouth of the River Torridge beside Bideford Bay in Devon.

Mavis moved out of Etwall Road and into new lodgings in Hunton Road, Erdington. Her new teaching post, was not quite what she wished as she was required to teach on the generality of subjects, but she kept herself occupied with musical activities in her spare time. She wrote to Miss Ackroyd at Rosemundy House:

"I STILL DON'T CARE FOR MY SCHOOL JOB – ALTHOUGH I LIKE THE CHILDREN, GENERAL SUBJECT TEACHING IS DEFINITELY NOT MY PARTICULAR SPHERE. HOWEVER, I HAVE PLENTY OF MUSIC AT NIGHT, AS BESIDES MY USUAL CHOIR AND RECORDER ACTIVITIES, I NOW PLAY FOR A VIOLINIST, A SCHOOL OF BALLET DANCING, AND A TEACHER'S TRAINING COLLEGE."

Mavis Frampton, 6th November, 1953

Secure in her employment, happy with her music and confident of Isaac's return and her future marriage, Mavis decided to tell her father of her love for the mining engineer who had turned her past year into a whirlwind of emotions. Mr Frampton had written to his daughter, concerned that she was now well again. His letter begged Mavis to pay him a visit to his Surrey home.

Mavis clutched at the opportunity to see her beloved father once more. She determined to tell her father all and end the suffocating secret between them. Uncertain as to how he would react, Mavis decided to write, stating all that she had been through and see how he would respond. She was delighted with her father's reply. One Dread was slain. Mavis mentioned it in a letter to Miss Ackroyd:

"MY FATHER AND HIS WIFE INVITED ME TO THEIR HOME IN SURREY, BUT I FELT I COULD NOT GO WITHOUT FIRST TELLING THEM THE TRUTH. IT WAS FORTUNATE I DID SO, AS MY MOTHER HAD ALREADY INFORMED THEM IN JULY! THEY DIDN'T INTEND TO MENTION IT UNLESS I DID SO FIRST, BUT I WISHED I HAD CONFIDED IN THEM EARLIER, AS THEY MIGHT HAVE BEEN ABLE TO HAVE HELPED. AREN'T PEOPLE SURPRISING? I WOULD NEVER HAVE BELIEVED MY RELATIONS COULD BE SO CALM, HOW DIFFERENT FROM MY MOTHER. I COULD WEEP WITH RELIEF TO KNOW I HAVE ONE 'SANE' AND REASONABLE PARENT.

Mavis Frampton, November, 1953

Mr Frampton expressed no surprise at the scale of the deception attempted by his daughter. He admitted that he half-believed his former wife's wild stories regarding Mavis. However, he still bore the scars of his former wife's deceitful behaviour and infidelity, and was not inclined to take Mrs Church's ranting too seriously. He explained to Mavis that he had trusted in his daughter telling him everything when she was ready. He was pleased that she loved the child and expressed the hope that she would get her wish and would marry her Isaac.

Mavis wondered whether her mother had really found out about her pregnancy. It was possible that Mrs Church had pressurised the police to tell her. However, Mavis had received no word of any further intrusions into her life by her prying mother and concluded that her secret remained safe.

What of Mr Frampton's reconciliation to Mavis's situation? Would my childhood have taken a different course had Mavis told her father beforehand and not been gagged by her shame? Perhaps, but there was no offer from her father to help look after Pip... or was there? Was Mavis content with the arrangement she now had?

It was two months and school half-term before she could visit her Pip in Tapley Park Nursery. She found the 400-mile return trip to Instow exhausting, even if it was enjoyable. On her return she wrote to Miss Ackroyd:

"LAST WEEKEND WAS OUR MID-TERM HOLIDAY, SO I TRAVELLED DOWN TO INSTOW OVERNIGHT, ON THURSDAY (OWING TO FOG I MISSED ALL THE CONNECTIONS!). THE TAPLEY PARK NURSERY IS A BEAUTIFUL PLACE, BUT TERRIBLY OUT OF THE WAY."

Mavis Frampton, November, 1953

Pip seemed in good spirits but she noticed that her child was developing fast. Leaving him was pain enough but she also feared that her long absences would lead to an estrangement. The letter went on:

"IT WOULD BE WORTH ANYTHING TO FEEL HE WAS MINE AGAIN, IF ONLY FOR A FEW DAYS.......ALTHOUGH PHILLIP SEEMS VERY HAPPY THERE I AM VERY TROUBLED ABOUT THE DISTANCE AND THE FACT THAT I CAN ONLY SEE HIM AT HOLIDAY TIMES. YOU SEE HE IS GROWING SO QUICKLY NOW THAT I AM AFRAID HE WILL FORGET ME. I WOULD DO ANYTHING TO GET HIM NEARER – EVEN IN BIRMINGHAM."

She requested of the Welfare Society matron in St Agnes that she could bring her Pip to stay at Rosemundy House over Christmas. Mavis wrote to Barnardo's to the same effect, also adding a plea that her son be moved to a home closer to Birmingham:

"I CAN ONLY SEE HIM ONCE IN THREE MONTHS – AND I AM SURE THAT YOU WILL APPRECIATE THAT IT IS A LONG TIME IN A BABY'S LIFE! IS THERE ANY HOPE YET OF A TRANSFER, A LITTLE NEARER TO BIRMINGHAM, PLEASE?...HE IS ALL THAT I HAVE.

"I AM HOPING TO HAVE HIM WITH ME IN A FEW YEARS TIME"

Mavis Frampton, November, 1953

Barnardo's duly granted the Christmas visit. In addition, they promised to look into the matter of a transfer closer to Birmingham.

And what was Pip growing into? The Principal at Tapley Park Nursery observed:

"VERY WIDE AWAKE LITTLE FELLOW. QUICK TO NOTICE PEOPLE AND MOVEMENTS. HAPPY NATURE, BUT HAS A HEALTHY PADDY WHICH STOPS IMMEDIATELY HE IS PICKED UP. PHYSICALLY WELL MADE BUT IS INCLINED TO BE CHESTY.
"LIKES TO BE THE CENTRE OF ATTRACTION EVEN AT THIS EARLY STAGE. HABITS NORMAL FOR AGE. WOULD BE SUITABLE FOR BOARDING OUT BUT WOULD STRIVE TO ATTRACT ATTENTION AND WOULD BE VERY EASILY SPOILT. VERY ATTRACTIVE CHILD."

Principal, Tapley Park, December, 1953

Mavis had a child she could love – and a man she loved. The news came through that I would be moved to a Barnardo's home in Shrewsbury, just 43 miles from Birmingham. Mavis was delighted. Dollars had just learned to drive and offered to take Mavis down in the car to Instow and on to Rosemundy House in St Agnes. After Christmas, they returned with Pip, delivering me to Miss Bodell, the matron of my new home in Shrewsbury, Barnardo's Shelton House.

Chapter 5

The Fall

"SHE WAS HOPING TO SAVE UP FOR THEIR HOME UNTIL ALL THAT WENT WRONG."

Dollars, 1968

I was five months old when I arrived at Shelton House, a large attractive mansion built in stone and close to the village of Bicton in Shropshire. Mavis resolved that she would see her Pip every weekend. She asked to see me immediately, explaining that she was still on her school holidays.

The matron, Miss Mary Bodell, was reasonably pleased with what she saw of Miss Frampton. But Mary Bodell was very much a matron. These Barnardo matrons, like Miss Bodell, were mainly of the middle classes and spinsters, who had long given up little white child-thoughts of their own. Mary Bodell was one of the more neurotic of their number.

That they looked down on the fallen women, who had abandoned their children to the Homes, I am certain. Miss Bodell believed that these fallen women and particularly, the la-di-dah, well-to-do ladies had, through their irresponsible behaviour, clearly forfeited the right to dictate the welfare of their children. Indeed, that is what all these mothers had signed away when Barnardo's took in their children.

"Besides, while the mothers might enjoy their visits to see their children, we are the ones who must care for these children when their mothers have left to enjoy their own lives," the matrons would say.

Hence, when after Miss Frampton's first visit to Shelton House, Miss Bodell noticed Miss Frampton's child to be in an irritated condition, the matron concluded that the boy would need some time to settle down without his mother. Mary Bodell reported:

"MISS FRAMPTON CAN VISIT WHENEVER SHE LIKES, BUT PHILIP IS IN A RATHER NERVOUS STATE AND HE SHOULD NOT BE VISITED FOR ONE MONTH."

Mary Bodell, 18th January, 1954

For Mary Bodell, one incident of note that served to paint Mavis in a very bad light that month of January 1955 was the circumstance behind my "christening" and the appointment of my godparents.

When Mavis first applied to Barnardo's she was informed that, to be brought up in the Protestant faith, little Phillip would have to be baptised. Mavis told them that her baby had not been baptised, to which Barnardo's replied that, if so, then they would arrange for the baptism and the appointment of godparents.

Mavis soon changed her story, stating that Phillip had been baptised. Barnardo's demanded the baptismal certificate as proof. For some months Mavis was unable to produce it. Under pressure from Barnardo's she finally sent in a letter. I had, it said, been christened on 27th September 1953 at All Saints Church in the Clifton district of Bristol. Unusually, I had two godmothers. For a boy normally has just one. Nobody knows to this day who or whether there was a godfather.

When I was much older, my godmothers spoke of my being christened in Bristol and sent me a copy of the certificate. However, to my knowledge, there is no one around who can remember the christening. Nobody can assert that it took place.

Because I was told that I had been christened in Bristol, for 30 years I assumed that I must have spent that autumn in a home in Bristol. For who is baptised in a church who does not live within its parish?

However, there is no record of Mavis, myself or my godmothers living in Bristol. Nor is there any record of baby Phillip being taken out of Rosemundy House to be christened 120 miles away. Mavis could not possibly have managed in one weekend to travel 200 miles to St Agnes, the 240-mile return journey to Bristol and then 200 miles to Birmingham to be ready to teach on the Monday morning.

My belief is that the christening never took place. This is the real story. In all the upset of leaving her stay and her child in St Agnes and taking up her new teaching appointment, Mavis omitted to secure the christening and informed Barnardo's that I had not been christened.

After some time, when I had reached Tapley Park Nursery in Devon, Barnardo's wrote to Mavis stating that they would arrange for Phillip's baptism and appoint his godparents. The matter was then dropped. It was Mary Bodell at Shelton House who reraised the matter with Barnardo's headquarters and Mavis:

"IS TAPLEY PARK NURSERY A BARNARDO HOME OR NOT? I UNDERSTAND FROM HIS MOTHER THAT HE HAS BEEN BAPTISED BUT THERE IS NO RECORD OF IT IN HIS PAPERS."

Mary Bodell, 18th January, 1954

Barnardo's wrote to Mavis:

"WE HAVE NO INFORMATION IN OUR RECORDS OF PHILLIP HAVING BEEN BAPTISED, AND I SHOULD BE GLAD TO HEAR FROM YOU WHETHER THIS TOOK PLACE."

Mavis panicked at the idea that her Pip should have strangers as godparents and relayed her fears to Dollars. Initially, Mavis stated that her child had been christened in November but at the time I was in Tapley Park, already in Barnardo's care and there was no record of Mavis taking me anywhere, least of all to be christened:

"DEAR MADAM,
PHILLIP FRAMPTON WAS CHRISTENED WHILE HE WAS AT A NURSERY IN BRISTOL, BEFORE HE WAS ACCEPTED BY YOU. I AM AFRAID I HAVE NOT GOT HIS BAPTISM CERTIFICATE WITH ME, AND SO I CANNOT GIVE YOU THE EXACT DATE. AS FAR AS I CAN REMEMBER IT WAS SOMETIME LAST NOVEMBER, BUT I WILL GIVE YOU ACCURATE DETAILS IF THEY ARE NECESSARY, IF YOU WILL LET ME KNOW."

Mavis Frampton, 21st January, 1954

One can imagine Mary Bodell's reaction, "Could this woman really not remember her own child's christening?" That was my reaction too.

Barnardo's replied:

"WILL YOU KINDLY LET US KNOW THE DATE AND PLACE WHERE THE BAPTISM TOOK PLACE?"

Barnardo's letter, 26th January, 1954

Mavis told Dollars and Pixie that she wanted them to be Pip's godmothers in case anything happened to her. She confessed that she had made a terrible mistake in telling Miss Bodell anything. Dollars agreed to be Pip's godmother but suggested that Mavis's "Old Chelt" friend, Martha Watson, be the other. Martha was by then living in London and, anyway, Mavis could always count on Pixie's support.

Deception was the order of the day and Dollars once more stepped in to aid her unfortunate friend. Oh what a tangled web we weave!

The headmistress searched her address book for kindly ecclesiastical contacts that might be in touch with a sympathetic vicar. Eventually, she was led to a worldly-wise canon in Clifton, Bristol. He agreed to christen Pip "in absentia." She told Mavis that he was the nearest one available. The cleric agreed to Dollars's proposal, prayed for forgiveness for his big white lie and arranged for Mavis's child to be given a backdated baptismal certificate by proxy. The baptismal certificate recorded that I was christened Phillip Roy on September 27th, 1953. My godparents were announced as Dollars and Martha Watson. Mavis only then was able to provide Barnardo's with her "proof." Last year, I contacted the church and was informed that I was on the records. There were no other details as to who was in attendance.

"PHILLIP WAS BAPTISED ON 27TH SEPTEMBER, 1953 AT ALL SAINTS, CLIFTON, BRISTOL."

Mavis Frampton, 30th January, 1954

Miss Bodell read through my records. Whether she believed that Miss Frampton had deceived her or whether the matron concluded that Miss Frampton was slapdash with regard to the welfare of her child is uncertain. Whichever way, Mavis fell heavily in Miss Bodell's esteem.

Mavis began visiting me regularly once the one-month's grace had passed. Every Sunday she came down, often with Dollars, Pixie or other close friends to visit me.

Mary Bodell became increasingly irritated by the well-spoken women, who giggled and chatted and stayed as long as they could to play with the mother's child then left him to be washed and fed for another week.

"Miss Frampton in particular," she thought, "gives herself far too many airs and graces for a woman with the shame she bears. She even called her child Phillip with two Ls when everybody knows that Philip only has one L. The poor child! Whilst he's in my care, he will have just one. He will be Philip."

What Mavis's friends found at Shelton House was not quite the image that Mavis had given them. One of her friends who visited wrote later:

"WHEN I WENT WITH YOUR MOTHER TO SEE YOU, I WAS SADDENED THAT BABIES SHOULD BE SITTING – JUST SITTING – IN THEIR CRIBS WITH SEEMINGLY NOTHING TO DO. EVIDENCE OF JOY OR AFFECTION SEEMED TO BE COMPLETELY LACKING.
"THE MATRON, AN UNEDUCATED WOMAN, OBVIOUSLY LOOKED DOWN HER NOSE AT THIS UNWED MOTHER WHOSE VISITS COMPLETE WITH GUESTS, SHE REGARDED AS HIGHLY INCONVENIENT. I JUST WISH I COULD TELL YOU THAT WE TRIED TO CHANGE THINGS BUT WE DIDN'T."

Joanne Marrs, January, 2000

But Mavis was oblivious to the matron's irritation:

"Surely the matron should understand that the child needs to spend as much time as it can with his mother?" Mavis would say later.

Mavis felt so much happier and wrote to Isaac informing him of the new situation and their son's progress. Isaac replied with his customary affection though his financial contributions had dried up. The couple remained determined to be reunited as soon as the engineer had saved up enough money to return and he wrote of how they could not wait to end their involuntary separation.

In March, Miss Bodell put an end to Mavis's weekly visits reporting:

"THESE VISITORS ON A SUNDAY ARE RATHER A NUISANCE – WE ARE USUALLY SHORT OF STAFF IN ANY CASE, PLUS THE FACT OF HAVING TO DO OUR OWN COOKING, AND OF GETTING CHILDREN OFF TO THEIR VARIOUS SUNDAY SCHOOLS LIFE IS HECTIC. WHEREAS THE MOTHER CAN VISIT ON ANY OTHER DAY, ...WE HAVE TO PUT UP WITH THE VISITS BUT MISS FRAMPTON AND HER FRIENDS DO SEEM TO GET UNDER OUR FEET. I AM LETTING YOU KNOW THIS IN CASE MISS FRAMPTON WRITES TO YOU, AS I THINK THAT SHE MIGHT..."

Mary Bodell, 10th March, 1954

It was Miss Ackroyd, the matron at Rosemundy House, who wrote in on Mavis's behalf saying that Mavis: "was unhappy about her visits to Shelton House and that she has been made to feel unwelcome by the Superintendent."

Barnardo's regional headquarters found in the Shelton House matron's (matrons were officially called Superintendents) favour. From visiting me every week for seven hours, Mavis was told that her visiting hours would henceforth be restricted to 150 minutes every alternate Sunday. The thread was weakening.

Mavis and her friends continued to visit through the spring into early summer. At the end of the summer term, she would, she told her friends, take Pip on holiday with her. "Just to spend a fortnight with him would be a dream," she declared. Once she had organised places where we both could stay, she wrote for permission from Barnardo's. Permission was granted but something happened that summer to end the dream.

I believe that the letter arrived from Isaac, the letter she never imagined would come through her door:

"Dear Mavis,

It is with great sadness and regret that I must tell you that my family has prevailed. I am to be married next year to a woman from my country. For sometime my family have been insisting that I have responsibilities here and that I cannot fail them in my duties. They are most adamant.

Please look after our Pip.

Your ever loving Isaac"

Mavis collapsed on her bedroom floor and 43 miles away I started to cry. I had lost my father. Mavis had lost her husband-thought, her lover, and hope. This time Mavis shed no tears. There was nowhere for them to go. There were no sobs. There were no ears to hear. All life was still, as dead as Mavis wished she were.

The blow was stunning, devastating, debilitating. The dream she had clung to, that had kept her alive and helped her to resist The Dreads, had vanished.

Whether Isaac was telling the truth about his family or not, I do not know. Whether he had lost heart in the prospect of returning to England or of returning to Mavis is also uncertain. Whichever way, the blow was decisive.

In the days that followed Mavis awoke, ate, taught and talked in a daze. The jilted lover was consumed in grief. Soon The Dreads began to circle once more, menacing, devouring Mavis's will to live, will to be a mother, will to embrace any pleasing thought lest it crumble in her hand.

She told Pixie and Dollars. They shook their heads and told her that perhaps it was for the best, that she would meet someone else and that she must think of Phillip and keep going. And she nodded her head and told herself: "I must keep going."

Her friends' kind words floated through her. There was no place for them to land. All the co-ordinates of her world had been tossed into the air. Certainty, probability and possibility became untraceable.

Distraught, the young teacher became listless. The days drifted by. She lost the holiday venues she had chosen through lack of desire to pick up a phone or write a letter. She summoned up strength for her Pip, picked new venues but lost them as well. It was only with the utmost effort that she managed to find a place to take me.

Barnardo's received letters from Mavis declaring that we were due to stay in Shropshire and Caernarfon, then in Shropshire and in Cornwall, then in Devon and finally near Stratford-Upon-Avon. She changed the dates from mid July to late July, to late August and finally, to July 29th.

Mavis collected me from Shelton House on July 28th. Again Mavis had changed our holiday stay. She informed Miss Bodell that we would not now be staying in the house near Stratford but in Stourton Manor at Shipston-On-Stour.

I have neither recollection nor knowledge of what transpired between my mother and me on that holiday, but I can only conclude that we were both in a state of distress. Of my condition on my return to Shelton House, the matron wrote:

"THE CONDITION OF PHILIP WAS NOT AT ALL SATISFACTORY WHEN HE RETURNED FROM HIS HOLIDAY WITH HIS MOTHER. HE SUFFERED FROM DIARRHOEA AND VOMITTING, AND HAD A LUMP IN HIS GROIN, DUE THE DOCTOR THOUGHT TO A STRAIN FROM PROBABLY BEING LEFT TO CRY FOR TOO LONG. ALL OF WHICH HAS HOWEVER RESPONDED QUICKLY TO TREATMENT. WE HAVE NOT GET HIS CLOTHES BACK TO A GOOD CLEAN COLOUR YET. HE HIMSELF DOES NOT APPEAR TO HAVE BEEN UPSET EMOTIONALLY IN ANY WAY."

Mary Bodell, 26th August, 1954

The two months that followed Isaac's letter were the saddest in Mavis's life. But she survived. As her friends said, she had to for her Pip. The new school year began and Mavis found herself being taken out by Pixie and Dollars to concerts and picture houses - that was when she had the time, for Mavis got back into her evening musical activities and still had to visit her Pip regularly. The joy of the visits had gone. The sight of Pip was the sight of her lost dream, her abandonment, my abandonment. After each trip The Dreads returned, dragging Mavis down to a terrible sadness.

But Mavis still loved her child. I was growing. By January of the following year I was one and a half years old. Miss Bodell filled in her annual report:

"FRAMPTON, PHILIP ROY.
HEIGHT: 30 INCHES WEIGHT: 23½LBS
HALF CASTE CHILD, DARK LARGE HEAD, SPINDLY LEGS, DARK SKINNED, HEALTH IMPROVED. WASHING.
MOTHER VISITS REGULARLY.
PHILIP HAS IMPROVED BEYOND ALL RECOGNITION. HE IS WASHING AND HAS SOME SPEECH. HE IS OF AVERAGE INTELLIGENCE. HE CAN BE VERY STRONG WILLED AND IS NOT FRIGHTENED OF ANYTHING OR ANYBODY."

Mary Bodell, January, 1955

Sometime late in 1954 or early in 1955, Mavis met a Norwegian student who in college went by the name of PK and, for propriety's sake, I will call him that or Mr Kay. Mavis found PK to be both kind to her and amusing. "In that respect," she told herself, "he is like Isaac. And PK is foreign too. But otherwise he is quite the opposite. Isaac towered above me whereas PK is smaller than me. Isaac was handsome. Isaac knew of the world and the arts."

Her liaison with PK eventually re-established the child-thought in Mavis's head.

The white child-thought returned but this time without the gleaming silver Bentley and balmy honeymoon in the West Indies. This time, she told herself, she would settle for a bicycle and a honeymoon in Bournemouth. And Mavis cherished the new white child-thought which soothed the wounds caused by The Dreads. But it sent her into mental anguish. Of that I am sure. Her mind would wash from left to right, forwards and backwards as she dealt with the most agonising of decisions whose shoots were sprouting as rapidly as the white child-thought.

All the while, Mavis sent in her monthly cash payments for my upkeep to Barnardo's. If I could, I would invite you to follow the monthly dramatic changes to Mavis's signature. From June 1954 until

June 1955 my mother's signature, always dashed out with a fountain pen, changed a dozen times. The F was printed, the F was embellished. The F pointed forward, the F pointed backwards. Curled, straight, it told of a mind in turmoil.

It was when Mavis began looking forward to seeing PK that she realised that she might fall in love again. This time she told herself to be more careful and allowed him only to court her in the most formal manner. In time, she grew more and more fond of the Norwegian student. But the student was not rich and he could not afford to help her look after Pip. And would he want Pip anyway and if he didn't what would she do?

Mavis went to the counsel of Etwall Road for advice:

"I really do feel I love him and I think that he is in love with me. But he is only a student and being in architecture will not earn money for some time. I have told him about Pip and he doesn't seem to think the less of me. But I am worried that he seems increasingly frustrated with my trips to Shrewsbury. We see little of each other as it is, what with my teaching, my music practice, my piano playing and tutoring."

"You are very lucky, Mavis," responded Dollars, "to have found someone new so quickly and it seems this young man will have fine prospects. However, as you rightly say, you must face up to the situation with Pip and your feelings for your child."

Dollars went on: "Frankly, I think that first you must decide whether you love this young man. If you do and you wish to marry him, will you want to take Pip in with you? You have to consider what taking Pip into your home would mean in regard to your job and the complications it might bring for your husband also.

"That is, of course, whether the young man would want to have the child in your joint home, particularly when you will have a small income between you. Personally, I cannot see him wishing to father another man's child, and a coloured one at that. If you really do love this man and you wish to marry him then you will have to make a choice between the two."

"You will have to have the child adopted," added Pixie.

The choice was put starkly. Mavis could stay with the child she loved and lose the young man she loved or go with the man and lose the child. At home, Mavis lay on her bed in mental agony, searching for the safe middle ground:

"Did life have to be so beastly? Why, if he loves me, can he not love my child? Does he really love me for what I am, a mother, or for what he wants to see in me? Of course Pip is not his child but Pip is part of me? Would I really lose my job if Pip were returned to me? We could make up a story that we had adopted him. I could take up other work. So could PK. But am I right to ask him to give up his career for me, for Pip?" The questioning went on:

"How will Pip fare with that horrid Miss Bodell? He would have to be adopted and then what will he think of me when he is older, when he knows that I abandoned him?"

She remembered Dollars's final words: "There are not two but three choices here, my dear. You must choose not only between Pip and PK. You must consider yourself and what is best for you."

It was that choice between her and myself that shook Mavis's handwriting, that straightened then twirled her F's, that twisted and stretched the cross of her T's and shortened and lengthened the twirl of her L's. By May 1955, the tempest was subsiding. In that calm I was set adrift. The words hurt. They were recorded over 40 years ago and left on paper to ferment into a bitter brew of angst, regret, selfishness, callousness and myopia.

I turned the pages and the brew exploded before my eyes. Once:

"LETTER FROM MISS LITTLE, MWW BIRMINGHAM STATING MOTHER WONDERS COULD WE PLACE PHILIP ON ADOPTION LIST, SHE CANNOT SEE ANY POSSIBILITY OF HAVING CHILD WITH HER AND REMAINING A TEACHER, SHE IS ALSO CONSIDERING MARRIAGE WITH A NORWEGIAN, WHO IS ALREADY JEALOUS OF THE CHILD. MOTHER REALISES SHE MUST CHOOSE BETWEEN THE CHILD AND THE NORWEGIAN."

Barnardo's report, 1955

Again:

"MOTHER FEELS SHE WILL NEVER BE ABLE TO HAVE HIM HOME. SHE IS CONSIDERING MARRIAGE TO A NORWEGIAN WHO IS JEALOUS OF PHILLIP."

Letter to Barnardo's, May, 1955

Again:

"SHE USED TO VISIT REGULARLY, BUT ON LAST VISIT ON ABOUT JULY/55 SHE SAID, 'WOULD I GET PHILIP ADOPTED SINCE SHE WAS GOING TO GET MARRIED AND DID NOT WANT PHILIP ANYMORE'. ORIGINALLY SHE WAS COMPLAINING THAT WE DID NOT ALLOW HER TO VISIT ENOUGH."

Miss Bodell, December, 1955

Again:

"MOTHER HAS NOW DISCONTINUED VISITS, HAS STATED THAT SHE WAS GETTING MARRIED AND DID NOT WANT ANYTHING MORE TO DO WITH PHILIP."

Miss Bodell, December, 1955

And Again:

"14TH JULY, 1955

"DEAR MATRON,
I AM VERY SORRY THAT I WAS UNABLE TO COME AND SEE PHILLIP (FRAMPTON) TODAY, BUT I HAVE BEEN IN A TERRIBLE STATE WITH HAY FEVER FOR THE LAST TWO DAYS. PLEASE WISH HIM A HAPPY BIRTHDAY FROM ME.
"I DON'T KNOW WHETHER YOU WILL KNOW FROM HEAD OFFICE, BUT I HOPE TO MARRY A NORWEGIAN (SOMETIME!) AND HAVE COME TO THE CONCLUSION THAT, IF POSSIBLE, THE BEST PLAN WOULD BE TO HAVE PHILLIP ADOPTED. I FEAR THERE IS LITTLE CHANCE OF THIS HAPPENING BUT I CAN SEE NO FUTURE WITH US TOGETHER, AS AT THE MOMENT I WOULD ALMOST CERTAINLY LOSE MY JOB AND MY NORWEGIAN FRIEND IS TOO JEALOUS TO ADOPT HIM, WHICH I CAN UNDERSTAND.
"I SHALL BE GOING TO NORWAY TO MEET MY FRIEND'S PARENTS AT THE END OF THIS WEEK, BUT I WILL COME AND SEE PHILLIP AS SOON AS I RETURN.
"YOURS SINCERELY,
"M.FRAMPTON"

I read the words and fell from the peaks of respect for my mother and PK, to anger. This man I still knew. Or you might say that I thought I knew him. He had made me a cuckold, as much a cuckold as had been her father before me. But I was not a man. I was a little boy, not yet two years old. He had forced her to choose, forced her to abandon me to the wolves and robbed me of my mother. Of such discoveries are human tragedies made. Little wonder that he had never sought me out, never made one effort to safeguard the future of his wife's love-child.

Then came my feelings of sorrow, my recognition of human frailty and jealousy. Rather than lose her chance of marriage, of feeling wanted again by another and making real her white child-thought, it was Mavis who had cut me adrift.

She had given: "all that I have" for another, swapped me for a new toy, tossed the one-eyed golliwog back into the cupboard and left me to be buried beneath the other unwanted toys.

As for her prospective partner one wonders whether he really did make her choose. Jealous of a two-year-old child! You might understand. I do not. In my anger I wrote confronting him with her damning words. He denied all: "I left Mavis to make the decision." The court will never sit.

Despite his denial, Mavis asserted that he was jealous, time and time again. Why? Because a mother knows? Perhaps it was the fact that he never offered to accompany her on her visits to see me. Perhaps it was the way he sometimes appeared to resent her leaving his side to go to Pip or the time she might have spent knitting or shopping for her son. Those "little things" would cross her mind. Those "little things" would chew her up with anxiety.

There were other considerations as to how his family might react to their son having a black stepchild and how they would face up to a world that might react in a hostile manner. Faced with the prospect of her continuing visits while he was sitting at home thinking white child-thoughts, was Mavis too frightened to confront her lover with the issues?

If, as he said, he left her to make the decision, Mavis would have had to read her partner's mind. She would have guided herself with that mother's intuition and drawn her conclusion. Or did she invent PK's jealousy for Barnardo's ears and hope that her lover would never read her words?

"What could he do?" the old ones say, "You were not his child."

Whose child was I? Nobody's.

Nevertheless, the attraction Mavis felt at the prospect of lifting the pressures of those secret trips to Shelton House and all the other burdens that were the consequences of her young foolishness triumphed. The prospect of a new "respectable" life had become irresistible.

Whether hay fever struck or not, Mavis was too frightened of herself to go and say goodbye to her Pip, to see him and know that she would not see him again. She was too ashamed to tell the matron that she would never see her child again. She had cut her Pip's umbilical cord and left me and her past dreams to drift off into an uncertain world.

It all seemed so brutal for Miss Frampton's child.

Mavis would never return, would never face up to the final goodbye. Are not so many of us like that, so fearful of our emotions at the decisive hour, so fearful that we pretend that the decisive hour has not arrived? Then we look back and realise that terrible moment has passed without us knowing and we breathe a sigh of relief. In armies people are shot for it. In our lives it corrodes our spirit, eats into our strength.

As to her Pip's future, Mavis was informed that the likelihood of a black child being adopted was doubtful in the extreme:

"I FEAR A NIGERIAN HALF CASTE IS ALMOST IMPOSSIBLE TO FIND ADOPTERS FOR. SO SORRY."

Barnardo's letter, 26th May, 1955

Barnardo's however said that, given that adoption would be impossible for such a poor specimen of humanity, I would have to stay in the home. Miss Bodell, at Shelton House, in triumph wrote:

"I AM ENCLOSING A LETTER WHICH I RECEIVED FROM PHILIPS MOTHER WHICH I THINK EXPLAINS ITSELF. IT IS RATHER IRONICAL IN VIEW OF THE FUSS THAT MISS FRAMPTON HAS MADE IN THE PAST. I DO NOT THINK THAT DR. LONGMORE WOULD AGREE TO ADOPTION, SINCE PHILIP IS SUCH A POOR SPECIMEN OF HUMANITY AND THERE IS SOME DOUBT OVER HIS INTELLIGENCE. HE WOULD PROBABLY THRIVE IN THE RIGHT B O HOME..."

Mary Bodell, 25th July, 1955

I laughed when I read that I was considered a "poor specimen of humanity" with "doubts over his intelligence." Yet, I must tell you that there are many children who have been in care and labelled as "educationally sub-normal" and left to rot. Among this number there are also many that have gone on to university, defying the prejudices of their carers.

But this poor, thick specimen was now Barnardo's problem.

PK had invited Mavis to travel with him to visit his parents in Norway. That, she thought, was proof enough of his love. At the same time a letter arrived from Isaac informing her of his marriage during Whitsuntide. Isaac had moved on. Mavis had moved on. All that was left of their encounter was a little black boy.

Sailing across the North Sea during that summer of 1955 was, to Mavis, a joyful symbol of her new beginnings. Try as she did however, she could not put her Pip far from her thoughts. She hoped and prayed that he would be found a good home. The one thing that she never did on that trip was portray her thoughts to her lover. PK was happy. She had made her decision and it was in his favour. He was now master of her affections and Mavis was loved.

Mavis enjoyed a wondrous journey across the mountains and fjords of Norway. Her lover's family lived in the northern city of Trondheim and, during that summer, darkness never seemed to fall.

By the end of August she was bewitched by her new beginnings. She wrote to my godmother, Martha Watson, who by now was working in Southern Rhodesia:

"I SPENT THE WHOLE OF MY SUMMER HOLIDAY IN NORWAY AND FIND IT A WONDERFUL COUNTRY. HIS PARENTS WENT TO LAPPLAND 12 DAYS BEFORE US SO WE WENT ROUND BY BOAT TO MEET THEM. WHAT A WONDERFUL 12 DAYS WITH A WHOLE HOUSE TO OURSELVES...NOTHING CAN COMPARE WITH THESE MOUNTAINS, ON WHICH I NATURALLY SPRAINED AN ANKLE. THEY ARE REALLY BREATHTAKING ESPECIALLY THOSE THAT STILL HAVE SOME SNOW ON TOP. WHEN I FIRST CAME HERE IT WAS LIGHT ALL NIGHT – MOST STRANGE, BUT WE WERE NEVER IN BED TILL 2 OR 3A.M...

"I FEEL COMPLETELY OUT OF TOUCH WITH ENGLAND NOW AND HAVE NOT THE SLIGHTEST WISH TO GO BACK. I SHOULD LIKE TO LIVE IN NORWAY AND PROBABLY – NO! I'M AFRAID TO SAY ANYTHING. LIFE HAS BEEN SO GOOD THE LAST FEW MONTHS. I'M AFRAID SOMETHING IS BOUND TO HAPPEN TO GO WRONG."

It was a long, long letter in which Mavis gossiped about their mutual friends, Elizabeth, Perry Cox, Pixie, Dollars, Barbara and Don. Of the child she had left behind, she merely said:

"BEFORE I FORGET, PIP IS FINE AND MANY THANKS FOR THE BIRTHDAY GIFT – I'M OPENING A SAVINGS ACCOUNT FOR HIM WITH IT. ISAAC WAS MARRIED THIS WHIT. AND STEVE (REMEMBER HIM?) HAS WRITTEN TO ASK HIM TO DO SOMETHING ABOUT PIP."

Mavis, 31st August, 1955

She made no mention of the fact that her Pip would never see her or, for that matter, the Savings Account again.

The only blot on the Norway visit was PK's father's refusal to countenance the couple's marriage while PK's studies were being paid for by his parents. But PK was determined to marry his true love and said that he would seek a loan from the government to cover his education and secure his father's consent. Mavis returned to England and back to teaching and the world as it was before Pip had turned it upside down. She was free – well almost.

In turn, Mavis took PK to visit her grandparents and her Uncle Reg. Now Uncle Reg was an eccentric character. None of the neighbours thought too much of the man in the dirty old raincoat who lived in the rundown house in their corner of Swindon. He was polite but hardly said a word to them. All they knew was that he would leave his house early in the morning with a suitcase and that he never returned till late at night.

Uncle Reg actually left early in the morning with his suitcase to take a train to London. On the train he took out his three-piece suit ventured to the toilet and changed. The man in the dirty old raincoat was off to the Stock Exchange to chance his arm. He made a fortune.

He used part of this fortune to secretly build a mansion for his equally secret mistress. As soon as PK could drive, his job was to take Uncle Reg to inspect construction work on the folly.

"I would drive and Uncle Reg would sit in the back. No one must see that Uncle Reg was inspecting the site in case they suspected him of involvement. He cut two holes out of a newspaper and, as we passed the building site, he would lift up the paper and peer through it to inspect the workmen's progress."

Mavis was truly back in the comfort zone.

"It's for the best," said Pixie and Dollars.

In preparation for her intended marriage, Mavis then requested, on account of the marriage and PK's situation, that Barnardo's drop their insistence on her weekly payments of 30 shillings for her Pip.

The Chief Executive Officer for the Barnardo's region wrote sympathetically to her head office:

"SHE HAS HAD A ROUGH PASSAGE THROUGH LIFE AND IN VIEW OF THIS AND HER FUTURE PLANS COULD WE REDUCE HER PAYMENT TO – SAY A NOMINAL 5/- OR 2/6 PER WEEK FOR THE NEXT 6 – 8 MONTHS IN THE FIRST PLACE."

Miss Merrison, 16th January, 1957

Miss Merrison added:

"I SEE A GOOD MANY SNAGS IN THE WAY AFTER MARRIAGE OWING TO FATHER'S JEALOUSY BUT CAN WE LEAVE THAT FENCE UNTIL WE GET TO IT."

Of Miss Frampton's situation and marriage, Miss Merrison opined:

"IT IS OF THE MOTHER'S CHOOSING, AND I DO FEEL THAT SHE IS EXTREMELY FORTUNATE IN THAT THE GRANDPARENTS HAVE ALREADY GIVEN HER THE MONEY TO PUT DOWN FOR THE PURCHASE OF A HOUSE.

"WE DO FEEL THAT THE MOTHER'S FIRST DUTY SHOULD BE TO HER CHILD, AND ALTHOUGH WE WISH TO HELP HER, AND WILL DO SO ONCE SHE IS MARRIED, WE REALLY DO NOT FEEL THAT WE CAN, IN EFFECT, FURNISH HER HOUSE FOR HER, PARTICULARLY AS THERE WILL BE NO PLACE IN IT FOR PHILIP, ONCE SHE HAS ESTABLISHED HERSELF THERE."

Miss Merrison, 9th March, 1957

Mavis's weekly payments were finally ordered to be reduced to 10/- in the event of her marriage. One year later, on July 25th 1957, Mavis Frampton became Mavis Kay. Her grandparents, my great grandparents, had given her the money to buy a house and the two happily settled down with their white child-thoughts at 38, Central Avenue in the Northfield district of Birmingham. PK was still studying at the Birmingham School of Architecture and life would be hard.

In July 1956, one of my godmothers, Martha Watson, visited me in Shelton House. She added a request that she be allowed to take Pip on holiday that summer. Miss Bodell remained extremely suspicious and rather contemptuous of Miss Frampton and her friends, none of which had bothered to visit for one year. The request was turned down.

July 8th, 1955 was the last time that any of the characters around Mavis would ever see the child Pip. They were out of my life.

Miss Bodell seemed quite content that it should be so. In December 1955 she reported on her charge, Phillip Frampton and, true to her oath she continued to write his name with one L since it was preposterous to give him two:

"FRAMPTON, PHILIP ROY
SMALL, THIN, HALF CASTE NEGROID BUT VERY PALE COFFEE COLOURED
PHILIP HAS MADE EXCELLENT PROGRESS PHYSICALLY AND MENTALLY. HE IS STILL VERY THIN – BUT APPEARS WELL. HIS SPEECH IS EXCELLENT."

Miss Bodell, December, 1955

And as she stared at her coffee, it appeared a little too dark for "Philip." So the matron added a little more milk and it was just right. "In the summer he will go terribly dark again," the matron noted, "I must remember to add a little less milk."

Miss Bodell decided that the small, thin, half-caste, Negroid, very pale, coffee-coloured boy was not ready to be put up for either adoption or fostering. But I was making progress from being the dark-skinned, spindly legged, half-caste, poor specimen of humanity with doubts about his intelligence, of six months previous. By March of 1956, the matron was prepared to describe me as ready for fostering and:

"BROWN SKINNED AND CURLY HAIR, THIN AND ATTRACTIVE.
"MEDICAL NOTES: HALF CASTE NEGRO.
TEMPERAMENT: A VERY GOOD TEMPERED LITTLE BOY - VERY POPULAR WITH OTHER CHILDREN – TALKS WELL, VERY AFFECTIONATE.
APPEARS OF AVERAGE INTELLIGENCE."

Mary Bodell, 12th March, 1956

Ten months later, Mary Bodell still considered the "very happy little boy" to be "too thin." She added:

*"APPEARS INTELLIGENT AND CAN BE QUITE OBSTINATE.
PROGRESS AT SCHOOL: EXCELLENT – GOOD POWER OF CONCENTRATION AND HAS IMAGINATION
MUSICAL, MOTHER IS L.R.A.M., SHOULD BOARD OUT WELL – BUT IS HALF NEGRO WHICH MAY BE A HANDICAP.
HAS MADE EXCELLENT PROGRESS – A NORMAL, INTELLIGENT CHILD"*

Miss Bodell, January, 1957

The matron almost gleefully commented on her former adversary's lack of interest in the child:

"CONTACT WITH BROTHERS AND SISTERS IN OUR CARE, WITH PARENTS AND OTHER RELATIONS: NONE THIS YEAR UNTIL MOTHER WAS REPEATEDLY ASKED TO WRITE – WHEN SHE SENT XMAS PRESENT."

It was to be the last Xmas present that I would ever receive from my mother.

Barnardo's headquarters were keen to see me "Boarded Out", which to them meant a range of situations including adoption, fostering and, for the elder children, lodgings. Their efforts, from the middle of 1956, to effect my placement all came to nought, as they had expected they would: "Who on earth wants to have a half Negro, coffee coloured poor specimen of humanity in their home?"

Actually, there were six people who came forward, all of whom were subsequently deemed unsuitable. Miss Bodell had grown fond of her little black boy, and was in no mood to give him up easily. She turned down two would-be foster parents herself and requested that headquarters place the boy close to Shelton House in the hope that she could still watch over him while she added milk to her coffee.

By February 1957, her superiors in Barnardo's were despairing of finding a home for the boy. Nowadays, the media treat advertising for homes for unwanted children as a novelty. But in the fifties placing appeals for would-be foster parents in the press was already a practice for last-ditch attempts to board out particular children.

Barnardo's ordered an advertisement to be placed in the personal columns of the *Uttoxeter News* and *Derby Evening Telegraph* regarding another black child and myself. My unwanted existence was made public:

"PHILLIP AGED 3½ AND ALICE AGED 6 MONTHS, LITTLE COLOURED CHILDREN WITH NO RELATIVES IN TOUCH ARE BADLY IN NEED OF A HOME AND INDIVIDUAL AFFECTION. MAINTENANCE AND CLOTHING ALLOWANCE PAID. WILL ANYONE HELP? APPLY TO WESTERN AREA, DR. BARNARDO'S HOMES, 18 STEPNEY CAUSEWAY, E.1."

Barnardo's letter, 22nd February, 1957

Eight weeks later and there was still no take-up of the advertisement. It seemed that the coffee-coloured boy would have to spend the rest of his childhood in a Barnardo's home.

Chapter 6

Suffer the Little Children

We were sat in the back of an estate car passing along those narrow winding roads, which pass through the mountains of North Wales. We were happy and singing away: "I love to go a wandering along the mountain tops..." and,

"I'm a H.A.P.P.Y. I'm a H.A.P.P.Y.
I know I am. I'm sure I am. I'm a H.A.P.P.Y.

I'm L.O.V.E.D. I'm L.O.V.E.D.
I know I am. I'm sure I am. I'm L.O.V.E.D.

I'm S.A.V.E.D. I'm S.A.V.E.D.
I know I am. I'm sure I am. I'm S.A.V.E.D.

I'm happy, loved and saved.
I'm happy, loved and saved.
I know I am. I'm sure I am. I'm happy, loved and saved."

Happy, we were. Saved we may have been. Loved we were not. I was now nearly four years old. This is when memory begins and competes with and sometimes complements my files. It is as if I woke up in spring of 1957 when the snow had melted from the peaks of the mountains of Snowdonia and daffodils blossomed in the valleys.

I woke up among the wolves in green nylon overalls. I had no memory of having a mother or father, no memory of brothers or sisters, uncles or aunts. But I was happy playing with the other children and being nurtured by the wolves.

One day in Shelton House, Matron got me dressed and combed my hair. The comb got stuck in my curls. That hurt. Matron said that a nice couple was coming to see me. Me and my friends were playing with a spinning top that kept falling over because we were in the garden. Matron called me inside to her room. Inside, was a tall man with a kindly smile, big bushy eyebrows and a white collar around his neck and his wife who was shorter and thinner and wore glasses like him. There was a tall boy there too, called Paul, and a girl, called Christine, who was even taller. They were the man and woman's children.

They talked very nicely to me then asked if I wanted to go for a ride in their car, which was small and grey. I said that I would, so they took me out in it. They were very nice and very kind. Before we went out, the man's wife straightened my tie, which had black and white stripes on it. The man with the dog collar let me sit in the front of his car and play with the driving wheel. He wouldn't let me drive but said that one day he might teach me if I wanted to learn.

They took me for a nice meal. The lady coughed a lot. She asked me if I wanted to wash my hands. I didn't want to but I thought she wanted me to. So I said: "Yes." and the man took me to the toilet.

When we came back to the home, Matron asked me if I had had a nice time. I said that I had. I said: "Thank you for taking me out," to them. Then they asked me if I wanted to go out and play with Paul and Christine and we went into the garden and played with a ball. Then the man and woman came into the garden and called to Christine and Paul. Paul had grass in his hair because he had been rolling in the grass with the ball and his mother took a comb out of her bag and told him to comb his hair because she said he looked like a "mucky pup." Then they said: "Goodbye."

After they had left, Matron asked me if I would like to see them again. I said that I would. Matron said that Mr Granville was a very good man because he was a priest and that meant he was very holy.

One day Matron asked me if I wanted to have a holiday with the man and woman who had come to see me. I said: "Yes." Matron said that she would take me. We would have to take a train because they lived a long way away in a place called Bolton. But on the day I left Matron was too busy. Nurse Coulson, who was fat and who I liked because she smiled and played with us a lot, took me on the train to Bolton to have a holiday with the man and woman. I was there for four weeks.

I liked their house. Their little boy and girl were older than me but I liked playing with them. I played with Paul's toy soldiers in the back garden. It was much smaller than our garden at Shelton House but I liked it too because it had a fence and on the other side were black and white cows and buttercups and daisies in a field. At the bottom of the hill, you could see the steam trains going somewhere.

I liked the food too.

Then they said: "Would I like to live in their house?" I said: "Yes." They said that they would be very happy for me to stay and that I should call them Uncle George and Auntie Florence. So I never saw my friends in Shelton House again and I never said goodbye to Matron because she was not there when I left for my holiday.

On April 18th, the matron at Shelton House finally got word that I had been found prospective foster parents. The willing would-be foster parents were a minister from the Protestant Congregational denomination and his wife. The Reverend George Granville with the letters BD after his name lived in Bolton, Lancashire, with his wife, Florence, 13-year-old daughter, Christine, and nine-year-old son, Paul.

The very reverent Reverend was keen to do his duty before God and take into his care one of the many unfortunate unwanted children of the times. In the years following the 1939-45 war the young George had read so many times of the long lists of orphans and unwanted children taken in by organisations such as Barnardo's and the Salvation Army. Successive governments played their part as they set up more children's homes and shipped thousands of the children across the oceans for "new" lives in the homes in Australia and Canada.

Now he and his wife were settled with two children of their own, the foster child-thought began to flourish in his mind. The minister wanted to play his part and take in a child. Florence had said that she didn't wish to bear any more children, so the idea of having a foster child grew on George. It was no surprise to Florence, for she and everybody around him considered him to be the kindest man they could ever meet.

She watched her husband clothed in his black cassock, white surplice and dog collar climb to the pulpit before the packed Sunday morning church service. Florence smothered a cough with her hand. The tickle in her throat always seemed to come at moments such as these. Over the years she had learned to live with her bronchial problems.

"Today," he began with a smile in his soft but resonant voice, "I should like to read from Paul's first letter to the Corinthians.

"In it Paul says, 'And I will show you a still more excellent way. If I speak in the tongues of men and of angels, but have not love, I am a noisy gong or a clanging cymbal. And if I have prophetic powers, and can understand all mysteries and all knowledge, and if I have all faith, so as to remove mountains, but have not love, I am nothing. If I give away all I have, and if I deliver my body to be burned but have not love, I gain nothing.

"'Love is patient and kind; love is not jealous or boastful; it is not arrogant or rude. Love does not insist on its own way; it is not irritable or resentful; it does not rejoice at wrong, but rejoices in the right. Love bears all things, believes all things, hopes all things, endures all things.'"

Florence, sitting in the front pew and wearing her new pink hat and one of those blouses of the time with padded, puffed-up shoulders, knew this was true of her George. So too did many of his congregation.

George Granville was not only a follower of the word of God but a lover of humanity. He was devoted to his church and the world at large. Whether his supremely kindly nature arose from his own heart or his readings and faith, will forever be a matter of conjecture. But, for this clergyman, his life was lived through his readings of the scriptures and the scriptures lived in him. He would die a "good" man.

Nevertheless, the minister enjoyed his more mundane activities as a man, doing odd jobs around the house, playing and watching cricket and football and filling in the crosswords in his daily newspaper. He loved all there was in the world to be enjoyed and hated all the suffering and misery he saw. Florence sometimes wished he wouldn't love the world so much since it left her alone in the house with the children, but she marvelled at his devotion.

He hardly touched a drop of alcohol – except for an occasional glass from the bottle of sherry, which he kept in his study and they shared together when the children were asleep. His pipe smoke was a bit of a nuisance but he kept it in the study and let it out through the front window. He was what any woman would want "for better, for worse."

When George read of the plight of black children in Africa and read in the church magazines of the difficulty of finding foster homes for "coloured" children in England, I set root as a black child-foster thought in his mind: "We have a settled home, a reasonable income. Why shouldn't we do what is every Christian's duty?"

The minister rose to his feet to deliver another Sunday sermon: "Today, let us heed the words of Luke:

'Now they were bringing even infants to him that he might touch them; and when the disciples saw it, they rebuked them. But Jesus called them to him, saying: "Let the children come to me, and do not hinder them; for to such belongs the kingdom of God. Truly, I say to you, whoever does not receive the kingdom of God like a child shall not enter it."' And he read it out loud and spoke on Christ's meaning. His congregation truly believed that he was appealing to them.

George Granville knew he was addressing himself and cherishing his black foster child-thought. Once again, as thought, I was loved. But this time there were no Dreads around to threaten my existence. For George was content – except in the moments after one of Nottingham Forest's players had been crudely fouled on the football pitch.

What better way to serve the Lord could there be than to take an unwanted waif and bring him into the home and care for him and feed him, bring him up loved and watch him take his place as a man in the world?

He talked the matter over with his cousin and, of course, with his wife, Florence. Florence was not so certain. Florence was a frail and quite nervous woman with perennial bronchial trouble who lived with the feeling that she could not live up to her mother's expectations. She had fallen in love with the tall, handsome, gentle and studious man almost at first sight. His courting had been immaculate and, though she knew that her George was destined for a life of service to the Lord, Florence was happy to join him wherever he might be posted.

The reason for Florence's apprehension regarding her husband's desire to take in another child was that her looking after her own children and carrying out the endless rounds of coffee mornings and jumble sales that were the lot of a clergyman's wife were strain enough. Besides, for a long time Florence had looked forward to getting the children settled at school so that she could escape the house by taking on a part-time job.

Now that her son and daughter were both happy in their schools, Florence could see her chance of going back to work passing by. Another child would mean more cooking, more washing, more tidying up and less free time. But George wanted it and Florence wanted George to be happy. For hadn't he made her so happy? Hadn't George been a model of care and devotion? As Florence's foster child-thought I was tolerated.

That February of 1957, George's cousin told him that there were two coloured children being advertised for foster homes in the Derby Evening Telegraph.

Florence winced when George, in his usual soft, gravelly voice, told her of his phone conversation with his cousin.

"A 3½ year old boy and a 6 month old girl, he doesn't think that I can look after them both does he?" thought Florence.

George put Florence's initial reaction to rest: "Don't you think that we might take one of them into our home?"

"If you are sure that's what you want, George," replied Florence.

"Which one should we have?" asked the minister, "I'm sure Paul would like to have a little brother around. It would give him someone to play with at home."

Florence knew that she would have to go along with the idea. Paul was too boisterous for her already and having the two of them careering around the house filled her with more apprehension.

"Yes he will enjoy it," said Florence, adding, "But you must promise to tell Paul that he must not drive the little boy into too much excitement. The little girl might be better for us as a family but she is just a baby and I really don't think that I could go through all that again."

Florence told George of her main concern: "At least the little boy will soon be old enough to be enrolled full-time in Paul's school. That way, I will be able to take on a job again and I think we will need the money."

"Oh, Dr Barnardo's do say that they will pay for the children's maintenance and for their clothes, so it shouldn't put us in too great hardship. You know," said George with a sagely pause, "I think that we will find that, with another boy to play with, Paul will not be under your feet so much. If he takes care of his little brother, it will be the best way for him to learn how to behave himself."

"But will he really be Paul's brother?" asked Florence, "Are you proposing that we adopt the child. If so, I don't think it will be a good idea. What if it doesn't work out as you hope and that we have to send him back? Then we should have to tell Paul that he has lost his brother. Better that we foster the child. They say that fostering is not such a lifetime commitment. If it does work out over a few years, then we could adopt him."

"Yes, I think you are right," said George, fearful of pushing Florence too far. He sensed her apprehension and knew he must restrain his enthusiasm. "Like son, like father!" he thought, chuckling to himself, "I know where Paul gets his spirit from."

"Florence, I am so grateful to you. You know how happy this will make me and I am sure that it will make the whole family happier."

Florence remained unconvinced: "George is such a kind man but he really can be quite impractical. We have no spare bedrooms. Paul would have to share his bedroom with the boy. What if Paul or Christine don't like the boy? They say that those orphan boys could be such handfuls. They say some of them are dirty and come out with the must foul things even when they are very young." Nevertheless, the evident joy that the thought had put in her husband's head secured her capitulation.

"Well George, you must telephone Barnardo's quickly, before someone else snaps the boy up. Do make sure that we can both see the boy before we take him in. And we must ask Paul and Christine what they think too. Paul will have to share his bedroom with him," declared Florence, with a little part of her hoping that both the Barnardo children had already been found new homes. Another part of her prayed that if the boy was not right then George would have sense enough not to offer to take him in.

George smiled: "I am sure that Barnardo's will want to see us and that they will want to see how the boy responds to us before anything is agreed."

When asked, Paul and Christine were both delighted by the idea, Paul especially. Now he would have someone to play with at home!

Their father phoned Barnardo's that same day. Within two days, Mr Granville was sat in his house in St Mary's Avenue, Bolton, entertaining Miss Wallis; an elderly, plump woman dressed in a grey woollen suit. She had been sent by Barnardo's to interview the Granvilles and inspect their home. What the Barnardo's local Welfare Officer saw pleased her. Of course, she didn't expect to be other than pleased, with Mr Granville, him being the minister at Mawdsley Street Church.

Most of the polished, dark brown wooden doors in the house were ajar, so the Welfare Officer was able to take a peek into each room. Each room was tidy to perfection. A faint smell of rich tobacco smoke came from one room whose walls were lined with books large and small. That room, she presumed to be the learned minister's study. A stack of magazines sat on a rosewood table beside an inkwell and blotter.

The dining room next to the kitchen seemed the most lived-in room. Miss Wallis didn't consider that the pink and red flower patterns on the cream wallpaper matched the rest of the room. The table was covered in a pretty, woollen, brown and purple tartan tablecloth on the top of which half a dozen cork tablemats were stacked. In one corner was a small television and in another an oak chest on top of which stood a large wireless set.

From the ceiling hung one of those clothes maidens that one would hoist up with a rope. White shirts, baggy men's and boys' vests, underpants and grey socks hung down giving off moisture that mixed with the last odours of a mincemeat and onion pie that Mrs Granville had presumably baked for the couple's lunch.

The Granvilles ushered the Welfare Officer into their living room, which had the customary three-piece suite, also decorated with flower patterns – this time of red roses. On the walls hung several small, wooden picture frames, most of which contained black and white photos of country scenes. On the mantelpiece, were stood copper rimmed mountings with photographs of various family members. The curtains in the bay window were a heavy, maroon velvet. Beneath the curtains was a mahogany foldaway table covered in a white tablecloth fringed with lime coloured floral patterns.

Apart from the underwear in the kitchen, the only sign that children might live in the house was the stack of boxes holding board games such as Monopoly, Totopoly, Cluedo, Ludo, Snakes and Ladders and the like. All was as she had expected.

Everything seemed in order. The family seemed to know what was required of them and the home was clean and tidy. Miss Wallis made the customary request to use the Granvilles' bathroom and that too was as spotless and smelt as fresh as she had imagined it would. "If only all vicars wanted these children then we wouldn't have a problem," she thought to herself.

Concluding the interview, Miss Wallis came to the question of Barnardo's maintenance payments given to foster parents to assist raising the foster children.

"As for maintenance, we normally offer those looking after our boarded-out children one pound a week. We offer an additional allowance of five shillings a week to buy the children clothes and a small amount for pocket money. In the case of a child as young as this one it would probably be only six pence a week," said Miss Wallis, asking the minister, "Would that be satisfactory?"

"That would be more than enough," replied Mr Granville, looking his wife in the eye. "We know that Barnardo's has to do a lot of work to raise money for the children."

Miss Wallis left in a happy mood. She had found a family, which would make a very nice home for a coloured boy. They were so keen to have one of these poor boys that she didn't have to mention that Barnardo's "normal" payments to foster parents for the coloured children was 30 shillings a week. The minister could obviously afford to dip more into his pocket and she had saved the organisation £25 a year of tin-rattling time.

Miss Wallis wrote a glowing report back to her head office.

On May 1st, exactly two weeks after responding to the Barnardo's advertisement, the Reverend was able to show his wife the letter that had arrived from the Barnardo's office.

"We have been accepted as foster parents," said the smiling George.

Florence leant over, put her arms around George and kissed him on the cheek: "And when might we see the child?"

"They say that we will be informed shortly. They wish their adoption officer to make a final visit to the home where the boy is staying. They naturally say that they have to make certain that the boy is suitable for fostering."

Miss Bodell at Shelton House received a letter from her head office on May 2nd:

"AT LAST WE HAVE POSSIBLE FOSTER PARENTS FOR PHILLIP...FOSTER FATHER IS A CONGREGATIONALIST MINISTER, A KINDLY TYPE OF PERSON, VERY FOND OF HIS CHILDREN. FOSTER MOTHER IS SAID TO BE A GENTLY SPOKEN PERSON, KIND AND UNDERSTANDING WITH A SENSE OF HUMOUR."

Chief Executive Officer, Barnardo's Western Area, 2nd May, 1957

Miss Wallis, who had visited the Granvilles, was despatched to Shelton House to check that the boy, Phillip, was ready for fostering. After an overnight stay at the home she reported:

"PHILLIP WAS IMMEDIATELY FRIENDLY AND EAGER TO SHOW HOW HE PLAYED. HE INVITED ME TO SIT BY HIM AT THE DINNER TABLE AND GAVE ME A BUNCH OF FLOWERS HE HAD PICKED FROM THE FIELD. HE SEEMS READY FOR THE CARE AND AFFECTION OF FOSTER-PARENTS. HIS QUIET SOFT VOICE CAUSED ME TO EASILY ASSOCIATE HIM IN MY MIND WITH THE GRANVILLES. MISS BODELL WAS SAYING HOW HE HAD DEVELOPED, AND IS SHOWING SOME SPIRIT WHEN THIS IS REQUIRED OF HIM. I THOUGHT HOW ALERT HE WAS TO HIS SURROUNDINGS AND ALL THAT WAS SAID TO HIM."

Miss Wallis, 15th May, 1957

Florence Granville was eager to find out what this Miss Wallis thought of the child her husband wanted to bring into her home. She also wanted to make sure that she would have a chance to see him for herself. In the same letter, Miss Wallis reported:

"MRS GRANVILLE WHO IS VERY KEEN TO HAVE A CHILD, HAS PHONED ME TO HEAR MY OPINION. I HAVE TOLD HER ABOUT PHILLIP AND THAT SHE WILL RECEIVE WORD FROM HEAD OFFICE OR MISS BODELL REGARDING THEIR VISIT TO SHELTON HOUSE."

The Granville family was told when they would be welcome at Shelton House to see the child and the visit duly took place. George Granville was pleased. His son, Paul, was delighted and his daughter, Christine, contented. His wife Florence was relieved.

On the 27th May, George wrote to Barnardo's thanking them and confirming that they would like to take the child:

"PHILIP WON HIS PLACE IN ALL OUR HEARTS FROM THE VERY BEGINNING, AND IT WAS A HAPPY THING FOR US TO FIND THAT HE SEEMED TO TAKE TO US QUITE HAPPILY.... WE ARE MORE EXCITED AND HAPPY ABOUT THE COMING OF PHILIP THAN EVER, AND WE LOOK FORWARD TO HAVING HIM AS A MEMBER OF OUR FAMILY."

George Granville, 27th May, 1957

Mary Bodell at Shelton House was happy to note that the minister also spelt Philip the way she did – the right way. She wrote to her superiors expressing her satisfaction with the Granvilles.

One week later, the Granvilles were informed that Miss Bodell would bring the boy, "Philip," to their home in Bolton. The letter went on to say:

"AT THIS STAGE, WE FEEL THAT IT WILL BE IN PHILLIP'S BEST INTERESTS IF WE REGARD THE FIRST FOUR WEEKS OF HIS STAY WITH YOU AS A HOLIDAY. TOWARDS THE END OF THIS TIME, OUR WELFARE OFFICER, MISS WALLIS, WILL BE CALLING TO SEE YOU AND WE SHALL VERY MUCH LOOK FORWARD TO HEARING THAT PHILLIP HAS SETTLED DOWN HAPPILY IN HIS NEW SURROUNDINGS AND THAT YOU WOULD LIKE HIM TO REMAIN WITH YOU UNDER OUR FOSTER HOME SCHEME."

Chief Executive Officer, Barnardo's Western Area, 5th June, 1957

So after one Barnardo's visit to the Granvilles and one visit by the Granvilles to see me, Barnardo's decided that I was suitable to be placed with the Granvilles. Florence Granville was still not quite sure. "But I'll give it a try if it makes George happy," she concluded.

I was told that I was going on holiday and then the holiday went on and on – but not for long.

Two days before her marriage, Mavis Frampton was informed by post that I had been "boarded out" and that all her letters and parcels for me should be sent via Barnardo's head office. Mavis was relieved. But no letters or parcels arrived from her.

What did arrive for my birthday were half-a-dozen presents sent by Martha Watson and various friends of Mavis. Florence Granville, however, was none too pleased at the plethora of gifts from people she did not know that came with the postman. She considered that she had arranged enough presents for Phillip from her family, friends and neighbours. Florence feared that the very people who had forsaken him would spoil the boy. Paul would demand as many presents. It would make life difficult. Far easier that these people were out of Phillip's life and not complicating hers:

"F.MOTHER (SIC) HAS BEEN VERY CONCERNED AS TO THE NUMBER OF GIFTS PHILLIP RECEIVED FROM VARIOUS PEOPLE FOR HIS BIRTHDAY. I TOLD HER THAT THIS WOULD NOT ALWAYS BE SO, BUT BEFORE HE CAME TO THEM PHILLIP HAD 'AUNTS' WHO TOOK AN INTEREST IN HIM...WHEN F.F. (SIC) CAME IN HE EXPRESSED HIS JOY AT THE NUMBER OF PEOPLE WHO HAD REMEMBERED PHILLIP'S BIRTHDAY. I THINK PERHAPS HE HAS A GREATER UNDERSTANDING OF THE NEEDS OF A CHILD WHO IS WITHOUT HIS OWN PARENTS. F. MOTHER IS INCLINED TO EXPECT THIS LITTLE BOY TO IMMEDIATELY TAKE HIS PLACE AS A CHILD GROWING UP IN A FAMILY, RATHER THAN A CHILD WHO NEEDS TO BE GRADUALLY WEANED INTO THE FAMILY CIRCLE."

Miss Wallis, 31st July, 1957

The tensions were beginning.

On my fourth birthday I got lots of presents. Auntie said that she would save some for later as I had too many. I played with my new toys all day, then I had a birthday party with candles.

The next day I woke up Paul and we played in the bedroom with my new toys. Then Auntie came in with round things in her hair. I asked her what they were and she said they were rollers to make her hair curly like mine. I said it hurt when I combed my hair and did it hurt when she combed hers? She said: "Never you mind! It is too early in the morning and you should both be asleep."

I liked my new toy farm. It was plastic with plastic cows and pigs. Paul went to school so Auntie said that I could go and play with them in the garden. She brought me some Marmite sandwiches. When Paul came home we played together. Then he went to have tea at his friends and I went to play with Christine but Auntie said that I should not because Christine was doing her homework:

"PHILLIP LOVES TO FOLLOW CHRISTINE, BUT F.MOTHER WILL ONLY PERMIT THIS FOR A SHORT PERIOD AS SHE FEELS CHRISTINE SHOULD NOT BE EXPECTED TO HAVE PHILLIP WITH HER. PHILLIP IS A FRIENDLY CHILD AND MAY BE MISSING THE CHILDREN AT SHELTON HOUSE. HE SAYS HE DOES NOT WISH TO RETURN THERE."

Miss Wallis, 31st July, 1957

Sometimes Auntie was nice and let me watch television. I liked watching *The Wooden Tops* and *The Flower Pot Men.* But sometimes Auntie said I couldn't because too much television was bad for me. So I played with my farm and toy soldiers. Then I played with my coloured wooden bricks, which had letters like A, B, C and D on them and I made words like CAT and DOG. And I took my teddy from our bedroom and I talked to teddy. Auntie made nice food for lunch and I asked her what it was. After lunch she wanted me to sleep but I couldn't so she let me go back to the dining room next to the kitchen and I talked to my teddy again or my plastic cows and pigs and ducks.

Then Auntie came in and said that I was a chatterbox and one day, I would have my mouth sewn up. And I told her about what Matron used to say at Shelton House when she told me to go to sleep.

Sometimes Auntie told me to be quiet, especially when I went with her when she was shopping. I liked going shopping with her because of the smells of nice food in the grocers' shops and because people came up to me and gave me sweets. Auntie said they shouldn't but they did. I liked talking to them and asked them about the shop and what they liked most and Auntie said: "I'm sorry, we must go now. Phillip is such a chatterbox, he will keep us here all day."

On Sundays I went with Uncle to his church. He put me in the Sunday school where we read books and said prayers and made things and they asked me where I was from and I said that I was from Africa. I went every week and I won a prize for my attendance. It was a Mickey Mouse book, which I liked.

Sometimes, when Paul was at home I played with the other little children in the avenue. I liked them but then Auntie said that I should come in because we were making too much noise and we would upset the neighbours.

"THE NEIGHBOURHOOD AND SUNDAY SCHOOL FOLKS ARE NOW MORE USED TO HAVING PHILLIP AMONGST THEM, BUT FOR A FEW WEEKS F.MOTHER WORRIED BECAUSE HE WAS SO MUCH THE CENTRE OF ATTRACTION. HE IS A LOVEABLE CHILD AND HE IS ABLE TO SHOW HIS AFFECTION TO BOTH F.PARENTS, ESPECIALLY F.FATHER. F.MOTHER THINKS HE IS QUITE MUSICAL, WHICH IS INTERESTING."

Miss Wallis, 24th September, 1957

I didn't like the neighbours next door. They never were nice to me. They had a big black dog with long curly hair, which they called Nigger. I knew what Nigger meant and it was naughty to say it. When they shouted Nigger, I never knew if they were shouting at me. I didn't like the dog and I was frightened. Uncle and Auntie never said it was naughty but I knew it was.

Sometimes Christine or Paul took me shopping and I liked that. At Christmas I went into the town to shop with Christine. I was in a shop with her then I walked out and when I went back in I couldn't find her. So I went outside again to look for her. I saw a woman who was in the butcher's shop and she took me to a police station. I didn't cry. Then Auntie came to pick me up and I cried.

"F.PARENTS HAVE DECIDED TO HAVE A SMALL IDENTITY DISC MADE FOR PHILLIP AS HE IS A CHILD WHO BECOMES SO COMPLETELY ABSORBED IN HIS SURROUNDINGS, AND HE MIGHT WELL DO THIS AGAIN. HE KNOWS HIS OWN NAME, BUT FINDS IT DIFFICULT TO REMEMBER THE NAME GRANVILLE ETC.

"HE RECEIVED MANY BOOKS AT CHRISTMAS, BUT F.MOTHER HAS PUT THEM AWAY FOR A LITTLE WHILE UNTIL HE IS OLD ENOUGH TO APPRECIATE AND USE THEM.

Miss Wallis, 31st January, 1958

Neither Florence nor George Granville had expected the permanent fuss that would be made over their little black foster child. George was too busy with his ecclesiastical duties to notice but poor Florence could not escape the little coloured boy dominating her conversations whether the boy was present or not. She couldn't come away from a coffee morning or a church service, couldn't walk into a local shop or walk around the neighbourhood without Phillip's welfare being the first enquiry people would make about her "family."

Not that there was any malevolence intended by her inquisitors. Far from it. The Granvilles, and the Reverend in particular, were held in such high esteem that genuflecting to the family's "wonderful gesture" came naturally. There being not much else of import to talk about in the town, Florence found herself surrounded by a suffocating wall of sympathy and admiration - a wall which didn't seem to allow her own children inside. They had become an afterthought in her friends' conversations.

When she first mentioned this matter to George, he had told her not to worry and that the novelty of having Phillip in the neighbourhood and at the church would wear off. He calmed her fears that Paul and Christine would become jealous of the boy:

"Paul gets on very well with Phillip. They are always playing together."

"Yes, too much for my liking. Phillip copies Paul too much and is always chasing after him. Paul seems to get far too excited when Phillip is around. If anything I think he has got worse since Phillip arrived," replied Florence.

George winced. He saw the warning signs: "Paul is growing up, dear. He has always been very lively and I don't think Phillip has changed that. The teachers say that he is the same way at school."

The fuss around Phillip never seemed to die down. For Florence, it meant what seemed like hours of hanging around waiting for the little boy to finish his conversations. It meant the return to loving a four-year-old as she had loved her own and this she could not do because this was not her own child, it was George's and it was wearing her down.

The more people gave the little Phillip attention, the more Florence questioned her own feelings about the child. What did they see in him that she didn't? Why didn't they pay her own children as much attention? Was she being unfair to the child? Was she giving him enough love? Were her own children missing out on her love?

The pressures of looking after George's child were proving too much for the frail, nervous Florence. The Barnardo's Welfare Officer, Miss Wallis, commented on her apparent reluctance to allow Phillip to go to play with other children in the neighbourhood. It wasn't that Florence disliked the children in the neighbourhood, only that she feared that the next step would be having them around her house and she knew that she would not be able to cope. And the children's parents would be making a fuss of Phillip too and he would become too spoilt. But after Miss Wallis had gently questioned Florence about the matter, Florence felt a torrent of guilt and self-doubt.

Florence managed to find me a place in the Brandwood Street Primary School nearby. When, after Easter, she took me for my first day, she felt a sigh of relief. At least now she would have her days largely to herself. I was happy in the school. But Florence was not happy. When a Barnardo's officer visited the Granvilles in May, Florence said of Phillip:

"HE IS A CHATTERBOX...HE DOESN'T SLEEP IN THE AFTERNOONS BUT DRAWS OR READS BOOKS...HE LIKES SCHOOL VERY MUCH. HE PLAYS WITH OTHER CHILDREN NOW...HE IS AN ACTIVE LITTLE BOY, AND CAN'T SIT STILL FOR LONG. HE IS NOT FOND OF MUSIC. HE COVERS UP HIS EARS WHEN ANYONE IS PLAYING THE PIANO!"

Barnardo's Report, 13th May, 1958

So that was my musical career over! More than that, the Barnardo woman's constant questioning of Florence as to whether Phillip was now being allowed to play with other children sent the minister's wife into a panic. She was not coping. She was not treating the child properly. She was being unfair not letting him be spoilt. But she had Paul and Christine to worry about as well. They had problems too. She had problems too. She had to make ends meet and cook and clean and go to coffee mornings and jumble sales and church services and she had to look her best and smile because she was George's wife and... It was all too much.

Florence sent me to play in the back garden, went upstairs lay on her bed and wept. I didn't see her tears. She never would let me – unless they were joy-tears. George saw her tears that night after we were all tucked in bed.

"I'm sorry but I can't cope any more!"

George sensed immediately the matter that was troubling her but Florence declared: "It's not just that. It's everything. I don't know what the right thing to do is for Phillip, or for Christine, or for Paul. Paul gets more of a handful by the day. Phillip is always talking. Christine is becoming older and wants different things. You are never here. I feel drained, tired all the time and want to burst into tears all the time. I know how much you wanted Phillip here but I just can't cope with everything else as well. I'm so sorry, George. I'm so sorry. I feel I've let you down."

"You have nothing to be sorry about Florence." replied George, "We will sort everything out. Don't be anxious now. Just rest."

George stayed seated on the bed, holding his wife's hand until she had fallen asleep. Her left cheek was on the pillow. Her mouth hung open with a grimace that spelt pain.

"I have never known her in this mood before. She looks so troubled! If she is in the same spirits tomorrow I will have to call the doctor."

In those moments, the minister was overcome with sadness:

"Has my happiness caused her so much pain? I have been so thoughtless. I really thought that she was enjoying having Phillip around. Or did I see the signs and selfishly ignore them, thinking that they were minor irritations? I knew that she had her doubts from the very beginning. She travelled with me but it wasn't her journey. Life has always been a little too much for Florence and I thought that her little expressed doubts and irritations meant nothing untoward.

"If Phillip is such a trial for her, then we will have to ask Barnardo's to take him back. He will be so upset and think that we have betrayed him. Paul will be upset too. He really likes having his little brother around. But if Phillip stays here Florence might get worse. Her health and temper have always been fragile. Then, what will happen to all of us?"

George Granville was strong. Now he was in tears. The past months of joy, of his joy, would now be as nothing to the sadness to come. He felt shame and guilt. At that moment the minister was consuming all the misery to come:

"Have I brought us to this?"

He slipped on his dressing gown and tartan, woollen slippers and crept downstairs to his study. He was searching for solace from the scriptures. He had always found Paul's epistle to the Corinthians to be a source of comfort and flicked through the pages until he read in Book 2:

"And to keep me from being too elated by the abundance of revelations, a thorn was given me in the flesh, a messenger of Satan, to harass me, to keep me from being too elated. Three times I besought the Lord about this, that it should leave me; but he said to me: 'My grace is sufficient for you, for my power is made perfect in weakness.' I will all the more gladly boast of my weaknesses, that the power of Christ may rest upon me. For the sake of Christ, then, I am content with weaknesses, insults, hardships, persecutions, and calamities; for when I am weak, then I am strong."

And George Granville knew he must bear his thorn. The comfort was brief. He knew of his sins but he felt weak and humbled. He prayed for forgiveness because he did not feel the strength to be able to boast of his sins. Yes, he might be a better man before the Lord. But how could he forgive himself for having sinned against those that he loved?

Florence slept through the next day, not eating and hardly drinking. George took it upon himself to get me ready for school. He cancelled his engagements and gave her apologies for a Women's Guild committee meeting. He stayed by her side, except to fetch her water and to call the doctor who arrived in the afternoon. Doctor McArthur, George's age, a Catholic but a portly, fellow member of the town's Rotary Club, diagnosed Florence's condition as high blood pressure. The minister had been by enough bedsides of the sick to know the implications.

"How long must she rest for?"

"'Until she feels 100 per cent. It could be weeks. It could be months. She must have absolute rest."

That afternoon a neighbour brought me home from school. Uncle George waited until we were sat at the dinner table and had said grace, to explain that Aunt Florence was poorly and that we would have to be very good in the next few days. He looked very sad; his mouth turned down as he spoke. His eyes faced down when he finished. Once he turned to look at me with a smile. It was a comforting smile.

The Reverend George Granville stepped up into the pulpit and adjusted his spectacles, glancing down at his huge Bible to the pages, which he had selected for that Sunday morning. He didn't wear his customary smile, indeed some of his congregation thought they could detect anguish in his face. Word of his wife's condition had quickly got around the worthies of Mawdsley Street. But even the worthiest were not aware of the dilemma their minister now faced.

> "Today let us read from Psalm 143, a psalm of David for guidance."
> He continued:
> "Hear my prayer, O Lord; give ear to my supplications!
> In thy faithfulness answer me, in thy righteousness!
> Enter not into judgement with thy servant; for no man living is righteous before thee.

> For the enemy has pursued me; he has crushed my life to the ground;
> He has made me sit in darkness like those long dead.
> Therefore my spirit faints within me; my heart within me is appalled.
>
> I remember the days of old, I meditate on all that thou hast done;
> I muse on what thy hands have wrought.
> I stretch out my hands to thee; my soul thirsts for thee like a parched land.
>
> Make haste to answer me, O Lord! My spirit fails!
> Hide not thy face from me, lest I be like those who go down the Pit.
> Let me hear in the morning of thy steadfast love,
> For in thee I put my trust.
>
> Teach me the way I should go, for to thee I lift up my soul.
> Deliver me, O Lord, from my enemies!
> I have fled to thee for refuge!
> Teach me to do thy will, for thou art my God!
> Let thy good spirit lead me on a level path."

His discourse on the subject of the psalm that morning was so packed with emotion and kindness, so near to the lives of those sat in the pews, that it brought out a few tears. Edna Hughes, who would have set up a George Granville fan club such was her adoration of the man, clapped her hands together - but just the one time before she glanced around and went as red as her hymn book.

George Granville wasn't aware of Mrs Hughes strangled applause. He was consumed in his own prayer; that his wife, Florence, recover to health as quickly as possible and lift the burden of the possible pain to come.

One day, I was playing in the garden with my farm animals. Then I read my *TV Comic*. Then I climbed on the fence, which was wooden. I was watching a steam engine in the valley. It puffed out smoke and you couldn't see the fields behind it. They were yellow. Uncle came out and sat on my stool, which was wood too and had three legs.

"Phillip," he said, "You know that Auntie Florence is poorly and she will have to go away for a while for a holiday so that she can rest. I will be here on my own and have to look after Christine and Paul and look after my church. It will be very difficult here. You remember that you were in Shelton House in Barnardo's with Miss Bodell and you liked it? Some kind people in Barnardo's in Southport have said that they will take you on holiday too for a while. Would you like that? Southport is where we went and had a picnic on the beach at Easter and you played with your bucket and spade and Paul and you made sandcastles."

"Yes," I said, "I would like that. Will I come back?"

"Yes," Uncle George said, "It will only be for four weeks while your auntie gets better."

"Will Paul come too?" I asked.

"Paul and Christine have very important work to do at school so they will stay here," he said, "But we will come and visit you as many times as we can."

Chapter 7

A "Communal" Child

So, one day when Auntie Florence was not so poorly, I helped her pack my suitcase and I got in the car with Uncle and Auntie and Paul and Christine and we went to Southport. They took me into a big house with lots of children playing in the garden. Then they said: "Goodbye, do be good!" and I said: "Yes, I will be good." And they left and Matron took me into the house, which was big, like Shelton House.

Florence had taken some weeks to recover her composure. George Granville was anxious to resolve the future. What he knew of the present was that the mention of my name to his wife did not raise a smile but rather it dimmed her eyes then lowered her eyelids, as if she were ready to sleep rather than contemplate returning to her recent trials.

The minister phoned Doctor McArthur for advice. The answer he received severed the thread that held up the Sword of Damocles: "Your wife has high blood pressure but her problems are being exacerbated by excessive nervous tension and her frail constitution. Total rest will restore her back to her previous condition but you must understand that her mind is such that having the boy there could lead to similar or even worse set backs for your wife in the future."

"Thank you, Gerald," George replied, "I understand. Florence sends her regards and wants to thank you for all you are doing. We'll see you next week then."

It was a few days before Florence was well enough for George to broach the subject of my future. He sandwiched the topic between talking about the children and talking about events at the church:

"Florence, I know that you have found it difficult dealing with Phillip and the children at the same time and I hope you forgive me. I never realised how much of a strain it was for you. I have been rather selfish and should have thought of you more before I set my mind on fostering another child. Doctor McArthur says that he is too much for you. Perhaps I should have been more help to you. I think that we should consider asking Barnardo's to find him a different home, don't you."

Florence was sat upright in bed. She put her hand on George's and said: "Thank you dear, but I think that I will be fine after a rest. I don't really feel that Phillip is such a problem. You and Paul have grown to love him and I know how upset you both would be to send him away. He can be such a lovely boy."

George was pleasantly surprised by his wife's change of attitude. But he reminded himself that he had been in a similar situation before. Florence had gone along with the fostering proposal to keep her husband happy. He was now of a mind to be much firmer:

"Doctor McArthur believes that you need four weeks' rest and that time by the seaside would be good for you. You need to be away from the children and the chores. I will organise that with one of your sisters, then we will see what further the doctor has to say."

"Well George, I am sure you are right but I will be fine after a rest. I don't want Phillip to be sent away any more than you. But if I go away how will you cope with the children?"

George replied: "I will ask Barnardo's if they can do something. Phillip could have a holiday with them too. He used to always talk about Shelton House and I'm sure he wouldn't mind going back there to see Miss Bodell."

In the days to follow, George clung to the hope that Florence would recover well enough and that the family life could continue. Florence held on to the same wish. Their lives would only be interrupted for a brief period and then they would continue. George would be more understanding of his wife, as mother, and Florence would spend less time in church committees.

George contacted Barnardo's explaining his wife's condition and requesting that I be taken back to Shelton House for a brief period.

"He did so like Shelton House and still talks of Miss Bodell."

The reply came: "Well we do appreciate your request and do hope that your wife can return to health as quickly as possible but Shelton House is fully occupied at the moment and, I am sorry to inform you that Miss Bodell passed away at the end of the year."

"Oh, I am sorry to hear that," responded George, "she appeared such a good influence on Phillip."

"But, we can look into another place for Phillip. Really, it should be somewhere nearby so that you can visit the boy, otherwise he might be quite upset. We do have a home in Southport. It's in Birkdale, a very pleasant part of the town. If you wish, I can put in a request that Phillip be boarded there for a while."

"That would be ever so kind of you," said George and the conversation drifted into possible arrangements.

On May 23rd a letter finally arrived for Florence from Barnardo's:

"I HAVE MANAGED TO OBTAIN A VACANCY FOR HIM AT OUR BRANCH AT 16/18 TRAFALGAR ROAD, BIRKDALE, LANCS. THE MATRON IS MOST UNDERSTANDING, AND WILL I KNOW GIVE HIM EVERY CARE. THIS IS I THINK THE NEAREST HOME WE HAVE TO BOLTON, AND I DO HOPE THAT PERHAPS MR GRANVILLE AND YOUR CHILDREN WILL BE ABLE TO VISIT HIM OCCASIONALLY, AND I AM SURE THAT YOU WILL SEND HIM A LOT OF POSTCARDS. THIS CONTINUOUS CONTACT IS VERY IMPORTANT, ESPECIALLY TO SUCH A LITTLE BOY TO WHOM TIME SEEMS SO LONG.
...MAY I AGAIN WISH YOU A SPEEDY RECOVERY..."

Barnardo's Chief Executive Officer, Western Area, 23rd May, 1958

The letter also informed Florence that Barnardo's would, as part of their statutory duties, have to seek a report from her Doctor McArthur and that their doctor would also wish to discuss the matter with the Bolton doctor.

Florence wrote back:

"I FEEL VERY GUILTY ABOUT ALL THIS AND KEEP WONDERING IF WE ARE DOING THE RIGHT THING, BUT I SEEM TO HAVE GOT TO A STAGE WHERE EVERYTHING SEEMS TO BE ON TOP OF ME AND I AM FINDING IT HARD TO COPE. I DON'T THINK THAT THERE IS ANYTHING SERIOUSLY WRONG WITH ME (I SINCERELY HOPE NOT). IT SEEMS TO BE MORE OF A CASE OF EXCESSIVE NERVOUS TENSION, BUT YOUR DOCTOR WILL LEARN MORE ABOUT THIS... I AM HOPING TO GET AWAY ON MY OWN FOR A WHILE AS WE THINK THIS WILL HELP MORE THAN ANYTHING.

"PHILLIP KNOWS THAT I HAVEN'T BEEN WELL FOR SOME TIME, AND WHEN I TOLD HIM THIS EVENING THAT HE WAS GOING TO A DR BARNARDO'S HOME AT SOUTHPORT UNTIL I WAS BETTER, HE TOOK IT VERY WELL...I AM HOPING THAT WE SHALL BE ABLE TO FETCH HIM HOME AGAIN READY TO START SCHOOL ON JULY 14TH, WHEN OUR LOCAL SCHOOLS START AGAIN AFTER THE ANNUAL WAKES FORTNIGHT, SURELY BY THEN I SHOULD BE FEELING BETTER."

Florence Granville, 25th May, 1958

Barnardo's set the wheels in motion, informing the matron in their Southport home of the circumstances of the little boy who was about to enter her care. The Character Form said:

"NAME: PHILLIP FRAMPTON HALF-CASTE. AGE: 5 YEARS (sic)
REASON FOR PRESENT TEMPORARY MOVE: FOSTER MOTHER IS UNWELL
GENERAL CHARACTER: AN INTELLIGENT LITTLE BOY, VERY FRIENDLY, FOND OF PLAYING WITH OTHER CHILDREN PARTICULARLY OUT OF DOORS. ALTHOUGH A CHATTERBOX, HE IS NOT A NOISY CHILD. HE STARTED SCHOOL AFTER THE EASTER HOLIDAYS AND SETTLED WELL THERE.
SPECIAL APTITUDES: HE LIKES LOOKING AT BOOKS AND PICTURES, SEEMS TO BE ARTISTIC. IS FOND OF DRAWING."

Barnardo's Report, 29th May, 1958.

The name, Phillip Frampton Half-Caste, seemed to follow me around Barnardo's and, had they actually overseen my christening, I expect I would have Half-Caste somewhere in my name – like the Mr Browns and Mrs Blacks of the world.

The Granvilles prepared to deliver me to the Barnardo's home in Southport on May 31st. It was a sad day for George as he packed my small leather suitcase into the boot of his grey Morris Minor. Paul and I played with our soldiers in the back seat, Florence occasionally turning round to tell us to make less noise and not be so silly. Within half an hour we saw the two gleaming gas towers which dominated the flat landscape of the coastal part of the Lancashire Plain. Trees bent by the onshore winds flanked our road.

The sunshine was such that we might have been off to spend an afternoon on the beach. Indeed, I did ask Auntie as we saw the fairground but we sped past into leafy Birkdale and arrived at Trafalgar House in Trafalgar Road.

George Granville was a little shocked by the appearance of the rambling house. His memories of visiting Shelton House in Shrewsbury had suggested that Phillip's temporary, and possibly permanent, home would be much more pleasant. He fussed over me while Florence stood aside trying to keep her son in check. They all gave me a little peck on the cheek then left.

Back in the car George said: "I do hope he will be happy there. I am sure that we have done the right thing." No one replied. Nobody was sure that it was the right thing.

"We must make sure that we see him every week and send him his comic," added George after a pause. He turned to Paul: "It will mean a nice trip to the seaside each week for you and Christine while your mother is away. It seems we'll all be at the seaside for the next few weeks."

The journey back to Bolton was otherwise silent. As George drove the car he couldn't help being consumed by deep remorse. The shock of seeing Phillip's ramshackle new home and the scruffy unkempt children with the look of the lost, filled him with a guilt almost equal to that he felt for having put his wife through so much torment.

Florence was seated at his side with the guilt she had taken on for having let her husband down. What made her feelings worse was that she knew that there were those of the minister's acquaintances who would now say: "We knew it was too much to take on a coloured boy. They say that they can be such a problem. Don't they come from savage stock? Mr Granville is a very kind man but sometimes he can go too far. Look how the boy drove his wife to a breakdown."

At the same time Florence tried to remove the burden of her guilt:

"George didn't understand. Phillip was too much for me to handle. I had to teach him so much. He couldn't even hold a knife and fork properly when he came. And who taught him that constant chatter? I'll never know. And he wound Paul up so that Paul became so uncontrollable when Phillip was around. In my condition I really couldn't be expected to take it."

You might think that Florence Granville was being unreasonable. So did Florence Granville and so too did her husband. But he knew that there was no alternative but this outcome and he had to bear the cross not for Christ's sake but for his family's.

"I ALWAYS HAD A FEELING THAT MRS GRANVILLE WAS EXPECTING A RATHER HIGHER STANDARD OF BEHAVIOUR FROM HIM THAN WAS POSSIBLE FOR A CHILD OF HIS AGE...
"I WAS NOT SO CERTAIN ABOUT HER AFFECTION FOR PHILLIP. I THINK SHE FEELS A GREAT SENSE OF FAILURE BOTH TOWARDS PHILLIP AND TOWARDS HER HUSBAND, BUT SHE SAID THAT HER BLOOD PRESSURE WAS PARTLY DUE TO NERVES AND IT WAS NOISE THAT SHE COULD NOT STAND, AND OF COURSE PHILLIP NEVER STOPPED TALKING. ONE FELT THAT SHE ALMOST BLAMED THE CHILD, ALTHOUGH SHE DID SAY THAT HE WAS REALLY PRETTY GOOD AND OBEDIENT.
"MISS WALLIS HAD SPECIFICALLY ASKED HER BEFORE THEY TOOK PHILLIP AS TO WHETHER SHE FELT THAT SHE COULD MANAGE HER BUSY LIFE AS A CLERGYMAN'S WIFE WITH TWO CHILDREN OF HER OWN, AND SHE HAD BEEN SURE THAT SHE COULD, AND HAD OVERESTIMATED HER POWERS...I HAD JUST WONDERED WHETHER SHE WAS RESENTING PHILLIP AND ONLY FALLING IN WITH HER HUSBAND'S SUGGESTIONS BECAUSE SHE FELT SHE WAS LETTING MR GRANVILLE DOWN."
Chief Executive Officer, Barnardo's Western Area, 18th September, 1958

Meanwhile, the matron at Southport was not fully in the picture. She told Mr and Mrs Granville that they could only visit me once a month. George contacted Barnardo's office to express his dismay and they wrote back to the matron:

"I WONDER IF YOU WOULD BE GOOD ENOUGH TO SEE THAT HE KEEPS IN DIRECT CONTACT WITH HIS FOSTER PARENTS AT LEAST ONCE A WEEK. IF NOT I GREATLY FEAR HE WILL FEEL REJECTED AND WONDER IF WE REALLY MEAN HIM TO RETURN TO THEM. IT IS NOT AS THOUGH HE WAS COMING IN FOR GOOD AND SO WE MUST GET IT OVER TO THEM AND HIM THAT HE 'BELONGS' TO MR AND MRS GRANVILLE."
Chief Executive Officer, Barnardo's Western Area, 11th June, 1958

To his relief, George was informed that the matron had accepted her superior's instructions and the weekly visits began. As to resolving the issue of my stay with the reverend, by no means everybody shared George Granville's views.

I was later informed of how the decisive moments on his day of decision arrived.

Dr McArthur was handling the situation with Florence Granville extremely delicately. In his opinion, the woman had suffered a nervous breakdown. In his weekly visits to see his patient he was thankful that her husband was not present. He already understood that the woman was prepared to hide her real feeling about the boy out of devotion to the minister.

As she continued to talk about the little coloured child returning and, "hoping that she would be able to cope," the doctor took it upon himself to invite George Granville to visit his surgery. He was certainly not of the opinion that she could cope with a coloured boy. "These coloureds can be wild," he thought to himself, "and the boy could drive her into the ground. Besides, at the Rotary Club some of the chaps are laughing behind Granville's back and that will make life even worse for the minister."

George Granville attended the surgery in a rather apprehensive frame of mind. He suspected and expected the worse. He sat till the appointed time flicking through the comic that he had just bought for Phillip, then was called in to Dr McArthur's office. The doctor was sat behind a large grey metal desk and surrounded by olive-coloured filing cabinets, some of which were half open with papers sticking out. On the doctor's desk was the untidy collection of papers that were Mrs Granville's files.

"Thank you for coming in George," he began, "I really haven't got a great deal of time but I do need to acquaint you of the position regarding your wife. Her illness has given me a great deal of concern and I am even more concerned that she is still holding on to the notion of having the coloured boy back in your home.

"Quite frankly, I have to advise you that taking the boy back could be a dreadful mistake. Your wife has had a breakdown on account of too much strain and the boy will probably be more of a handful in the future."

"What makes you say that?" asked George, "He is a very well behaved child."

"Well, that is not the view of your wife," replied the doctor, "She considers him to be too much of a handful. She might not say these things to you because she knows you are devoted to the child and she does not want to upset you."

George nodded and the doctor continued: "She complains to me that the boy wakes too early in the morning and never stops talking all day.

She says that his table manners are rather uncouth and that he is a bad influence on your son, Paul. If that continues then she could have a real handful on her plate."

"Paul is as much a problem now as when Phillip arrived," interjected George, "I don't think you are being fair to blame the behaviour of a ten-year-old boy on a four-year-old."

"It is not me who is saying that, George. It is your wife," the doctor retorted, "You have to consider the implications of what Florence is saying. Her condition has improved slightly and she is prepared to have the boy back but I must advise against it. The alternative is for your wife to suffer another breakdown in health and that could be much more serious for her and your family as a whole. Your affection and wish to do good for the boy is obvious but you must put your family first."

The doctor's words stung George into submission. He wanted to cry out that his Phillip was part of his family. Otherwise whose child was he? Nobody's? He didn't cry out. He knew that Florence did not consider Phillip to be hers and clearly had only tried to cope with him on his behalf. The minister lay down his sword and submitted:

"Very well then, Dr McArthur, I do expect that you will be making a report on these lines to Barnardo's. I think it is best if you leave it to me to break the news to Florence."

"Yes, I think that will be for the best," the doctor concluded. He rose from his chair and the meeting was at an end.

One more incident that caused George Granville consternation was the occasion of the Granville family's second visit to see me in Southport. They arrived when I was playing soldiers and hide-and-seek in the garden with some of the other children. Hiding in the bushes or climbing the metal banisters that ran up the back of the house was such fun. I was so carried away with our game that I had forgotten that Uncle and Auntie were coming that afternoon. I really didn't want to leave the game and I wanted to go out to the park with the rest of the children.

"WE HAD TEARS LAST SATURDAY BEFORE THEY ARRIVED BECAUSE HE WANTED TO GO OUT WITH THE OTHER CHILDREN AND WHEN THE GRANVILLES BROUGHT HIM BACK AT FIVE, INSTEAD OF SIX O'CLOCK, THEY SAID HE DID NOTHING BUT SAY HE WANTED TO COME BACK TO THE HOME."

Matron, Trafalgar House, 12th June, 1958

It had been George's decision to deliver me back to the home earlier than the scheduled time. He could see that his wife was getting more and more tense as the boy talked forever about the little children in the home and his games and how he wanted to go back and play there. The whole incident saddened him.

You may have thought that George would have been relieved at my having apparently settled so well in the Barnardo's home but there was something else on his mind, which he mentioned to Florence when the family had arrived back in Bolton:

"I do hope Phillip wasn't acting like he was because he feels that we have let him down. It will make him so sad in the future. I'm wondering whether he will trust us again. We must make sure that he understands why we have had to leave him there."

"I think the matron might be spoiling Phillip," replied Florence, "He really did behave quite badly today."

Florence then went silent, leaving the minister to ponder as to whether he had brought misery and pain into two people's lives.

"Has Phillip really rejected us so quickly," he thought, "Perhaps he understands more than we think. Poor Florence can not help showing her impatience with him and I think the boy picks it up."

Two visits later, George did not know what to make of the situation: "Phillip seems happy. He never gets upset when we leave and never asks whether he can come back to stay with us. I wonder if he wants us in his life after what we have done. Still, at least he seems happy there."

"HE HAS NEVER ASKED ABOUT COMING BACK, AND WHEN WE PART FROM HIM THERE IS NO SIGN OF UNHAPPINESS AT STAYING BEHIND."

George Granville, 8th July, 1958

On July 4th, Barnardo's officially informed George Granville that, in the opinion of Dr McArthur, Phillip could no longer stay in his charge, as Florence Granville could not be expected to look after the child. Dr McArthur went further, advising Barnardo's that his patient should not foster again.

The door was well and truly slammed shut.

George Granville was beside himself. Little Phillip would once more be without a proper home. But he knew that he and Florence had already taken that decision. There was nothing to be done but to try and help the boy by staying in contact with him at the Southport home.

That would mean Phillip being kept in the home. For, if the boy were to be boarded out again, then the Granvilles would surely not be permitted to stay in contact with him. To this end, the matron of the Southport home helped him. Miss Stewart had become particularly attached to the little coloured boy with the mop of black and sun-bleached curly hair, just as she became attached to all her children so long as they were not too much of a handful.

Her job was to care for the children in her charge and if others were not up to raising these children then she believed that she should be left to raise them herself. In this respect she was no different to Miss Bodell at Shelton House and many of the other matrons of the time. She therefore constantly expressed her wish to her superiors that the boy be kept with her at Trafalgar House rather than being "boarded out" again.

"MISS STEWART IS VERY ATTACHED TO PHILLIP, AND AS SHE HAS A VACANCY AT THE HOME, SHE HOPES YOU WILL DECIDE AT HEADQUARTERS TO LET PHILLIP STAY ON THERE INDEFINITELY. IF THIS SHOULD PROVE POSSIBLE, IT WOULD ENABLE US TO KEEP IN CLOSE TOUCH WITH HIM, BOTH BY VISITING HIM THERE AND BY HAVING HIM OVER HERE FROM TIME TO TIME."

George Granville, 6th July, 1958

Regarding continuing to be my foster parents, the minister added:

"WE BOTH FEEL THAT IT WOULD NOT BE RIGHT TO PHILLIP OR TO OUR OWN FAMILY FOR US TO CONSIDER HAVING PHILIP BACK."

The Reverend Granville's words seem clear enough but Mary Stewart would take off her spectacles whenever she read over this part of his letter.

George Granville and Miss Stewart conspired together with the aim of me being kept in the home. They had a mutual interest. Though, I might say that it seems that the minister's desire to make good the harm he felt he had done to me blinded him to the fact that, by denying me another foster home, he might be doing me further harm. Was he working out his guilt? Was he right? Today's current thinking on these matters would suggest that he was wrong. Barnardo's area headquarters were not so certain. As we shall see, it became a matter of debate very pertinent to the care for today's unwanted children.

Barnardo's Western Area Chief Executive Officer was a Miss D C Merrison. Of Miss Merrison, all that can be said is that she appears to have been a very shadowy character, a Miss M. Like James Bond's 'M', she was hardly ever seen, hardly ever put a pen to paper, never sent out a letter signed by herself and often sent out letters which, while being on her behalf, carried totally illegible signatures.

Miss Childs-Foster was one of M's assistants. M joked that, with a name like Childs-Foster, her assistant had been born to the post. With that double-barrelled name, I imagine she was rather tall, portly and, at 55 years old, blessed with that white, almost boyish, straight hair that characterised the elderly spinsters in the Barnardo's administration. Her spectacles were plain and hung on the end of her nose, allowing more emphasis to be put on her eyes than her heavily wrinkled face. She wore the customary cream bonnet when she was off on her visits and each week swapped between the grey and the chocolate woollen dress suits that were her travelling outfits.

On the day when she took the train up from London to see the Granvilles and Miss Wallis in Bolton concerning the minister and his wife's continuing contact with the boy they had fostered, she had chosen her grey suit as she would have to travel through that grimy city, Manchester. Miss Childs-Foster loathed having to travel up north. She ached for the rolling green fields of her native Wiltshire and believed every child should be brought up in the countryside. And these poor little waifs in her charge deserved more than being raised amid the grime and smog of Manchester's dark satanic mills.

As the train left London, Miss Childs-Foster dipped into her soft brown leather briefcase to acquaint herself of the case of the little boy, Phillip Frampton. The case intrigued her. It wasn't the first "half-caste" boy she had had to deal with. In those years she had got used to young women discarding themselves of their unwanted illegitimate black babies.

These children were the result, as she saw it, of silly young college women throwing themselves on African students. It was a mark of the times; a trend, which she believed, had begun in the war years when men and women seemed to throw themselves at each other like there was no tomorrow. Black American servicemen were as much a target for the women of the day as were white. But then these irresponsible harridans had black babies and abandoned them.

Phillip's mother seemed a case in point. What a shame for such an educated woman! But then hadn't Miss Frampton's mother, herself, had an affair with a soldier during the war? Miss Childs-Foster did feel that

Miss Frampton's mother could have shown her daughter sympathy. Instead, the mother appeared to have behaved disgracefully but what did Miss Frampton expect of society? Sympathy?

Now poor Phillip had been rejected once again – though it seemed the situation was rather unfortunate. Everyone spoke well of his foster father, the Reverend Granville, who appeared to her to be an educated man. He had gained his Bachelor of Divinity at college and his home would have made a fine place to bring up a boy whose mother was an LRAM and whose father was a highly qualified engineer. This boy might be expected to go to university when he was older but he could hardly expect the homes to give him the support he would need to get through his exams: "After all, who of our children ever went to university?"

"What a shame," she mused, "that the mother, who was from Swindon, could not have raised him there, close to the countryside."

Miss Childs-Foster knew of a Dr Lathom who lived in Newent in the Forest of Dean. The Doctor and his wife were keen to adopt or foster and, having spent some time in Kenya, were not averse to taking in a black child. She had agreed with M that Phillip seemed of the right stock and with this background, he might expect the support necessary to get him through his school exams in his teenage years. An upbringing in the countryside and in Dr Lathom's large house would be ideal:

"PHILLIP COMES OF INTELLIGENT STOCK, HIS FATHER WAS A MINING ENGINEER, HIS MOTHER LRAM AND A MUSIC TEACHER...I HAVE NOW BEEN TALKING TO MISS MERRISON ABOUT HIM, WHO SAW PHILLIP AT BIRKDALE THIS WEEK. SHE AND I AGREE THAT HE JUST MIGHT BE A POSSIBLE CHILD FOR DR_____ AND MRS_____..."

Miss Childs-Foster, July, 1959

The problem Miss Childs-Foster had was that both the Granvilles and Miss Stewart in the Southport home were requesting that the boy be kept in the home. Miss Stewart reported that he had settled very well. He didn't seem to miss the Granvilles at all and was happier being in the company of lots of children. Before her was a letter from Miss Stewart to M:

"HE EVIDENTLY HAD SUCH HAPPY MEMORIES OF SHELTON HOUSE THAT HE TOOK IT FOR GRANTED THAT HE WOULD BE HAPPY HERE. HE IS SUCH A DEAR LITTLE BOY, WE ALL LOVE HIM, AND IT IS A CASE OF TRYING NOT TO GET TOO ATTACHED TO HIM: I THINK HE LOVES HAVING CHILDREN OF HIS OWN AGE TO PLAY WITH. MR AND MRS GRANVILLE ARE EXTREMELY NICE AND UNDERSTANDING."

Miss Stewart, 12th June, 1958

It was clear that the Reverend Granville wanted to be able to keep contact with the boy but knew that he could never have him back. Miss Childs-Foster resolved to talk the matter over with Miss Wallis when she reached Bolton.

The train arrived into Bolton railway station ten minutes late. Rain hurtled by the blackened chimneystacks and the swirling wind sent the smoke from the factories in all directions. Bolton was all that the woman from Wiltshire had feared. Miss Wallis greeted her and took her outside quickly. There they hailed a taxi, reaching Miss Wallis's office via streets lined by cloth caps and brown dungarees.

When tea and biscuits had been served and the pleasantries were over, Childs-Foster began with a sigh: "Well this matter of the boy Phillip is rather complex, and – I might add – rather sad."

"Yes," added Miss Wallis, "I have spoken to Mrs Granville and she feels she has failed both the boy and her husband. The Reverend Granville seems to have taken it rather well and is very supportive of his wife but she still seems in a very poor state. You will see later that she looks thin and drawn and swings between blaming herself and blaming the boy for what has happened. Her husband will have nothing to do with the idea that the boy is to blame and, though he won't say it in his wife's company, he is more inclined to suggest that his own son's boisterous nature was more the cause of her condition."

"It's interesting what you say," replied Childs-Foster, "but I was rather more referring to the boy's situation."

Miss Wallis knew that she had betrayed her sympathies for the boy's former foster family and tried to excuse herself: "I really am so sorry. I didn't mean to be insensitive to little Phillip's situation. It's just that the Granvilles say that he does seem to be quite happy in Southport. He has never asked them if he can come back to Bolton. The matron there seems to be of the opinion that he is a child more suited to living in a home and Mrs Granville said that, when he was with her at first, he never seemed to stop talking about the matron at Shelton House and the children. So when he went back there, it seemed quite natural to him."

Childs-Foster replied: "Yes, but you do know of this child's parents and their background. He is likely to be a quite intelligent child and if he is to have any success in later life, he really will need support through his schooling, and that, I'm afraid, our homes are not equipped to give. That is why it is such a pity that the Granvilles weren't able to keep him."

"They were hoping that they would be able to see him regularly and have him to stay at their house during school holidays." Miss Wallis explained, "I know that the Reverend is very fond of the child and feels terribly disappointed at the outcome. Mrs Granville does want to see the child too and I think that, when she is fully recovered, it would be a good thing for her. She needs to overcome her sense of failure."

Childs-Foster was surprised at the Welfare Officer's concern for the minister and his wife, which, despite Miss Wallis' excuses, seemed to be at the expense of the boy: "Thank you for the explanation. I understand your compassion for the Granvilles but we really must approach this issue from the point of view of the welfare of the little boy. It is very hard to place coloured children and, if we have an opportunity to do so, do you think that Phillip will take to another family?"

Miss Wallis, feeling rather contrite but unable to move her sympathies, replied: "He really does seem to adapt to wherever he is put but I wonder if Mrs Granville found his constant chatter about Miss Bodell and the children at Shelton House unnerving. If he is placed with another family, he might have the same effect on the foster mother. If he has affection for the Granvilles, and that does appear to be the case, would it be wise to test him out again and confuse him as to whom his parental figures might be?"

"Well it's true that we wouldn't wish to create any problems for our prospective fosterers. That couple are really special," said Childs-Foster agreeing with one of the Welfare Officer's points, "And I am not so certain that moving a child from family to family is a good thing. From all the reports, Phillip does seem to be a child who is happiest in the company of other children and quite suited to community life. There are children in our homes who seem to settle well and enjoy them. However, I still can't help feeling that we are missing an opportunity for this boy to fulfil his potential."

Miss Wallis sensed that Childs-Foster was coming round to a point of view that was not fully her own but favoured the Granvilles: "Well, you have seen the reports of Miss Stewart and it may be for the good of all that Phillip be kept at Southport for some time. Couldn't we then see how it works out?"

"Miss Stewart," she added, "believes that Phillip is happier in the home. She has told me that it is her opinion that he is happier being around children of his own age."

Childs-Foster was slightly taken aback by Miss Wallis's continuing offensive and re-asserted: "But we still have to consider whether he wouldn't be better growing up with a family like the Granvilles. If we held on to every child who preferred to be with other children all day long then our homes would be stacked full. The world would become a Neverland full of Peter Pans and Wendys. Perhaps Miss Stewart thinks that's what her home is."

"I do think that Miss Stewart is trying to do of her best," said Miss Wallis, evading a clash with her superior, "The Granvilles are quite a special family and I am not sure that we will find the like elsewhere. Phillip is after all a half-caste child. I am sure you know the problem we had with boarding him out before."

"You put rather a lot of trust in the Granvilles, Miss Wallis," replied Childs-Foster, "What if Mr Granville is called to preach in another church, 200 miles away? Then he will not be able to see the boy on more than the odd occasion. We would be leaving Phillip with nobody at all."

"Personally," answered Miss Wallis, "I can not see the minister moving, what with his children being settled in the local schools."

"I am not so sure that you are right," remarked Childs-Foster, "I will have to meet this Mr Granville of whom everybody speaks so highly and then perhaps I can make a more informed judgement. In the meanwhile, do you think that the Granvilles continuing to see Phillip will be of benefit to him? Is Mrs Granville well enough to make him welcome and does she really want to have him in her home?"

Miss Wallis was quite certain: "Yes, they would both dearly love to have him to stay. They continue to visit him regularly and send him his comic weekly. Their son Paul has even asked when they can have him back. I think that you will find Mrs Granville still is not of good health and we must be careful as to the frequency of Phillip's visits or we might risk a further breakdown. The situation is rather delicate."

So there I was, the child "more suited to communal life" – a Romulus raised by wolves and a strange breed for today's social workers and child psychologists. In today's world of mission statements and stringent budgeting, the family has won out as the automatic place for any unwanted child. Families are normal and families are cheaper than children's homes and every unwanted child is to be placed with a family.

Whether the family is the best situation to bring up children who have often already suffered rejection does not seem to be given consideration. Families are neither professional nor dedicated to the needs of particular children. Parents muddle on, normally through unconscious studies of how their parents muddled on to raise them. Furthermore, what many unwanted children require above all is not parental love but domestic stability. Foster families neither guarantee stability nor the avoidance of further rejection. At best, they may give parental love but that is a random, unplanned and uncontrollable element of a child's life. Current government policies involve thousands of unwanted children being shunted regularly from one foster home to the next – Wanted, Unwanted, Wanted, Unwanted, Wanted, Unwanted, Wanted, Unwanted. It is calculated psychological abuse of the cruellest, most destructive form.

I therefore had mixed feelings when reading Childs-Foster's words. Perhaps the term, "more suited to communal life" was a momentary improvisation to suit dealing with my situation but, even though they condemned me to a childhood spent in institutions and robbed me of a placing with a well-to-do family, the words struck a chord.

The current government's mission statement to attempt to place all unwanted children in families is misguided and furthermore, stigmatises all those children who end up in children's homes because they are deemed to be problem children. In reality, it is often the families that they are placed with that are the problem. The differing needs of each child must be taken into account. But you may judge for yourselves as this story unfolds as to the origins and validity of my concerns.

Back to our story. Suffice to say that, when Miss Childs-Foster met the Reverend George Granville, she too was so overwhelmed by his charm and his wish to maintain contact with the boy.

Of Mrs Granville, she remained unconvinced. The minister's wife was clearly far from having recovered from her breakdown and, at times in the meeting, still complained about the boy.

However, wooed by the Reverend's grace and kindness, Childs-Foster allowed many of her reservations, over what the reverend, Miss Wallis and Miss Stewart had proposed, to subside. Even the point that the minister might be forced to move churches, with which Mr Granville concurred, was passed by.

Childs-Foster in any case entered the discussion careful to avoid rejecting the Granvilles' wishes in their entirety. The discussions with the other prospective fosterers might take some time and with Miss Stewart and Miss Wallis so adamantly in favour of the Granvilles, Childs-Foster herself might be brought to account if a further foster placement for the boy were to fail.

"Isn't the Reverend such a kindly fellow?" remarked Childs-Foster as Miss Wallis accompanied her in the taxi back to the railway station, "I do feel much more inclined to support his case and will discuss it further with Miss Merrison."

"10.9.58. I VISITED WITH MISS WALLIS AND SAW MR AND MRS GRANVILLE, AS THEY HAD ASKED ME TO CALL NEXT TIME I WAS IN THE NORTH. MRS GRANVILLE LOOKED ALMOST ILL, TERRIBLY THIN AND PALE, VERY TENSE. I SHOULD SAY THAT SHE IS A WORRIER BY NATURE AND POSSIBLY A LITTLE RIGID BUT GUIDED BY THE HIGHEST PRINCIPLES...MR GRANVILLE IS AN EXCEPTIONALLY NICE MAN, A WARM PERSONALITY, MOST REASONABLE. I FELT THAT HE HAD A REAL LOVE AND CONCERN FOR PHILLIP AND HE HAD BEEN DEEPLY UPSET AT HAVING TO PART WITH HIM.

"...I TRIED TO POINT OUT THAT AS IT IS SO DIFFICULT TO FOSTER COLOURED CHILDREN. IT WAS NOT VERY LIKELY THAT WE COULD FIND ANOTHER FOSTER HOME FOR PHILLIP AND THEREFORE THEIR CONTINUED CONNECTION WITH HIM WOULD BE EXTREMELY VALUABLE. THEY FEEL THAT HE HAS SETTLED DOWN VERY HAPPILY AT BIRKDALE AND SO WE AGREED THAT PERHAPS HE IS A LITTLE BOY WHO TAKES EASILY TO COMMUNAL LIFE.

"I FELT IT VERY IMPORTANT FOR THE PEACE OF MIND OF THE FOSTER PARENTS THEMSELVES THAT THEY SHOULD FEEL THAT THEIR CONNECTION WITH PHILLIP HAD NOT BEEN A COMPLETE FAILURE, AND THAT THEY COULD STILL PLAY A USEFUL AND IMPORTANT PART IN HIS LIFE..."

L M Childs-Foster, 18th September, 1958

When Childs-Foster reported back to M, M was not as convinced as her assistant and so the debate over my future continued for another 13 months. Nevertheless, Childs-Foster wrote to the Granvilles to reassure them:

"I KNOW THAT YOU HAVE BEEN WORRYING A GOOD DEAL ABOUT PHILLIP, BUT I DO HOPE THAT YOU WILL NOT DO SO ANY MORE. HE SEEMS TO BE A CHILD WHO IS HAPPY LIVING A COMMUNAL LIFE, BUT I AM SURE THE CLOSE CONNECTION WITH YOU AND YOUR HOME AND FAMILY WILL ALSO BE VERY GOOD FOR HIM."

Childs-Foster, 18th September, 1958

The opportunity for my placement with Dr Lathom disappeared. Then, a year later, the question of my adoption or fostering was again broached. This time it was with a family of not such a respected status as the Lathom's. Once again Miss Wallis from Bolton took a hand in my fate but this time she used the social status argument of Childs-Foster's in favour of the Granvilles. She wrote to a Miss Wolstenholme who had taken over Miss Childs-Foster's role:

"MISS SIM FEELS PHILLIP SHOULD BE BOARDED-OUT AGAIN AND AS SHE KNOWS OF A COUPLE WHO ARE EAGER TO HAVE A COLOURED BOY, SHE WONDERS ABOUT PLACING PHILLIP THERE...WHILE IT CAN NOT BE RIGHT TO DEPRIVE A CHILD OF A FOSTER-HOME AND ALL THIS MEANS, I AM NOT SURE IF PHILLIP MIGHT NOT BE BETTER REMAINING IN CLOSE TOUCH WITH THE GRANVILLES...I AM CONCERNED LEST LOSS OF CONTACT WITH THE GRANVILLES, ESPECIALLY MR GRANVILLE, MIGHT NOT AGAIN BE LIKE THE SEVERING OF A VITAL ARTERY TO THE CHILD. IT IS DIFFICULT TO KNOW IN A CHILD LIKE PHILLIP...

"IN EXPRESSING MY IMMEDIATE REACTION, I WOULD STRESS THAT IT IS ONLY IN THE INTEREST OF PHILLIP AND HIS FUTURE. IT IS NOW A FEW YEARS SINCE I SAW THE SMITHS AND I AM WONDERING IF WE MIGHT NOT HAVE SOME REGRETS IN LATER YEARS, IN CASE WE MIGHT NOT HAVE DONE A LITTLE BETTER FOR PHILLIP. THIS WITHOUT ANY THOUGHT OF SOCIAL STATUS, BUT MOST CERTAINLY WITH HIS BACKGROUND IN MIND. HE DOES SEEM IN TUNE WITH THE TYPE OF BACKGROUND THAT THE GRANVILLES HAVE TO OFFER...

Miss Wallis, 8th November, 1959

Miss Wallis was aware of a recent incident where I had been staying at the Granvilles and said that I did not want to go back to the children's home. If this was reported then it might contradict my being portrayed as a "communal child." To cover this point, she added:

"P.S. ... PHILLIP SAID TO PAUL AND MR GRANVILLE THAT HE DID NOT WANT TO GO BACK, BUT AS THE STAY HAD BEEN RATHER SHORT FOR HALF-TERM, MR GRANVILLE THOUGHT THAT HE REALLY MEANT HE WOULD LIKE TO HAVE STAYED A BIT LONGER. HE FEELS HE NEVER REALLY MINDS GOING BACK THERE."

Miss Wolstenholme in turn sent a note to M, her superior, raising a series of points:

"1. NOT KNOWING PHILLIP AT ALL, I WONDER WHETHER HE HAS STRONG AFFECTIONS TO THE GRANVILLES – IF SO, HE WOULD FIND IT DIFFICULT TO MAKE ATTACHMENTS ELSEWHERE.
2. IS HE THE TYPE OF CHILD TO BE HAPPY IN A BRANCH HOME WITH OUTSIDE CONTACTS OR THE TYPE WHO REALLY NEEDS TO LIVE IN A SMALL PRIVATE HOME.
3. ARE THE GRANVILLES THE TYPE OF PEOPLE WHO LATER COULD HAVE HIM BACK. WHAT ARE THE SUPERINTENDENT'S VIEWS?"

Miss Wolstenholme, 16th November, 1959

Once again, the issue was put. Did the boy "really need to live in a small private home" or was he more suited to communal life? It appears a strange question today. Regarding the final question, the answer was clear, the Granvilles could not have me back. Regarding the first question, it is a wonder to think how Barnardo's could make themselves believe that a child who had spent all but 10 months of his young life in care, could form a lasting filial attachment to a couple with whom he had spent only 10 months.

Regarding the matter as a whole, I for one was not made aware of it until I secured my files, 40 years later. The coat was cut to suit the cloth. Miss Stewart was written to for her opinion, which, given that she was the Superintendent or matron in Southport appears to have been considered decisive. She wrote:

"PHILIP (SIC) HAS ALWAYS BEEN VERY HAPPY WITH US AND AT THE BEGINNING WE HAD TEARS WHEN HE HAD TO GO OUT WITH THE GRANVILLES. NOW HOWEVER HE IS FEELING QUITE SETTLED, AND REALLY LOOKS FORWARD TO SEEING THEM AND LOVES GOING TO HIS LITTLE HOLIDAYS. I FEEL THAT PHILIP IS DEEPLY ATTACHED TO HIS 'UNCLE' BUT JUST LIKES HIS 'AUNT', AND THAT HE REALLY LOVES ME TOO, AND I CERTAINLY AM VERY ATTACHED TO HIM…
"SO FAR AS THE PRESENT IS CONCERNED, THE ARRANGEMENT FOR PHILIP SEEMS TO BE MOST SATISFACTORY, BUT OF COURSE I REALISE THERE IS HIS FUTURE TO CONSIDER…I KNOW THAT PHILIP FEELS THAT IT (THE GRANVILLE'S HOUSE – PF) IS HIS HOME, WHICH HE LIKES TO KNOW IS THERE FOR VISITS THOUGH I THINK HE ACTUALLY IS HAPPIER TO BE HERE WITH MORE CHILDREN OF HIS OWN AGE TO PLAY WITH, DURING TERM TIME."

Miss Stewart, 27th November, 1959

What little 2 L's Phillip thought of the Granvilles, the home and Miss Stewart was very far from what Miss Stewart argued, as you will soon see. But what I actually wanted and where I considered to be my home, was not of any real significance since I had no voice in this matter and no rights. What mattered was what Miss Stewart, Miss Wallis and the Granvilles wanted, so I was happier to be in the home than with the Granvilles and their comfy house and nice food and playing with Paul.

On the 4th of December 1959 I was sentenced to remain in the home in Southport at Barnardo's pleasure.

Chapter 8

On the Inside Looking Out

So, I was four when I was told that Auntie Florence was poorly with having to work and look after three children and Uncle George had two churches to run. I would have to go away for a holiday in a home with other children like the one I was in before.

One day, they said that Auntie Florence was too poorly and that I would have to stay in the home. I don't recall crying. They did What Adults Do. I was in their house and they told me to leave. I didn't really know what I had done to be carted off. I hadn't done anything. Maybe that was the problem. Anyway they fostered me and unfostered me. They took me out of a children's home and put me back in one. We were quits. I didn't owe them anything. Little one-eyed golliwog crying no one-eyed tears, tossed back in the cupboard.

I was always on the move, me - a little black Pinocchio - St. Agnes, Instow, Shrewsbury, Bolton, Southport. I had nobody so I had to move - little black bastard love-child. Child of love. Child of pain.

I wasn't to know at the time but anything resembling family was now over for the rest of my childhood. I would never want to be fostered again. Nor was I prepared for what was to come. I was off into the bleak; back to the social dustbins which They called homes.

"THE LINO FLOORS, THE POLISHED SHOES
AND POLISHED DINING TABLE.
THE BROKEN CHAIRS AND SPLINTERED DOORS
AND SCREAMING BABY'S CRADLE.
THE BREAD THAT BLOCKED THE STINKING LOO
THE KITCHEN FULL OF FLIES
THE TOELESS SOCKS AND WHEEL-LESS TRAINS
THE MOTHERS AND THE 'WHY'S'.
A HOME FOR A CHILD OR A PRISON?
AN "AUNTIE" TWICE A DAY.
THEY MUST HAVE HAD A REASON
TO SHOW THEIR LOVE THIS WAY."

Phillip Frampton, 1966

My heart sank as I entered the place where I was now to be Looked After. Funny phrase, 'Looked After'. I joined the 40 other children being Looked After – Looked Through, Thought of After. Look Before. Look Now. Look After. Sometimes children were lucky and went away to be Looked After by someone else.

They sent me to sleep in a big dormitory with lots of other boys. They sent me to sleep to wet the bed.

Sometimes children came back after being Looked After for a while.

They Wet The Bed too.

We were there because we had nobody else to be Looked After by.

We Wet the Bed.

We wet the bed and we were punished because wetting the bed was naughty. Sometimes we were smacked; sometimes we had to stand in a corner facing the wall. That would teach us not to wet the bed and to go to the toilet before we went to bed. But in the dormitories we still wet the bed and we didn't know why and we never stopped wetting the bed.

We woke up in the darkness with a warm wet patch beneath us that smelt like old fish and it was wee. And we took off our pyjamas which were wet and cold and lay on the edge of the bed till morning to keep out of the wee, which went cold because we weren't lying on it any more and keeping it warm. And if we put our blue blankets on top of the wee to cover it up, the sheet turned blue. If we wet the bed too often, an orange rubber sheet was placed on top of the mattress and we woke in our piss because, like us, it had nowhere else to go.

And in the morning we were shamefaced and tried to hide it but the sheets were wet and smelt like wee and They could smell rotten fish. They got very cross. The older boys were cleverer and they disguised their wet beds till they could sneak up to the dormitory and switch their mattresses for ours. And we got the blame. And we were punished. Sometimes we wet our pants and knickers too and we were punished for that as well.

I was four years old and in my best grey short pants in Trafalgar House, Trafalgar Road, Birkdale, Southport, Lancashire, England, Europe, The World. A Doctor Barnardo's Home. The home held 40 children. From babies to teenagers they, we, were all equally scruffy.

Everything that I found in the ramshackle old Victorian mansion depressed or intimidated me. It was a horrible place. Children hared down grimy corridors that were graced with chipped cupboards and broken chairs. The cream painted walls of the rooms were variously adorned with crayon or pencil marks or grubby fingerprints. Elsewhere, the paint was scoured to fading by efforts to erase graffiti.

The toilets sported yellow-green pools of undirected urine; their walls carried the remnants of unwelcome faeces that had found its way on to little fingers.

Everywhere reeked of the terrible fetid smells of institutions deprived of care and social attention. Odours of Neglect and Poverty. Stenches of urine, stale food, ammonia and damp were matched by the furniture and fixtures, none of which could appear unblemished. Blankets had patches faded by bedwetting, stuffing hung out of the comfy chairs, doors sported cracks and tables bore scratches. Here a wheel-less train. There a toeless sock.

I ate, slept and played in a whirl of activity that never stopped until I was sent to bed. And then when Nurse, in her orange nylon overalls, turned the dormitory's lights out, we sat up again and talked and played or read our comics lit up by a torch beneath the sheets. Then Nurse came in again and told us to be quiet and confiscated our torch and comics and told us that we would get a smack if we didn't go to sleep.

They fed us with stale bread and stale cheese, half-washed lettuce, dirty potatoes, cold lumpy porridge, cold fried bread, cold gravy, cold tea and warm sour milk. Oliver Twist asked for more. We contrived to starve.

At least, in the daytime and evening time, we had the great big garden to play in and the cream, metal fire escapes that climbed up and down and all over the back of the house. Playing was great and I loved to play with Matron's pet dog. But one day it came into the garden with another dog and they started chasing us and we ran away and they bit us and we cried. The more we ran away the more the dogs caught up with us and bit our legs. I didn't like dogs after that.

The other dog never came back again. Someone said it had been put in a bag and put in the sea. So now we could play in the garden again. And in the garden the boys fought and the girls fought and whoever lost cried. And the boys were naughty and the girls were naughty and when they were punished with the cane, they cried. And lots of children cried. Some cried that they wanted their mothers.

"Shut up! Your mother doesn't want to see you. That's why you're here."

Nobody wanted us. We were the unwanted. Being there was our punishment for being born.

We Lived There.

So They said.

Did I want to be there? No. I had arrived from a comfortable lower middle class home. I had had nice food and lived in a nice home and I didn't wet the bed. But that home was not my home. It was where I lived because I had been sent there. Now I had been sent to this place. I hated it. But what could I do?

The people who looked after me didn't want me any more, so I had to go. The kind white vicar had taken me into his home to Look After me. I called them "auntie" and "uncle" but they were not Mine. They were just kind to me. Everybody was kind to me. Everyone was kind to us all. They were kind to us even when they beat us. Because we had nothing.

I had nobody but I didn't cry. I had never known having anybody. I had lost nobody. Having somebody was as much a mystery to me as having nobody is to wanted children.

The Granvilles were nice people because they came and took me out to the beach sometimes and we went for an ice cream or some nice food in a café in the town. That was good. They sent me a comic to read every week too and that was good. And I learned to play with some of the other children and made some happiness out of it all – as children do. I still Wet the Bed.

I was taken to my new school and I was allowed to read while the other children had to have a nap in the afternoon and I liked that. I liked reading the books the school gave us; *Janet and John*, *Little Black Sambo* and all. And I read the *Turn About* story in a big book with lots of pictures called *My First Book of All* and published by Thomas Nelson & Sons. The story had two pictures. One was of a black boy chasing four white geese and the other was of the same geese chasing him up a tree: "When Sam ran after the geese he said it was a bit of fun. When the geese ran after Sam it was no fun for him at all."

And I read Little Black Sambo. But the book wasn't about me. It was about a little black boy who lived in a very poor country far away and all the people were poor because they had not learned to make things like the people in this country, and we sent them missionaries like Uncle George to educate them and teach them about Jesus and all. But if I were there I'd be a Little Black Sambo or a Sam because I was black too.

It was good to do well in the infant school and you got stars if you did good work and sweets off the headmistress if you got enough stars. Sometimes I did good work so I liked that. And the school dinners were always better than we had in the home. So I liked them and I liked school and I hated Trafalgar House.

The nurses walked us to school everyday. Those of us at Birkdale Infants and Junior Schools went together. We walked together, all Doctor Banana's kids, with DBH scrawled in black ink on white cotton tags sewn into Our socks, Our trousers, Our underpants, Our shirts, Our jumpers, Our coats, Our Everything. Just in case you get lost. Just in case you die. So that we can get Our clothes back.

Just in case you run away and take all your clothes, we'll also give you a Barnardo special pudding basin haircut or let your black curly hair mat and knot so everybody will know where to return you. And run away we did and get caught we did. There weren't really any kids like us in that neighbourhood so we never got far.

That neighbourhood, which our tribe trouped through to school, was the wealthiest part of Birkdale. And the Darkest. Light seemed almost hidden by huge mansions, and tall ancient sycamores, beeches and oaks whose summer leaves would bat away the sun. The sycamore trees' leaves twisted in the wind tossing off the greenflies that found their way into your mouth and into the lettuce in the Spam salad.

In autumn the sycamore trees scattered their seeds that twirled like dervishes as they flew to the ground. Then their leaves would fall, dark and crispy, like brown snow to darken autumn's sodden pavements and turn into a soft mush that clung to your shoes and got you told off for not wiping your feet.

In that first summer, I joined the rag-tag band of children assembled in front of the home by Miss White. She was one of the staff. We were to Go For A Walk. We lined up then Went For A Walk with Miss White. Out of the home we went, marching, skipping and shuffling past the other big houses that were lived in by other people like Matron; old people, rich people with their own gardeners and big gardens and big cars.

This was the domain of a smug upper middle class England with vast, leafy, unkempt gardens, rambling houses, huge lawns besides which long drives led to garages with Rolls Royces and Bentleys for the retired dowagers, businessmen and colonels. Doubtless the warren of rooms in which we were hidden away at Trafalgar House were once the patrol ground of butlers and maids for masters whose family were only finally parted from their house by death or decadence.

Two-by-two we came out of our Ark, we traipsed along, the boys in baggy hand-me-down, knee-length trousers and the girls in their ill-fitting hand-me-down dresses, a skinny, ragamuffin troupe of ten or more. The old ladies, with their walking sticks and little dogs, smiled at the poor little urchins. The swarthy, grey-haired gardeners scowled at the thieving little wretches who stole from the old ladies' orchards and came round offering to do little jobs which the old ladies agreed to, then found that their purses had gone missing.

Our Birkdale was dark and intimidatingly large. Leaving it was like entering into a bright world where children were free. Overhead the seagulls hovered, monitoring our progress, squawking continually and warning the townspeople: "Here come the ugly ducklings! Here come the ugly ducklings!" Returning home was a foot-dragging, coat swinging misery. The seagulls squawked on warning of our return. We were back off parole. We were back on the inside looking out.

And at night we were told to pray: "Lighten our darkness, we beseech thee O Lord…" for we were in the darkness of Birkdale, hidden away. We were the great unwanted, orphans, love-children, kids from "broken homes" and families that "couldn't cope" with us anymore. Like the outcasts of old, some of us would be shipped off to Australia. Some of us would be sent down south to learn a trade and become gas fitters and mechanics and tool fitters. And some boys would be sent to a "remand" home because they were too naughty, so they were remanded in a home and then went to prison.

Five days a week we tramped to school along Birkdale Road, the wide main street in the foliated, sedate village of the same name. The rows of shops on either side of the street were split by a railway crossing adjacent to the village railway station It let trains pass to Southport and to a big city called Liverpool and to take us away and bring us back and take us away again.

Everything about the shops seemed posh, stuck-up, not ours, nothing to do with us except when we had pocket money. There was a toyshop in the village where you could put little toys up your jumper or in your coat when They weren't watching you and waiting for you to put little toys up your jumper and in your coat. There was a newspaper and sweet shop where you could put sweets in your mouth when They weren't looking. The man who owned the shop would give you money for delivering his newspapers around the big houses when you got older and could ride a bike properly and got permission from Them.

So we learned how to get things from Them that we wanted and could never get. Take it from Them. They have it and you don't and your pocket money can't buy enough sweets for one day and you'll never have anything till you're old enough to get a paper round or sing in the church choir.

It wasn't the best school of crime. Someone was always getting caught for doing this or that. Everyone who ran away was always brought back. Mark Lancaster was seven and Mickey Thompson was eight when they ran away with two other boys and not a day older when the police found them at the railway crossing's lights. Go…Stop. Back to the place to be beaten and fight and scream and be locked in a room till you have calmed down and lost your pocket money for another week.

Matron, Miss Stewart, was a spinster – like most of the Barnardo's management. Tall and thin, she was well-spoken, on account of her private school education. The daughter of a vicar in rural Buckinghamshire, she had deemed herself destined for life in the wealthiest of circles. Now and then her thoughts would drift back to the occasion on which, as a young, high society debutante, she was introduced to King George V.

Only Miss Stewart knew who and what had crushed her dreams. Some say she once had a lover but it all went wrong; that he ran off with a woman with better prospects, leaving Mary Stewart to devote herself to the poor waifs of the world.

She exiled herself from the South of England after a spell working as a nurse at Stoke Mandeville hospital in her home county. Then she had become a Barnardo's "nurse". All the junior staff were women and had to be called Nurse this and Nurse that. One day it changed to Aunt This and Aunt That but we'll stick to Nurse for the story.

In 1945, Mary Stewart was promoted to run Trafalgar House. Now in her late fifties, she had lost hope of ever marrying. Instead, she had brought her elderly mother up North so that she could take care of her. We were told to call her mother "Granny." Granny came and tended the garden with Mac, the grumpy, old, white-haired man who also kept the boilers running. Granny was as thin as Matron and tucked her grey hair under her bonnet like Matron did when she was outside the home.

Mary Stewart tried to do her best for the poor little children she looked after but they were such a handful. They had to be dealt with very strictly because there were so many who had come from "very bad homes." When some of them went away to see their families they would come back unwashed and smelling so badly that even a good soaking could not get rid of the smell. They came back upset, using the most awful language and wetting their beds again. She often thought that it would be preferable for these children if their parents left them alone altogether.

She was fond of some of the children and knew that Miss Merrison in London considered her too fond of some. "Be careful of having favourites," M would say, "You will make a rod for your own back." But Mary Stewart believed in rewarding the good and children needed carrot as well as stick. Besides, the children had to live in this terrible home which was far too big to handle and for which there was never enough money to maintain. She told M that the situation would be much improved if she could have a smaller home to look after with a lot less children.

When I arrived, Miss Stewart had just been to inspect a new house where she would be in charge of less than 20 children. Trafalgar House and its grounds were to be sold and the children divided into two. Miss Stewart tried to make sure that she would take the best behaved of the children with her to the new house. The other half would be sent to Liverpool.

The complication was that she had several children who had brothers and sisters in her home. Some she did not want to take. But, though Barnardo's often despatched siblings to homes hundreds, sometimes thousands, of miles away from each other, Miss Stewart was loath to do so. She knew that she could not bear to face the hurt of those children she wished to remain with her.

"Good Lord!" she exclaimed to any of her staff when the issue arose, "If I split up their little families, I would never be able to forgive myself."

I had spent just six months in Trafalgar House before I was told that I would have to go back to the Granvilles for a time while all our things were moved to the new home, Tudor Bank, with Matron. I was pleased because I would be in the same home as boys I liked. They were mainly older than I was, but I liked to play with Mark Lancaster and Michael Ingham and Mickey Thompson. They were fun and taught me games and how to get sweets from the sweet shop when no one was looking.

In November 1959, the Granvilles took me to my new home, Tudor Bank. I liked it. It was like new. We were in Neverneverland. It might have been Peter Pan's Neverland but ours was a fantasy world where the lost children could never say never, where we lived on the never-never. One day we would have to pay for it all.

Everything sparkled and shone – the polished floors and banisters, the stained glass windows criss-crossed by strips of lead, the red bricks and the white, painted front of the house. The gardens were so big that it was more like there were four of them. They had grassy banks you could roll down and trees you could climb and swing on and a great big pitch to play football and kick-the-can and that. Across the road was a big park with swings and roundabouts and lots of trees to play hide and seek in. The park led to the beach, which had sand dunes to slide down and play soldiers and sand you could build castles out of and a sea that washed up messages in bottles and things you could take home and make things with.

And I was there, at Tudor Bank, 2, Beach Rd, Birkdale, Southport, Lancashire, England, The World, with my friends. I was happy being sent there.

Tudor Bank was a mansion, given its name because it was designed with a mock Tudor exterior and surrounded by green banks. The house was also set on a bank so that, while the basement doors at the front of the house opened out onto a garden, the rear basement constituted a cellar from which steps led up to daylight.

It was built in the late 19th and the early 20th Centuries. The front entry to the house was via two huge oak doors on a balcony, which were reached by ascending either of the twin flights of grand steps that formed part of the façade.

The oak doors led into a stone porch big enough to fit all 18 of us children inside. More doors led to a large hall. To the left was our dining room with four wooden tables that could between them seat 24 people. On one wall hung a copy of Picasso's *Child With Dove* and in another was set a large bay window that looked out onto the front lawn and the setting sun.

A mahogany set of drawers, on the right as one entered the dining room, was used for serving up. Beside it was a hatch, which opened onto the pantry and the kitchen. A door to the right of the dining room led to the pantry and the kitchen. The pantry was tiny. It was where we had to take turns to wash and dry up and put the crockery and cutlery away. The kitchen was large enough to seat us all. In its centre was a large oak table, around which we sat, sometimes seven at a time and ate our supper. The room had surfaces and cupboards on two sides, on which were piled great big iron cooking pans and blackened oven trays for the huge greasy oven.

One door at the end of the kitchen led outside to the back garden. Another led to the larder full of food that we would visit on raids at night. Besides the larder was the cook's bedroom. On the right side of the kitchen were two more doors. One that led down steps to the boiler room and the laundry room and the other that opened on to a narrow, winding staircase leading to Matron's room, the Sick Room and the staff bathroom.

Matron's office or The Study, as we would call it, was immediately to the right of the porch. That's where we would be sent to so that we could be told off or caned if we were naughty. That's where we would have to queue up for our pocket money – if we had not been naughty. Matron had a big wooden desk with a folding ledge to write on and the drawer that kept the cane for beating us.

Here, Matron had the safe that had our money in it. She also had a stained glass window that looked out onto the balcony so she could see who was coming to see us. The stained glass window was pretty. On it was a picture of Jesus and his sheep; it said: "The Lord is my shepherd I shall not want…" Once I thought it said: "I shall not be wanted." Then someone said it meant that we should not say: "I want" but, "Please can I have." Anyway, it was pretty and had a yellow sun rising above the hills in the background.

Her office had three small comfy chairs and a wooden chair around a small fireplace. That's where she talked to the important people, like people from Headquarters and policemen and the mayor.

The hall itself was almost bare. There was wood, wood, everywhere. At the end on the far right were more wooden doors. These led into a large room with wooden panelling along the walls. It would be our upstairs playroom. Around the sides, on the floor, were lots of wooden lockers for us to put our toys in. Two wooden bookstands held all the books that had been "sent in" - donated second-hand to the home. They were old and tatty and had "To Elsie, Love Peter," and things like that written in them.

At the centre of the room was a large table for us to draw on and play board games like Ludo, Snakes & Ladders and, if we were older, Monopoly. We were given an old gramophone, which was placed on a locker in the left hand corner. Sometimes it played and sometimes it didn't. The gramophone head was so heavy that it soon wore out and, it not being automatic, we soon scratched the records. The records in those days were made of heavy shellac and we'd drop and break them. That's what happened to *Oklahoma*, Caruso, Maria Callas and the Coldstream Guards' Band.

Some of the older girls bought records with songs by the Everley Brothers and Buddy Holly and Elvis Presley and Cliff Richard. David Langley and Brian Reynolds were older so they put lots of stuff in their hair and made out they were like Teddy Boys. When Cliff Richard's song, *Summer Holiday* came on, we would all sing along: "We're all going on a summer holiday…". We went on summer holidays – to Birkenhead and Bradford and Liverpool and Leeds and lovely places like that. And we sang, "We're going where the sun shines brightly, we're going where the sea is blue." We were in Southport and the sea looked more like it was brown to me.

The two bay windows, which looked out onto a sandpit, Beach Road and the morning sun, were as large as the window in the dining room. They were big enough for us to climb through. We were told not to climb through them, but we did because it was fun and it was the quickest way to get out since we weren't allowed to use the front door.

The right wall of the playroom was a folding wooden screen that had a door in it. This door led to the staff room with its two comfy chairs, a large settee that swallowed us little ones up, a wooden desk and a soft carpet in the middle. The chairs were set around the grand fireplace. This room also had a stained glass bay window and looked out onto the front lawn and the setting sun. A writing table was placed beside the window for the nurses to write their letters to their boyfriends and mothers and fathers and real people.

The staff room was out of bounds for us but it had the only television. We could enter to watch the television but only if we had their permission. It also had a piano on which Matron would play and sometimes we would be told to come in and sing with her.

The only other door leading off the hall was beneath the main staircase. It led to the downstairs boys' and girls' toilets and a staircase. The small stairwell went down to a cloakroom on the right where we hung our coats and kept our shoes. To the left was a narrow passage to the garage where we could keep our bikes if we had them and where Mac, the gardener, who was also the boilerman and handyman, kept some of his equipment and did little jobs. Somewhere along the walls there was a hatch leading to a shallow cellar beneath the house. The cellar was dirty and damp but one day we would sneak in with a torch and discover its secrets.

Between the entrance to the garage and the entrance to the cloakroom was another large playroom. We called this room, which had large black metal and glass doors looking out onto the front lawn and directly beneath the front door, the downstairs playroom. Some of us had to have our lockers down there because there wasn't enough room upstairs.

The downstairs playroom was where Matron would organise jumble sales. All she had to do was put an advert in the paper and lots of kindly people brought their jumble – discarded clothes, toys and the like. Then Matron took out the best of the discarded clothes and discarded toys for us and put them aside for our Christmas and birthday presents. Lots of old ladies and poor people came to the jumble sales and gave us money then the older boys and girls had to escort the pensioners back home.

The downstairs playroom was also the place where we received and kept our big Christmas presents, like the second-hand white rocking horse with one ear broken off and the scratched, out-of-tune piano with some keys missing that some of the older ones could play a tune or two on. We didn't use the room much because it was cold in the winter. We did use it sometimes for messing about which led to fights and tears.

Sometimes the downstairs playroom was used for little tea parties, and it was where we had our Halloween parties and played bob-the-apple. We would get our heads soaked as we put our heads in the big bowl that the cook used for making Yorkshire Pudding, and tried to fish out the green apples from the water with our teeth. Then the candles in the turnips were lit and the lights turned out and we all hooted and scared ourselves till we laughed – or cried.

Finally, off the hall and opposite the porch rose the main stairs. They must have been six-feet wide and in polished dark wood. The banisters were made of wood as dark and had a knob on the end to stop us falling off when we slid down. That wasn't allowed either but it was fun. Daylight passed through a large stained glass window sporting the red rose of Lancashire above the staircase. We climbed up to a door with wire-enforced glass that led to the upstairs corridor. The side of the corridor that looked down onto the main hall also had wire-enforced glass panes along its length.

The corridor, normally so deserted during the day, became a hive of activity during the evenings and just before breakfast time as we went to wash and toilet and played around while we waited for our turn. It was this corridor that linked three staff bedrooms, Matron's bedroom, the boys' and girls' dormitories, the boys' and girls' bedrooms, the boys' bathroom and toilet, the girls' bathroom and the staff bathroom.

The only other way to get upstairs or downstairs was via the back stairwell that led to the kitchen. We weren't allowed to go up the back stairwell unless we asked permission. It led to Matron's room and we didn't need to go up there did we? We did when we were raiding the larder at night and when we were playing hide-and-seek. But we didn't ask did we?

All the bedrooms had floors covered in green linoleum. It washed easily after we had peed on it. Matron had the best bedroom. It was right beside the staff bathroom and away from our rooms almost at the north end of the L-shaped corridor. She could get peace and quiet. The three nurses' bedrooms were designated to be beside our rooms so that they could keep an eye on us.

The nurses had a room each and their rooms were as big as the boys' and girls' bedrooms which each slept three elder children. The boys' and girls' dormitories were at the front of the house on the south and north wings. Both dormitories slept six of the youngest children and smelt most often of rotten fish.

The girls were lucky because they had a toilet in their bathroom. They were warm when they got out of the bath for a pee. But we boys were lucky because we had a separate toilet and when someone made a smell, it didn't smell the bathroom out. Our bathroom, with its two Royal Doulton white porcelain sinks and flannels hung up for wiping our faces, smelt of smelly socks and sweaty feet. Sometimes it also smelt of smelly underwear too. We were allowed a change once a week – unless we wet ourselves - so our bodies got sores and our skin was often chapped – like it was natural.

So that first night in our dormitory, when Martin Williams and myself were sent to bed and the lights turned off at six o'clock, we ducked under our fresh, white linen sheets. We were alone in the room because Mark Lancaster was seven and so he could go to bed at seven o'clock. Michael Ingham, Tom Chorley and Mickey Thompson were eight so they could go to bed at eight o'clock.

If you were nine you could go to bed at eight thirty and when you were ten, like Brian Reynolds who slept in the bedroom for the older boys, you could go to bed at nine o'clock. Jimmy Langley and David Bryant were also in his room. They were older than ten but they still had to go to bed by nine o'clock. They were big boys and soon they would go to Goldings, the Barnardo's home in Stevenage to learn a trade and maybe go to Australia or join the Merchant Navy. But they still had to be in bed at nine o'clock. Those were the rules. Everyone had to be washed or bathed and in bed by nine o'clock

I was tucked up in bed under my sheets and blankets for two minutes before I got up and went to the window to peer outside at our great big new playground outside. That night was a full moon and its light pierced the light, cream, cotton curtains showing up their patterns of children at play with whipping tops and red and blue footballs and green and red skittles. I pulled back the curtain enough to peep through and the moon lit up my face. Martin joined me by my side and he pulled the curtain back a little more.

Below us was the front lawn. "Matron 'as called it the Pitch," I said to Martin, "because it's where we can play football. She said we could play cricket and rounders on the Pitch too but in the summer."

"It's big in' it?" said Martin pressing his nose on the cold wet pane, "I bet the boys will 'ave races on there.

"And fights," I added. "We can play kick-the-can on there too and take our toys out there."

"Look at those big banks," said Martin, "We can ride our bikes up and down 'em. It'll be great."

"Bet you won't get your bike up there," I challenged him. He was two years younger than I was, so I could say what I liked to him, "It's too steep an' you'll fall off."

"Bet I won't."

The object of our conversation was a tall green grassy bank that surrounded the house and was topped in some places by wire and in others by wooden fences through which we would peer at the outside world and through which the people outside would stare at us. A smaller bank split the grounds at the front of the house. It formed the boundary between the Pitch and a patch of ground with fruit beds and apple trees. The tall bank to the right was topped with a grassy pathway and edged by a wire fence.

"What's on the other side of there?" asked Martin, pointing to the wire fence.

"I dunno but I've seen a big 'ouse in there, bigger than ours."

"Is it fer children like us?" Martin asked.

"I dunno. I've only been 'ere one day. I dunno everything you know. Brian Reynolds says he's been there before and there's a rich man lives there with 'orses and a big Rose Royce."

"What's a Rose Royce?" he asked.

"It's a car, stupid."

"I'm not stupid."

"You are if you don' know that."

We looked in front of us and there was another big bank. It was the same size. The grassy pathway from the bank on the right ran along it behind the trees. The moonlight shone through the winter-stripped sycamore trees that climbed up the side of the bank. The light showed up a tall wooden lattice fence that ran the length of the walkway.

"What's behind that fence?" asked Martin.

"The road, silly. Matron says its called Rotten Row. She says we're very lucky because it's very pretty in the summer with lots of flowers on it and very colourful. Brian Reynolds says there's a gate in the fence and some steps that go down to the road. 'e says 'e climbed over the fence an' rolled down the 'ill an' ended up in the flowers. 'E says it's great."

"I bet I can climb the fence."

"I bet you can't. You'll fall off."

Our chattering ceased for a while as we gazed at our Neverneverland and imagined the fun we would have and the treasures we would find.

Then Martin asked: "Can we go to the park?"

We had been told that there was a park on the other side of Rotten Row and were all very pleased.

"I dunno. Maybe Miss White will take us for a walk on Saturday or somethin'. Brian Reynolds says there are swings there an' roundabouts an' things."

Martin pointed to the small grass bank that ran along the left side of the Pitch: "I bet I can ride my bike up there."

"I bet you can too. Anybody can. Even a baby," I teased. "See on the other side. Matron says that's Mac's garden."

"Who's Mac?"

"The gardener, fool. The old man who wears overalls all the time."

"The grumpy one?"

"Yeah. You wanna watch 'im. David Bryant says he'll pull yer ear off if 'e catches yer nicking from 'is apple tree."

"Is it 'is garden?"

"Matron says it is."

"Why?"

"I dunno. Matron says he'll grow apples and strawberries and raspberries and pears and lettuce in there for us. So we can 'ave lots of fruit and lots of salad."

"Yuk! I 'ate salad," said Martin, letting his mouth hang open.

"Me too. Shhh..." We heard a faint rattle of the doorknob and scampered away from the curtain as the dormitory light was switched on.

"Get in to bed this minute," said the tall and plump Nurse Pat as I stood transfixed by the side of mine. "And where is Martin Williams?" she asked looking around the room.

"I dunno."

Then the blonde-haired, bespectacled 40-year-old caught sight of the blonde hair of the four-year-old. She marched over to a bed by the window, leaned down and pulled him out from beneath the bed by his hair. Martin screamed and Nurse Pat smacked him hard on the legs.

"If I catch you two out of bed again, I'll give you both what for," she threatened as she left the room.

The light went off and Martin was left to sob in the dark. We were always left to sob in the dark. Martin was a crybaby, so I thought. He was always crying for his mummy but his mummy never came. But I cried too sometimes. I cried when the older boys hit me.

That night I waited for Tom Chorley, Michael Ingham, Mark Lancaster and Mickey Thompson to come to bed and talk and tell me more about my new world. Michael, like his younger brother and sister, was mixed-race Asian. His younger brother, Dick, was still away staying with some people. When Dick returned the nurses would have to bring another bed. He used to sleep in the girls' dormitory with his sister, Mary, in the old home but now he was four and would be put in the boys' dormitory.

Michael Ingham was my best friend. We used to play together a lot. I had been given some toy soldiers and a fort and we played with them in the garden. Bang! Bang! Duhduhduhduh! Boom! Bang! Duhduhduhduh! Boom! Bang! Bang! Duhduhduhduh! Boom! Duhduhduhduh! Boom! Boom! Till all the soldiers had fallen to the ground. And we played Bang! Duhduhduhduh! Boom! All day long.

Michael was one year older than I was, so sometimes he played more with the bigger boys but I liked him. When the Granvilles came to take me out with them on a Saturday, I would ask them if he could come too and they said yes. We liked playing together and he liked their Marmite sandwiches when we had a picnic on the beach. He said Auntie Florence's sandwiches had nice soft bread and warm butter and weren't stale at the edges like Molly, the cook's.

Michael was the same age as Tom Chorley and Mark Lancaster. Tom was white and Mark was mixed-race with black curly hair like me but his skin was much darker. Mark was very strong and when he got into a fight he could even beat the bigger boys. Sometimes the nurses were frightened of him. When he got into a temper, it took two of them to hold him down. He was kind to me and never hit me. He taught me lots of things about animals and birds and that.

Tom smiled all the time but he didn't teach me about many things – just cricket and trains. He loved trains and went to the railway station in Birkdale on Saturdays to watch them go up and down the line. One day he went missing and they found him at the train station in Southport. It was eight o'clock and he was sat on the platform sleeping. He loved cricket too and batted and bowled all day long in the summer holidays. If nobody would play with him, he would bowl his tennis ball at anything then went and picked it up, tossed it in the air and hit it with his bat.

I liked Mickey Thompson too. Mickey was white with mousy hair and looked wise. He loved football and we played football on the Pitch as soon as we arrived and were allowed to. He supported Nottingham Forest because he was from Nottingham and I supported Bolton Wanderers because I was from Bolton. He went to watch Southport play football with Brian Reynolds and the big boys. Mickey ran away a few times but he was always caught and brought back.

Nurse Pat, who had the room next to us so that she could keep an eye on us, came in the dormitory again and switched on one light. "Make sure you are quiet," she told the other boys, "Phillip and Martin are fast asleep. Fold your clothes neatly and make sure you all brush your teeth and say your prayers."

Mark, Mickey, Michael and Tom got undressed and changed into their striped, cotton pyjamas.

"Oooh! It's really cold up 'ere," said Michael as he took off his white cotton vest; "I'm puttin' on me dressing gown."

"So am I," added Tom.

The dressing gowns with their belts were made out of the same coarse, woollen material as our blankets. We knew our own dressing gowns by the differing colours of the cotton stitching around the edges.

"That's mine!" cried Mickey as Tom reached for the gown with the red stitching.

"No it's not, it's mine," replied Tom clutching it to his chest, "Matron said I could 'ave red this time."

"Well it's not yours. Mine's red. In' it Michael?" Mickey shouted, wrestling the dressing gown from Tom's hands, "Go an' find yer own."

Mickey pushed Tom over and Tom started to cry.

"Cry Baby! Cry baby!"

In came Nurse Pat and little Tom blubbered: "He's taken me dressing gown and pushed me over! Matron said I could 'ave the red one."

Nurse Pat went over to Mickey and took the dressing gown off him then went over to the door where she found another dressing gown with red stitches: "This is yours Mickey. Now any more arguing and you'll be punished."

Mickey and Michael disappeared into the bathroom. In the bathroom they found the bright new tins of Gibbs powder toothpaste stacked, each with a boy's name scrawled on it. Cream metal pegs with names written on sticky tape beside them were fastened to a yellow piece of wood on the walls. Each peg held a boy's towel and flannel. By the time that they had finished, the bathroom floor had pools of water around it and the linoleum in the toilet next door had a yellow snake of urine.

Mickey was the first to kneel by his bed, hands clasped and pointed to the ceiling, for his prayer: "Our father who farts in 'eaven, 'arold be thy name, my kingdom come. Thank you. Amen."

And they giggled.

Mark followed: "Matthew, Mark, Luke and John, don't wet this bed tha' I lie on."

And they giggled and giggled.

Then came Tom: "For wha' we're about to receive that the pigs 'ave just refused."

And they giggled and giggled and giggled.

Michael could hardly say his piece for giggling but finished off: "Lighten our darkness we beseech thee, O Lord, so I can read Mickey's *Lion* comic."

And they giggled till their sides felt like splitting.

It was ten past eight when Nurse Pat turned out the light and ordered the boys to sleep, as they had to go to school the next day.

As soon as she had gone, Mickey sat up and leaned under his bed to find his torch. He started reading his *Lion* comic under the sheets. Then Michael sat up and hissed to Mickey: "Give us a read of that when yer finished will yer?"

Tom appeared from under his blankets too and I waited under mine for the boys to start talking. It was Mark who finally began the chatter, saying: "It's grea' this place. I asked Matron and she said that, if we're good, we can keep pets in the old shed at the back."

"Miss White said she lives in the 'ouse just behind the back," Michael volunteered, "So it means that she can take us for more walks."

"Matron says we can go into the park on our own so long as we mind the road," added Mark.

I stuck my head up and said: "I like the sandpit and the swing."

The sandpit and swing were on the right-hand side of the house. That area was on the right of the Drive. The Drive was wide enough to drive a car down and paved with stones that ran from the garage to the main gate on Beach Road. On the other side of the drive was Mac's Garden. Small grass banks lined both sides of the drive and as they tapered out, were replaced by a rockery.

"Matron says that's Granny's Rockery," said Mark.

"Why?"

"Because Granny will grow some flowers there and water 'em and that."

Granny was Matron's mother and Granny was very, very old. She could do what she pleased and she pleased to do the Rockery when the weather was good.

"Let's go to the beach after school and get some old rope," said Mickey, as he finally picked up our whispered chatter, "There's always some around and we can make a rope swing on the trees."

"I can climb all the trees 'ere," said Mark.

"Bet I can too. And we can get some wood too and make a den in the trees," added Michael. Then he turned to Mark: "Come on Mark, tell us one of yer monster stories."

"All right," Mark assented, "but let me think of one first."

Mickey Thompson turned off his torch and put his comic down. Then we all lay down facing Mark's bed beside the window.

Mark began: "Once upon a time there was a big green 'ouse where lots of boys lived. They played football and soldiers all day an' ate sandwiches, strawberries and ice cream and jelly every day. They didn't 'ave to go to school because they could read and write already. The 'ouse 'ad ten televisions an' the little boys went to bed at ten o'clock and the big boys went to bed at midnight when the ghosts came out.

"The ghosts were white an' scary an' made the little boys cry. Even the big boys cried sometimes because one ghost was a witch with a man's 'ead in 'er arms and a baby stuck to 'er toes. She said she wanted to eat little boys and girls but she never did. One day a big fat monster, with two big red noses an' yellow teeth and bad breath smelling like

Tom's farts (we giggled), came to the 'ouse and said 'e would get rid of the ghosts if the boys let 'im in.

"So the boys said: 'Come in monster. We 'ave never met nice monsters before.'

"The monster said 'e wanted a 'undred plates of jelly an' ice cream to eat so 'e would be strong enough to get rid of the ghosts. The boys 'ad no supper that night, only cocoa. The little boys went to bed early because they were frightened by the monster. Then, at midnight the monster did an 'ead stand, twirled round fifty times then made 'is 'ands go so big that 'e caught all the ghosts fer one 'undred miles around an' threw them into the sea.

"When the big boys saw this they clapped an' cheered. Then they asked 'im if 'e wanted a reward. The monster said that they must go to the town and get 'im some sweets. But it was midnight and the big boys 'ad to go a very long way. 'My legs are tired,' they all said. They couldn't find any sweets so they went to tell the monster that they would get some from the shop in the morning.

"When the big boys got back to the 'ouse. They couldn't find the monster or the little boys just lots and lots of bones in the dustbin."

"Was it the little boys' bones in the bin or the monster's?" asked Michael.

"I'll put you in the bin," threatened Nurse Pat, as she opened the door, "Lovely story that but will you be quiet or I'll send you all to Matron in the morning."

We were left to face the darkness and the monsters and the bones.

Nurse Pat sat in her room next door and perused the bags she still had to unpack. All things considered, she was happy with her new room with its cream coloured wallpaper studded with pink, rose patterns. On her wardrobe, waiting to be put away, were her nylon women's overalls – one green, one orange – that she would be expected to wear on alternate weeks. Being nylon, it was easier to wash off the children's wee from their sheets and the grubby finger marks and snot-stains, which appeared whenever the kids leant against her or grabbed her.

She was pleased with the house. It was grand enough and clean enough not to cause her anxiety if her boyfriend visited. At 34, Pat Thomas was desperate to get married and out of her current job. It helped her save up for a house, she told herself, but it was a job that lasted day and night.

Still, she mused; Miss Stewart had not done too badly in her choice of children out of Trafalgar Road. At least the woman had got herself free of the worst thieves and bullies. The little boys in the dormitory were little tinkers but some were quite sweet. She could take little Martin for her own. The older boys, in the bedroom on the other side of her room, were rascals but they were not bullies. Brian Reynolds was quite attractive and, if he was older, she was certain that she would have fallen for him.

Pat Thomas, though plump, was an attractive woman and only the interference of her father had led to her still being a spinster at 34. "How Miss Stewart could still be unmarried at 55," she would sigh to her boyfriend, "I will never know."

Mary Stewart unpacked her cases too, pulled out a gold locket, gazed at the face of her last love and put it away. She peered round the room and resolved to decorate it in white with pink curtains and pink carnations. Of course, the carnations would only be real once in a while but she loved pink carnations and roses.

Miss Stewart believed she had done well with her choice of children. "I only have a few years left with Barnardo's and it should make things easier. The other place was unmanageable," she told herself.

She sat at her pine dressing table and finished off some of the reports on the children. She had postponed completing them because of the move and now they were late. Some reports she liked to write. Others she didn't. When she got to little Phillip's she smiled. Little Martin, Dick and Michael were all lovely children as well. How could mothers ever treat their children this way? "Of course it's mainly the lower classes who can't cope and fall on difficult times. And the war did mess a lot of people up but mothers should know better!"

She heard a soft tapping on her door and went to see who it was at 11.30pm who wanted to speak to her: "Maybe it is ___________." It was and she let her visitor enter then closed the door.

The next morning we woke to a cold and crisp November day. The windows were slightly frosted up and the grass on the Pitch was singed almost white. I woke early and waited for Nurse Pat to come and tell us that we should get up. I always woke early and it was fine in the summer when daylight shone through the curtains and I could read but in the winter I just had to lie there or find Mickey's or Tom's torch.

When Nurse Pat entered the dormitory to tell us it was time to get up, I was the first to climb out of bed. I was always the first. I liked it that way. That way I could be the first to get into the bathroom to wash my face and brush my teeth. I was the first to go downstairs too. There I could play with my toys.

Barbara Carson came down the stairs and went into the kitchen. At 13, Barbara was the oldest girl in the home. Matron liked Barbara because Barbara helped with the little children and sometimes took them for walks. On winter nights, if it was dry, she would arrange games out on the Pitch for us. Today Barbara was making the toast for the nurses and Matron. Making the toast was a treat. If you were allowed to make the toast, you could have toast with real butter on it and not have to eat the stale bread. Making the staff toast was the one time we were allowed to eat toast. When I was older I would ask to make the toast.

That day was Mary Ingham's turn to ring the first bell. Mary was six and the same age as me. She was late for her chore and almost tripped up as she ran down the stairs in her blue woollen slippers. "How many times have I told you not to run around the house!" declared Matron watching her from the dining room door. It was already twenty past seven and Matron gave the brass bell with its wooden handle to Mary, saying: "Hurry up or everyone will be late for breakfast."

The first bell was the summoning call for all the children to be dressed and ready, forming a queue on the landing behind the glass swing door at the top of the main stairs. I watched Mary as she tried to hold the bell with one hand but it was too heavy. She was a girl and not as strong as us boys. When it was my turn to ring the bell, I would use just one hand because I was strong. The clang of the 7.20 bell started a flurry of activity upstairs. I ran back upstairs to take my place in the queue.

"You've got odd socks on," said Nurse Joan to Mickey as he stood behind me.

"I can't find any others. They've all got 'oles in," replied Mickey.

"Holes or not, they'll have to do for now," declared Nurse Pat, directing Mickey back to the dormitory.

Toeless socks had to do for now and a long time after. For as soon as a nurse would darn one sock, a new hole would appear somewhere else.

At 7.25 Mary rang the second bell. When the second bell rang we had to queue up beside the dining room door and wait for a member of staff to allow us to pass through the door to take our breakfast. That day I was the first in the queue. Then the routine inspection began as two nurses arrived and ordered us to hold out our hands and turn them over as they checked that our hands were washed and our fingernails were clean. It was a routine we were long used to and the bells, queues and inspections occurred at every mealtime.

As I entered the dining room, Nurse Pat pointed to the table where I was to sit, and there I sat looking at the green and white chequered tablecloth with strands of green and white cotton issuing from a rip that one of my toy soldiers could get through. The tablecloth had a brown gravy stain at the end of the tear and I recognised the tablecloth as having come from Trafalgar Road.

When we were all seated, Matron came in and took her chair on the table closest to the set of drawers from whose surface the food was served. She glanced round at us all then placed her hands together, closing her eyes. We followed suit as she began: "For what we are about to receive, may the Lord make us truly thankful."

But we weren't thankful as the breakfast was put before us. We might be in a new home with shiny floors and sparkling windows but the food was as horrid as before. On this first morning we went up to collect our cold fried bread and cold sausages. On other days we would have fried bread and cold, leathery bacon or fried bread and cold beans or fried bread and cold, fried tomatoes.

It was Donna's turn to pour out the tea, which she did from a big jug. She stirred the tea. It already had milk in it. She stirred it to break up the thin skin that had settled on the top.

The only saving grace was that the tables on which we ate had fold up tops with a compartment beneath. That morning, when Nurse Bates wasn't looking and most children had left the dining room, I lifted up the tabletop, took hold of my half eaten sausage and slipped it into the compartment. Then I stuffed a piece of fried bread in my mouth and pretended that I was chewing the rest of the sausage.

We were ordered to eat two pieces of bread and margarine with our breakfast. Today the bread was stale, as was usual. Not wanting to risk being seen sliding it under the table, I stuffed that in my pockets. That was usual too. Our pockets were always full of crumbs. I finished off the fried bread by smearing some marmalade on it. Breakfast for me was always marmalade and fried bread.

For us young ones, not finishing our food at breakfast meant being force-fed. The older boys and girls would have their uneaten food presented at every meal until they ate it. The only palatable alternative was to dispose of it in whatever receptacle we could find.

My plate finally clean, I was permitted to leave the room and headed for the downstairs toilet. The stale bread came out of my pocket and went into the toilet to be flushed. Almost anything that couldn't get into the compartment beneath the dining room tabletop ended up in the toilets. It didn't always flush away easily either, what with unflushed toilet paper and sweet papers blocking up the loo. On that day, I found two half-eaten sausages already floating on the surface.

Arms swinging, I marched back to the dining room piled up some of the lime green plastic cups and saucers and took them into the pantry where Mickey was washing up and Tom was drying.

"Hurry up!" ordered Nurse Joan. "You'll make everyone late for school."

I was on the breakfast rota with Dick, Mickey and Tom, which meant that today Tom and I were clearing the tables. Nurse Joan said I had to clear the tables because I was too slow washing up and when I dried up I didn't put the plates away properly. After we had cleared the tables, we had to lay them for the next meal.

Sometimes I liked clearing the tables because it meant that, if nobody else was in the room, I could remove whatever unwanted food I had placed under my place at the table and place it in the compartment under the table at a place where someone else would normally sit. The table compartments were not checked very often and sometimes I heaved and was almost sick as I lifted the tabletop and looked inside at the blue and white mould.

Since the meals and routine were repeated at teatime, we grew up to be quite thin. Our saving grace when we were young was school meals. For the older children, their saving grace was being paid to sing in the choir or for doing a paper round. That way they could buy chips and fritters. So the oldest boys survived but, by their teenage years, they all had their pallid faces speckled with pink and purple spots.

The tables cleared, and washing-up and drying completed, the three of us went downstairs to get our macks and put on our shoes. Martin had a grey, woollen duffle coat that his stepmother had sent for him. The rest of us had navy blue or black cotton mackintoshes that were always too big for us and came down to well beneath our knees. Mickey and Tom went up to be inspected again.

"After the first week, the older boys and girls will be allowed to walk to school on their own," said Matron, "but until we are sure that you won't get lost, Nurse Pat will take all the children at Birkdale Juniors to school. Make sure that you are all on your best behaviour. Remember we are in a new area and we don't want any complaints… Mickey pull down your collar and Barbara, will you please straighten Phillip's tie for him."

"Now, queue up in twos. Michael, stop pushing. Now, off you go."

"Bye!" we all chorused and lined up behind Nurse Pat to be led out down the drive and through our new neighbourhood.

We were still in Birkdale but closer to the town. Our neighbours still appeared very wealthy, with their huge houses, Rolls Royces and Triumph sports cars. We turned left down Beach Rd and left again until we came to a capstan and the place that would now be our dentists, Drayton House. On the other side of the dentists we paused to cross the busy Lulworth road. Nurse Pat shouted in her friendly voice: "Now children! Look left. Look right. Look left again." The road remained clear. "Now cross. Walk Michael! Do not run!"

We were now on Aughton Road, which would take us ten minutes to walk down until we turned right at a level-crossing which Tom told us was the line which went between Southport station and Birkdale station. He would say that wouldn't he? He was mad about trains.

When I was older I would take that walk without the nurses too. It was a long tedious walk. To save time we would take a short cut through the dentist's grounds. Sometimes they told us off but most times nobody was there when we passed through. Then we crossed Lulworth Road, taking care to look left, look right and look left again. The road would take us past the stable yards that would one day be the home of the great steeplechaser, Red Rum. Immediately before the stables we would pass by the home of Victor.

Walking past Victor's house sometimes frightened us and sometimes made us cackle with laughter. We thought his name was Victor but we didn't really know. Mary Ingham said Victor had big tits: "I seen 'im walkin' and his titties were so big they were swinging from side to side, like windscreen wipers."

Sometimes we used to see Victor in the park or in the sand dunes where he hid behind the bushes. When we got nearby, he would get out his willy and rub it up and down so that we could see him. Mickey said he was wanking. When Victor saw the girls or us he didn't stop. He kept on wanking. Mickey said he was wanking to get up spunk and spunk was white and made babies. Then Mickey or Brian Reynolds shouted: "Wanker!" and we ran off laughing. Sometimes we'd be in a big gang on our bikes and we'd ride at him, hooting and jeering. Once we were all in a big group and we chased him right off the beach and into the fairground.

Brian Reynolds said he could wank too and that he had shagged Donna Brotherton who was in the home and almost as old as Brian. Mickey said shagging was sticking your willy up a girl's fanny and he had seen Donna's fanny. It was hairy and brown. Brian said he had shagged lots of girls at school. But he didn't want to shag Barbara Carson because he didn't like her. She was Matron's pet.

Brian Reynolds said Victor had a gun and he lived in that house by the stables with his mother. Sometimes Victor would appear with his black, swept back hair, big swinging tits and beady eyes at the window and one day he would shoot us.

After Victor's house, the stables and the level-crossing, we came to some shops where, when we returned from school, we could buy sweets and fritters and chips if we had any money. We then turned left into an area of quiet streets lined with two-storey terraced houses where nobody had Rolls Royce cars or sports cars and everyone seemed to have vans. There were small builders' yards there and garages where mechanics crawled under cars. Shops appeared on the occasional corner before we came to a busy street with lots of shops on it and buses running along it.

Over a zebra crossing, where a kind old man in a white coat held out his lollipop and sometimes gave us real lollipops to suck, and we were at the gates of Birkdale Junior School. At Bury Road, we once more passed into the wanted world. The world where children were wanted by their parents and lived in proper houses and went on real holidays and had real Christmas presents and their own people to bring them to school.

They didn't arrive two-by-two and get smacked if they got out of line when they were walking. And they were white and me and Mark Lancaster were black with fuzzy brown hair that the other children liked to rub. They said that their mummies told them that we were black and had fuzzy hair because we were from Africa. But we were from Tudor Bank, Two Beach Road, Southport, Lancashire, England, Europe, The World.

White or black, we were different. They were different too. This was the place where the wanted met the unwanted, ate the same dinners, drank from the same bottles with their iced up milk in winter and warm milk in summer, and had the same teachers to please, the same tasks to master. But they went home to real families and on the school's Open Day, their mummies came to look at their drawings and stuff but nobody came to look at ours.

Mark Lancaster had already passed from the infants' school to the junior school and there in the grounds of the one-storey school built from red brick at the turn of the century, Mark became the best fighter. We could all fight well, us kids from the home. We were tough because we fought in the home. The boys punched and kicked each other and the girls punched and kicked each other and the losers cried and the winner ran off and hid to avoid being punished. We were tough and it made us better than the kids from proper homes and Mark was the cock of his year. He fought the cock of the year above him and still won. But Mark was kind and he looked after us. One day he wanted to go to university.

When school was finished, we waited around in the playground for Miss White or another nurse to pick us up and traipse us back to the land of the unwanted. We didn't mind going back because that was our world. We daydreamed through school to get back to our unwanted world and play with our toys and play games on the Pitch. We were on the inside looking out. Looking out at their world.

We returned to the home for tea at four thirty. The routine was the same as for breakfast except this time we queued up for our inspection outside the dining room. Afterwards we could play. It was almost dark and we only had time for one game of hide-and-seek before we were ordered inside. On those dark nights I would read my comic and then look in the bookcases in the upstairs playroom for other things to read. There I found *Beano* and *Dandy* and Lion annuals with pages torn out or scrawled over. When I had got through these I started on the books without pictures, reading stories of tribes in Africa fighting the Foreign Legion in the mountains or the British in the jungle. I read Enid Blyton's *The Three Golliwogs*:

"Once the three bold golliwogs, Golly, Woggie, and Nigger, decided to go for a walk to Bumble-Bee Common. Golly wasn't quite ready so Woggie and Nigger said they would start off without him, and Golly would catch them up as soon as he could. So off went Woggie and Nigger, arm-in-arm, singing merrily their favourite song -- which, as you may guess, was Ten Little Nigger Boys."

I didn't read it for long. Most of the pages had been crayoned over or ripped out. I read her *Five Runaway* book and imagined what fun and excitement it would be to run away. One day I would run away but maybe I wouldn't get far – like Tom and Mickey and Mark Lancaster. On the first night we were all ordered to bed early, as we were tired so They said. On the nights to come Matron would sometimes let us watch the television in the staff room but sometimes it didn't work properly and the picture was fuzzy so I went to read a comic or a book.

It came to six o'clock and Nurse Pat told me to go to the kitchen to get my supper. I didn't want my supper but we had to have it – a cup of tepid milk and a ginger biscuit or sometimes a plain biscuit. I gulped down the milk trying not to taste how horrible it was, then wiped my milk moustache and waited to go upstairs. I waited because Pamela Brotherton and Mary Ingham were supposed to go to bed at the same time as me but Pamela was three days younger than I was and Mary was three months younger. I wasn't going to bed before them because I was older and that's what I told Nurse Pat.

Nurse Pat eventually came up the stairs with me and told me to undress, put on my dressing gown and get ready while she ran my bath. Bath times brought the same routine as in Trafalgar Road. It was winter and I shivered wrapping my dressing gown around me, while Nurse Pat ran the bath. She filled it up with enough hot water to reach my willy if I sat in the deep end of the bath on the plughole.

"That's all the water you can have," said the nurse, "There's lots of people to have baths after you and we have to save water."

Baths were horrid cold things.

I climbed into my bed. The hard white sheets were cold and I shivered before leaping out of bed and running to get my dressing grown. My dressing gown had blue stitches and was fading where I had stained it one night when I'd wet my bed. But tonight I would go to sleep in my dressing gown again. It was too cold. I shivered.

Chapter 9

Neverneverland

I lay in bed wondering whether there would be a "grub" raid on the larder that night. Mickey and Michael had talked about it while we played outside. Mickey said it was easy: "We'll sneak past Matron's room an' down the back staircase an' see what's there. We'll get some ginger biscuits an' some Sugar Puffs."

"Bet you'll get caught. Those stairs always creak," I said.

"Bet we won't. We've never been caught," replied Mickey. "We'll go when everyone's asleep."

Mickey was right and they came back with ginger biscuits and Sugar Puffs crammed into Martin's woolly bobble hat. That was fun. Soon I would join them on the raids. We never got caught. Sometimes we'd get our hands on a bit of leftover sponge cake from the staff's afternoon tea. Sometimes we found only fig biscuits in the larder. After one night of stuffing fig biscuits, the moan would go out if we returned with those horrible things that gave you the runs: "Not fig biscuits again!"

We yawned our way through the next day and so life went on through the week as we looked forward to Saturday when we got our pocket money and could go to the shops in town – if we were allowed. I said that I wanted to go with the older boys but Nurse Pat said I was too young and she would take the little ones and me if she had time.

Saturday morning came and after breakfast, we were ordered up to change the white linen sheets on our beds. Every week we would remove the grubby, bottom sheet and replace it with the top sheet. The bottom sheet went into a heap of sheets in the bathroom and whoever was supervising would give us each a crisp white clean sheet to use as the top sheet. If the nurse wasn't looking, Mark would pick through the sheets to find one that wasn't torn or already stained with piss marks.

"Remember your hospital corners, Phillip!" Nurse Pat would say to me, "If you don't make your bed properly, you'll have to stay till you've got it right."

And that was a punishment because today was for playing and spending our pocket money. On this day especially, we wanted to get out quick. We had a lot to explore in our new home.

As soon as we had finished, the boys went out to play football on the Pitch. We put our gabardine macks and duffle coats down to make posts and kicked the ball all over the place. We kicked it into Mac's Garden and went to see his fruit beds but it was winter and there was nothing there to eat. We kicked the ball over the fence into the garden next door with the great big house and went to see the Rolls Royce but a gardener came out and told us to get back before he set his dog on us.

Pamela Brotherton came out and with her first kick sent the ball into a pile of nettles beneath the sycamore trees at the bottom on the bank opposite the front of the house. "Girls can't play football," said Tom who went off with Michael to find a fallen branch for the purposes of retrieving the ball. The ball rescued, our game lasted only a little longer – till the moment when Mickey kicked the ball into the tops of a sycamore tree, and we heard a loud hiss.

Then Brian Reynolds and David Bryant came back from the beach with a long rope, tied half a washed-up plank of wood to it and made a swing tying the rope to one of the trees at the top of the highest bank. It meant that we could swing from the grass bank high into the air above the Pitch. It was fun and I got a funny feeling in my feet when I swung out and looked down. Mickey swung out and jumped off and almost fell when he landed. Martin said he could do it too. But Mickey and Bryan said he was too young. Martin cried and we shouted: "Cry baby!" Nurse Pat came out and took him inside.

At ten o'clock we had to go to Matron's study and line up for our pocket money. The older children went first – that way there was no pushing. I went in. Matron was seated with her pink plastic spectacles hanging on the end of her nose. She wrote: "Philip Frampton…6d." Without a word, she handed me my sixpenny piece. I clutched it in my hand and marched out of the room.

That day we had roast beef and roast potatoes and cabbage at dinnertime. Dinnertime was at twelve thirty. The roast beef was cold with lots of slippery fat on it. The gravy was cold and lumpy and the roast potatoes were soft and greasy or hard enough to break your teeth. Mickey said he put them in his pocket and would play Conkers with them at school. Mickey made us laugh.

After dinner we could go to the shops. The big boys and girls went on their own. We went with Nurse Pat. I had sixpence pocket money. When I was seven I would get nine pence and when I was ten, I would get a shilling. With sixpence I could get enough sweets and chewing gum to keep me supplied all Saturday afternoon.

Sometimes we would get back and get out a toy tea set and pretend that we were having a party with all our sweets. At other times, the films man would come and show us a film on his big white screen that he erected in the upstairs playroom. The nurses would pull the curtains closed then sit on the chairs. We were already sat on the floor, waiting for the big lion to roar and Laurel and Hardy to appear.

Then it was tea time and time for prayers and bed.

If Saturday was a fun day then Sunday was a day that promised endless tedium. Sunday meant no shops open and our being escorted to church where we would be expected to sit through the hour-long service and be stared at by girls dressed in frilly frocks and boys in grey suits with gleaming white shirts and fancy ties. We stared back. These children with their immaculately combed hair, clean finger nails and shiny shoes were from the grand houses of the parish.

Before we trouped off to church to stare and be stared at, we had a couple of hours to play between breakfast and ten o'clock when we had to get ready. That first Sunday at Tudor Bank, a steady drizzle came down from the grey sky. It being too wet to play outside, Michael said: "I know let's go to the downstairs play room an' play some games."

"What will we play?" asked Tom, picking a bogey from his nose. Tom always picked his bogeys after breakfast. Sometimes he rolled them up and stuck them under chairs and sometimes he flicked them at us and we had snot fights. Mark couldn't join in because his nose was so snotty; his snot was always too slimy.

"We can play 'ide an' seek an' soldiers," answered Michael, "There's lots of rooms down there."

So off we went hurtling out through the wooden door and down the stairs. I stopped at the bottom by the huge chest where Matron kept old clothes and pulled out a green beret to wear on my head. Mickey dashed into the cloakroom and found a shoe brush, made out it was a pistol and shot me. Bbdumph!

"Ah!" I screamed, clutching my arm and falling against the wall. Mickey retreated behind the door and Tom ran past into the playroom. There he and Michael grabbed two large beer skittles donated to the home, marshalled them like machine guns then took guard on the door.

When Mickey Thompson made his entrance, running in from the cloakroom, the two sentries turned their machine guns on him and gave him a Dahdahdahdah! Dahdahdahdah! that sent him sprawling to the ground.

"I'm only wounded!" cried Mickey as he jumped up, rushed to a table on which was sat a plastic doll. He tossed the doll at them. Gebumph! Gebumph!

I joined up with Michael and Tom, and then Mark came down and went on Mickey's side. We retreated to the cloakroom, collected as many Wellington boots as we could carry then charged back into the room, flinging them at our assailants.

"Babambambambam!"

Mark and Mickey retreated behind a settee with its stuffing hanging out. Suddenly, they darted out, picked up the settee cushions and threw them at us. The cushions' fluffy innards were scattered across the room. Pamela Brotherton walked in then ran off crying after a Wellington boot caught her on the side of her head. But we were having great fun. We retreated into the garage where we hid in the dark, waiting for the enemy to fall into our trap.

The door opened the minute the garage light went on and a voice shouted: "What on earth has been going on down here! The place is a pigsty!"

It was Nurse Joan and she wasn't happy. "Stand up!" she barked, "Who else is down here?"

"Dunno, Nurse Joan."

Nurse Joan came up to us and slapped the three of us on the legs: "Now go up to Matron's study this minute!"

We slouched upstairs in silence. I hoped that we wouldn't get the cane. We stood waiting for Matron for all of 20 minutes while the other children passed by whispering to each other and winking and smiling at us. Matron appeared then disappeared.

She returned with a scowl on her face: "Come into my office, all of you."

I was relieved at our punishment. It was about the mildest that we could expect – a Punishment Walk. Punishment Walks were long walks to get us out of the house and out of Matron's hair. They were long walks to anywhere and nowhere. Often the non-nursing staff, like the cook, Molly Broughton, and Miss White would take us.

We liked Miss White. She had white hair. She lived in a little flat at the big house that stood to the rear of the home. Sometimes we would see her climbing the fire escape to reach her door and we would wave to her, "Hi Miss White!" Sometimes she waved back but she was a bit deaf was Miss White. As old and as bandy-legged as Molly Broughton, she was smaller in height than Molly but much the pleasanter and by far the gentler of the two. On our punishment walks she'd sometimes pull out a sweet for each of us to suck on and crunch up. "It keeps them quiet," she would tell Molly.

Miss White worked part-time in the home, coming in for two or three days of the week or for odd hours. Often we'd chatter away to her as she sat in a corner of the upstairs playroom sewing our buttons back on or darning our socks. Mary Ingham said she was Little Miss Muffet and I was the spider sat beside her.

But when Molly took us on our Punishment Walks, she was always grumpy. Molly was almost 60 years old, still smoking profusely and so unfit that she had to sit down on a street bench several times on the return journeys to the home.

"You will go out with Molly Broughton this afternoon. Now go and tidy up downstairs. When you have finished you can go and sit on your beds until it is time to get ready for church." Matron gestured us out of her office, holding the door open and giving us one more warning: "If I catch you making a mess downstairs again, it will be the cane next time."

Going to church was more of an endurance test than any punishment walk. The older children were allowed to go on their own and expected to be there when Matron scanned the church and did a head count of her flock. Brian Reynolds, David Bryant and Mickey Thompson sang in the choir and went off on their bikes. But, being one of the youngest, I was called to line up with the other children under eight who weren't in the choir. Having been inspected by Matron we were then ordered to march out of the house along the drive and out between the big oak doors of the main entrance.

Outside the gate we were back in the rich, mysterious world of Birkdale. A large detached house stood opposite. The walls of the house were so high that Brian Reynolds said that even David Bryant, who could climb over every other house in the area, couldn't get over them. Mr Briscoe and his family lived behind those walls. We hardly saw them except when the big red Jaguar car, sat engine purring, while someone opened the gates to their house. The Briscoes were millionaires, so we all said.

We turned left to leave Beach Road. The road was so small and the grounds of each house on it so big, that I counted only two houses on each side. Then we came to Westcliffe Road, where, instead of turning left to go to school, we now turned right and walked for five minutes past leafy gardens and mansions and the St Wyburn's girls' private school.

The St Wyburn's girls wore maroon and navy uniforms and hats and never talked to us. We never talked to them. They stared at us and pulled faces of disapproval – black children, dirty children, scruffy children, poor children - children that Harriet and Camilla had read about in *The Water Babies* and *Oliver Twist* – children that nobody wanted.

We stared back at the very white children, clean children, smartly dressed children, children of the rich – children I had read about in *The Beano* and the *Hotspur*.

"My mummy said that I would be sent to a home if I was naughty," said Harriet to Camilla as she searched in the brown, leather satchel hung over her shoulder. Harriet brought out a black, wax crayon: "Look," she giggled, "I can make your face just like that black boy's."

Mickey turned his nose up and his eyes down and started to walk with a wiggle of his hips and shoulders, like he'd seen the posh woman do in Charlie Chaplin. We laughed. Camilla and Harriet, stood across the road, turned their noses up too. But they were scowling as they turned their heads away.

Ours were very different worlds – the world of the Wanted and the world of the Unwanted.

A left turn and a right turn, and there we were at the Parish Church of Saint James with its spire and big rose window dominating the eye. St James still stands. It is a modest edifice for a Church of England parish that, at least then, was said to be one of the richest in the land. A small group of people stood huddled beneath their umbrellas outside the church.

Matron was in her pink see-through plastic mackintosh (the type women would wear over their Sunday best) and her blue bonnet – her Sunday bonnet. As we passed the huddle of umbrellas and grins, she lifted her head and returned a smile. She was back on the outside with her people – people with education, people who read the Daily Telegraph and the *Daily Express* and took tea in the afternoon and crocheted for charity.

"These Barnardo's women are a tribute to Christianity. Such dedication and sacrifice! What other nation would look after these children from the darkest corners of the earth?"

But Mary Stewart knew that they were wanted people and she was unwanted.

"Good Morning!"

"Good Morning!"

"Mornin'!" we chirped back in unison.

We followed Matron like a gaggle of geese or ugly ducklings, through the church doors and down the aisle past the stained glass windows of this saint and that. I was just tall enough to see over the tops of the rows of wooden pews and catch sight of Mr Drayton, the bald headed organist who someone said was really Arthur Askey. The huge grey pipes above him blew his tune – Derrrrderrderrrrrrderder!

It was as if the organ had been sounded to announce our entry.

"Look Mary," I said to Mary Ingham in her yellow woollen dress, "There's yer brother, Michael, and Emily Brotherton."

Michael and Emily were sat in the choir stalls next to Mickey, Tom and Brian Reynolds. Each of them wore their white surplice over their blue cassock. Around their necks they had a frilly white ruffle that would have made them look like angels if it weren't for their hair that Mary said looked like haystacks.

"When I'm seven I'll be in the choir too an' I'll be paid one pound an' five shillings a quarter."

"So?"

"You can't 'cos you can't sing. I can an' I can buy fish an' chips an' things. See that Pamela Brotherton, she told on me and yer brother before, I bet she did. Just 'cos Mickey threw a welly an' it 'it 'er on the 'ead. We're gonna get 'er later."

After a minute of fidgeting and being told to be quiet, the organ went silent. A bald-headed, portly man dressed in a black cassock over which he wore a white surplice and a white dog-collar, strode to the pulpit. He paused for one second, as if contemplating whether he had remembered to bring his reading spectacles. Then climbed up into the pulpit where he stood behind the brass eagle's wings that shot out from each side.

"Hymn 355," declared the Reverend Canon Jones.

I knew that because it said so on a large wooden board, which announced the numbers of the hymns like the runners at a racecourse.

" 'E, who with giants fight, foller the master!" We sang away. I thought of David and Goliath and all those lots of exciting stories of war and magic in the Bible. For when Canon Jones began his lengthy sermon on this and that, I took out one of the maroon Bibles in a ledge on the back of the pew and read away. Then I played with the shiny new sixpence that Matron had given me to put in the shiny brass collection tray that we would watch with envy as it was passed round full of green pound notes. We watched each other too – to see who was keeping their sixpence instead of giving it to the church. Finally someone poked me and it was time to rise for the last hymn and go home.

Going home from church on Sunday meant Sunday dinner. Sunday dinner meant roast beef with lumpy cold gravy, tinned carrots and peas and a sponge cake burnt at the edges, with cold custard so insipid that it poured like water. It was raining outside and I went to play in the sandpit, taking an empty matchbox and sailing it on a pool of rainwater. It was a battleship or a Viking boat about to land on a beach and despatch its warriors. And that's what I would have done all afternoon if it hadn't been for us having to go on the Punishment Walk that Matron had ordered.

Molly Broughton lay on her bed in her room sandwiched between the kitchen and the larder. She was peeved at Miss Stewart for ordering her to conduct the Punishment Walk. It seemed so unfair to Molly that, after spending two hours preparing the Sunday dinner, she then had to take those children out in the pouring rain and cold. But she had expected it since she had avoided going on the walks for a month.

Molly looked forward to her Sunday afternoon naps. In the summer she would collect a deck chair from Mac's Cellar (the boiler room) and place it on the grass bank outside the kitchen and doze off. If the children were all out she would fetch her transistor radio and listen to the *Third Programme*:

"The sun has got his hat on. Hip! Hip! Hip! Hooray!
The sun has got his hat on and he's coming out to play.
Lots of little Niggers out in Timbuktu.
The sun has got his hat on and there's nothing else to do."

In winter, Molly would lie fully dressed on her bed listening to plays or stories on the *Home Service* until the soft voices sent her into her dreams.

"At least I don't have to take the whole lot of them out," she consoled herself, "Normally Miss Stewart tells me to take every child no matter who has been naughty. Then taking them is like shepherding bedlam."

Molly passed a brush through her hair. She didn't bother to look in the mirror. If she had she would have seen her stringy grey hairs were turning silver with a matt of grease picked up from her toil over the stove. Just as her greasy hairs found their way into our food, so the filth in her kitchen found its way through the cook's hair net. Her appearance was almost as dirty as her kitchen. Her thoughts passed to the nice young grocery boy who would arrive at her kitchen door to make the weekly delivery the next day. Molly looked forward to Mondays.

She put on her face powder and re-sprayed her room with a musk scent that she had bought on holiday in Eastbourne. The odours of the kitchen would never enter her room. As soon as they neared the door they were met with a wall of musk. So were we.

She hated having to work and live in the home. But she had no other home to live in and nowhere else to go. The exact circumstances behind her arrival at Tudor Bank, we were never told. But she loathed the place with a vengeance. Molly's only respites were her trips to other seaside resorts – Eastbourne, Bridlington, Margate, Bournemouth. She sent Matron postcards from her rooms in Bed & Breakfast guest houses around the country.

Being beside the kitchen, Molly's bedroom in the home was on the ground floor at the back of the house. Soon after she had taken occupancy of the room, Molly caught a glimpse of four brown eyes and two white foreheads at her window. "The little blighters are peeping in!" From that day on, through summer and winter, her window curtains remained closed. She smoked her cigarettes in darkness, listened to *The Archers* in darkness, planned her seaside holidays in darkness.

She finished her ablutions and asked Nurse Joan to collect us up, get us into our mackintoshes and wellingtons and order us to wait in the hall. Molly collected us and took us right, out of the main gate, then left onto Rotten Row, the famous road that from springtime till late summer is adorned with glorious flowerbeds. It was the road that we peered down at from behind our lattice fence as the people on the outside, the wanted people, walked by.

That winter's day Rotten Row sported no flowers just pools of rainwater.

"Can't we go in the park?" I asked Molly.

"No. I don't want you running off. This is a punishment, not a party," Molly did wish we would run off so that she could go back into her warm, dry room. We followed her, sometimes ran in front of her, up the road as it climbed to a road bridge that crossed a disused, overgrown railway line.

Molly's bandy legs and four foot eleven inch frame were already creaking. She took us across the bridge then down a grass bank and we were on the old railway track surrounded by blackberry bushes, nettles and sand dunes.

"Where did this railway line go to Molly?"

"I don't know but I think it went to Preston."

"An' after that?"

"Scotland."

"An' after that?"

"Nowhere."

"Ireland?" I asked. We had a great big globe that stood on a cupboard in the upstairs playroom. The more I read of other countries, the more I studied the globe with its pink bits that Matron said were all the places in the British Empire. Ireland was not in the British Empire anymore. No country was. But Mary Stewart was still in the British Empire, still looking after the Empire's children.

"Trains can't run to Ireland," said Tom, "because Ireland is an island."

"So are we," I replied.

"Trains can't cross the sea silly." Tom knew a lot about trains. A lot more than me.

"When can we go back?" asked Tom. It was his turn to ask the question that Molly Broughton hated most. If it was Molly's wish she would turn back immediately or just leave the little wretches in the pine trees and let them see if *Babes in the Wood* was a nice fairy tale.

Molly kept up a continual scowl. Most of her head was covered with a plastic see-through hood that allowed a glimpse of the hairnet she wore almost permanently, as if only the Eastbourne and Scarborough world of her annual holidays were fit to see it uncovered.

As a derelict railway station came into sight, Michael ran ahead. He came out with three sticks of wood and the three of us took one each. We carried them like soldiers on parade as Tom said: "Hup, Two, Three, Four. Hup, Two, Three, Four Hup. Two, Three, Four."

Molly tried to keep up with us but gradually saw us disappear into the distance. We would have lost her for good had it not been for the wind getting up and the rain driving into our faces. We sought shelter beneath another road bridge and Molly finally arrived. As she did, Tom asked: "Can we play for a bit?"

"All right," said Molly, "but don't go running off."

We scampered into the dunes with our stick of wood-cum-rifles. "Bam! Aargh! Derderder! Boom!"

When we were out of sight, Molly lit up a Park Drive cigarette and cursed her luck.

In the dunes we continued our war games until we found a sand dune so steep that we could shelter beneath it from the driving rain.

"I bet it was Pamela Brotherton who told on us," said Michael as we sat taking a break from our desert battles.

"Tom tale tit."

"Tell tale tit."

"We'll get 'er later."

"Let's draw for it," suggested Tom.

"Stone, paper, scissors?" I asked. Michael nodded and we thrust out our hands in increasing fury until it was decided that I would be the avenger.

We got back early that day. Often, Punishment Walks would take two hours as we traipsed across the town to Hesketh Park or the Botanical Gardens.

"You're all back early," Matron commented as we appeared in the hall after changing out of our coats and wellingtons.

"The weather was too awful," answered Molly, "I couldn't have kept them out there any longer. They would have caught their death of cold."

We could have stayed out there all day. That Punishment Walk was fun, for us of course, not for Molly Broughton. The cook retreated to her room by the larder and lay exhausted on her bed. She took out another Park Drive cigarette. Her punishment was over.

We went to find the other children. They were sat around the fire with Nurse Pat and Nurse Elaine in the Staff Room. Nurse Elaine had been away on holiday in Bridlington with her boyfriend. She had been a child in the Trafalgar Road home once and now she was looking after us. Slight of figure, five foot two with auburn hair, she had left school without any qualifications and working in the home seemed to her the best life she could expect. Still, we liked Nurse Elaine. She was one of us.

Sat on her knee was little Sheryll Jacobs whose black curly hair she was combing. Sheryll, just three years old, was wincing and grimacing as the comb attacked her knots.

Not a word was said as the other children glimpsed our entry then returned to watching the film on the television. The television was black and white of course. Well ours was more dark grey and fuzzy grey as the aerial swayed in the strong winds that blew from the sea. Doris Day was riding in a wagon train and being chased by "Red Indians." Nurse Pat passed around a large tin of walnut toffees that some kind soul had donated to the home to improve the gaps in our teeth. We were happy. The only dampener was that it was school next day and who looked forward to that?

But I had a job to do and as the film finished and we were ordered out of the Staff Room, I ran behind Pamela Brotherton and hissed: "Tom tale tit."

"Well!" replied Pamela.

Little Martin had heard me and turned to her: "Tell tale tit! Tell tale tit! Yuh mouth will burn and yuh tongue will slit!"

As Pamela made to run off, I jumped in front of her and punched her in the stomach. Her wails were so loud that all the nurses came running. As Pamela stood doubled up pretending that she couldn't breathe, the nurses asked: "What's the matter?"

"Phillip 'it me in ma poorly stomach," she cried.

"Yes, 'e did. I saw 'im," said her sister, Emily.

I said nothing. Nurse Joan grabbed me by the ear, twisted it and took me grimacing to stand with her outside Matron's study.

Nurse Joan knocked on the door and Matron asked her in. I was dragged in almost in tears from the agony my poor sticky-out ear was suffering. After Nurse Joan had recounted what she believed had happened, Matron reached for her cane: "Well I have told you before, I will not have bullying in this home. Now, hold out your hand."

Being six years old, I knew I would get six strokes of the cane. It came down hard and fast. But I didn't cry. Only softies cried. Each stroke stung me harder than the last and when the sixth stroke came, I withdrew my hand.

"Put it back here!" shouted Matron and since I obviously wasn't going to play along, Nurse Joan came over, grabbed me by the ear and wrenched my hand from behind my back and into the reach of Matron's cane. Swish! Aargh! My punishment was done. Nurse Joan held her hand and winced. She had inadvertently taken some of my punishment for me.

I was sent to my bed early. Alone in the dark, I cried a little. When the other boys come up I told them: "I got the cane but I didn' cry."

Vengeance was done. Rules were rules. Neverneverland had its own rules. The staff were our crocodiles and set their boundaries.

You didn't tell tales or else you got punished. That was one of our rules.

Hit another child and you get caned. That was one of the crocodiles'.

The next day, I was happy. Pamela Brotherton had been caught stealing. Matron kept a Barnardo's Collection Box on a shelf in the hall beside the dining room. It was there to encourage visitors to put their donations in. Not that we knew where the money ever was supposed to go. Often, we knew where it actually went. It was always going missing and the nurses would search in the nettles and on the grass banks behind the trees. This time Pamela had been caught behind the sheds, trying to empty it. She would get the cane for that.

Christmas was coming and we began to look forward to the round of parties and presents that the boys who had been in the previous home longer were used to.

"We go to lots of parties an' play games and get ice cream an' jelly an' blancmange and sweets too!" enthused Mickey Thompson, "Last year I got a new bike. Well, it was second 'and but it was really good."

"I got a Tommy Gun," added Michael Ingham.

"An' I got a train set," said Tom.

We chatted and dreamed for hours about what we wanted. "I wanna kiss Emily under the mistletoe," said Mickey, "I wanna feel 'er titties."

The conversation about titties went on and on.

"Why do girls 'ave bigger titties?" I asked.

"To 'ave babies when they're older, fool," replied Michael.

His brother Dick had recently been moved into our dormitory after staying in the big girls' bedroom while space was made for him in our room.

"I seen Matron play with a girl's titties," Dick said excitedly.

"Fibber!" cried Michael.

"Whose?" asked Mickey.

"Can't remember," replied Dick, remembering the feel of Matron's hairbrush on his bare backside after the last occasion that he'd spoken out of turn.

"Liar, liar, yer arse is on fire," chimed Tom.

"I bet you seen Father Christmas too," I added.

"I seen Donna Brotherton's tits last year," Mickey said, "when I went into their bedroom."

I didn't believe him either. Some did. They knew more than I. But in Neverneverland you believed what you wanted to believe and saw what you wanted to see.

"We got to get dressed up next week, 'cos the mayor's comin'," said Mickey getting the subject back to our Christmas-time.

"What for?" I asked.

"I dunno. The mayor comes wi' lots of posh people an' they come into the staff room an' the upstairs playroom an' we do a bit of a show for 'em. That's why we got singing practice tomorra night. I think they bring presents for us but we don' see 'em 'til Christmas Day. "

Sure enough, the following night, we were all ordered to be in the staff room for six o'clock for singing practice. We sang, *The Little Drummer Boy* over and over again. I was proud because I was told that I would have a drum hung around my neck and would have to bang it when everyone else sang: "Perumahpumpum." But that was because

Matron said it was better if I didn't sing. Then we practised singing, *Noel, The Twelve Days of Christmas, Hark! The Herald Angels Sing* and a few other tunes before being packed off for supper.

Before the Mayor's visit came school parties and more singing practice. Part of practice was to be taken choir singing around the large houses in the area and collect money for Barnardo's. "It's not for you," Nurse Pat said, "It's for poor little boys and girls around the world."

Mrs Rod, the tall, fat, hairdresser came to cut the boys' and girls' hair. She came with her big scissors and comb, every month. We waited our turn to be called to "the chair" that she placed in the middle of the upstairs playroom. Then she snipped away until we all, boy or girl had the same pudding-basin haircut. She hurt me as her combs dragged through the knots in my curly hair.

Mr Metcalfe, the shoe repair man, came with his sack full of our repaired hand-me-down shoes, emptied it on the hall floor and watched as we scrambled to find our shoes with new heels and new soles. Brian Reynolds and David Bryant had shoes which looked the same and started fighting, rolling around the floor. Nurse Elaine and Matron pulled them apart by twisting their ears. Then Matron fetched two pairs of boxing gloves from her office and marched them outside onto the Pitch. Brian won. He was bigger.

The nurses put up the Christmas lights around the rooms and we helped decorate each room with the ceilings criss-crossed with twisted lines of yellow and red crepe paper and windows sprinkled with mock snow. Each windowsill had stretches of fluffy cotton wool laden across it and little ornaments displaying Christmas scenes placed upon them. So that when the mayor turned up with his troupe of fur coats, glistening jewellery and dress suites, we were already in our Christmas Neverneverland and happy to sing away.

After the night of the Mayor's visit came parties in big public halls and hotel ballrooms - musical chairs, pass the parcel, moving statues and fights with the other children who were there from the local Sally Army Home and the National Children's Home.

On the Saturday the girls put on their party frocks again and we put on our Sunday Best jumpers and short trousers. We climbed into a coach and went off to a theatre in the dark, dingy city of Salford to see Mother Goose with hundreds of other unwanted children just like us. They screamed: "Oh! Yes, 'e will!" and "Oh! No, 'e won't!" just like us.

Christmas-time was an endless whirl of fun and games and nice things to eat that culminated on Christmas Day when we woke as early as six o'clock to sneak down in our pyjamas and look at our presents.

In the upstairs playroom, I found my pillowcase hung on my locker and stuffed full of little wrapped up packets. I'd feel each one and guess whether it contained sweets or crayons or toys. Then we went to the downstairs playroom where our big presents were waiting for us. But the door was locked with a curtain over it and we could only peep through a gap in the curtain and guess at what might be ours.

I crept back to bed and awaited seven o'clock when Nurse Pat arrived and ordered us up. We hid under the bedclothes until she left the room; whereupon we leapt out of bed fully clothed and ran to the bathroom. A quick rub of our faces with the flannel and we hurtled downstairs.

What we found in our pillow cases was generally what we expected – sweets, chocolates, crayons, pens, drawing books, Dinky toys, toy soldiers, dolls and the like. Some packets had labels saying Auntie This and Uncle That. I always had one that said: "To Pip. Love from Aunt Martha." I didn't know who Aunt Martha was but she sent me nice presents on my birthdays as well. We ripped all the wrapping paper off our presents with equal expectation.

The clanging of the bell announced that we must queue up for breakfast before we could see our "big" presents. Only after we had finished eating, clearing the tables and washing up, could we queue outside the downstairs playroom for the grand opening. That year came freshly painted bicycles. In the corner were a big doll's house and a huge cuddly teddy bear. "These are for everybody," declared Matron.

Michael and I wheeled our new bikes outside into the crisp wintry morning and went for a ride around the deserted streets passed houses with windows lit up by Christmas lights and doors pinned with garlands of holly. We turned and went passed Tudor Bank and into the park where we rode and rode until it was time to get ready for church.

In the afternoon, Donna Brotherton and Brian Reynolds came into the upstairs playroom with their new pop records and we all got up and danced rock 'n' roll to Billy Fury and Elvis Presley. Matron said Mickey and I danced very well and maybe we would one day be the pick of the ballroom.

Later on, we were allowed into the Staff Room to watch Bing Crosby's *White Christmas*, where Nurse Elaine cried and the girls did too because girls could cry. Well, that night, it did snow and the next morning we woke to see the Pitch covered in a blanket of white, and snow nestling on the branches of the trees.

After breakfast we dashed down to the cloakroom, put on our Wellington boots and coats and had the fight of all snowball fights. A huge snowman went up at the centre of the Pitch and another one went up in the area beside the sandpit. We slid on our coats down the banks all afternoon until the snow had turned to ice and Martin's head hit the ground with a thump. Martin cried. Martin always cried.

We spent Boxing Day scribbling away at our Thank You letters to all the Auntie Thises and Uncle Thats who had sent us presents. We didn't know who Auntie This and Uncle That were and didn't really care but Matron said we had to write Thank You letters otherwise they wouldn't send any presents next year. So we wrote away seated around the table in the upstairs playroom: "Thank you for my crayoning book. It was very nice." And Matron collected all the letters and we never heard one thing about Auntie This and Uncle That till the next Christmas-time.

Donna Brotherton wouldn't write her Thank You letters: "I bloody, bloody won't!" she shouted at Nurse Pat. Our heads jerked up in expectation. Nurse Pat grabbed her by the hand and tugged Donna off her chair and Donna scratched back at her with her nails.

"Yoooooooou little so-and-so!" Nurse Pat hissed.

We knew what would happen to Donna Brotherton. Donna Brotherton had sworn. She would have her mouth washed out. She would be taken up to the girls' bathroom and held down while a lime green bar of Fairy soap was stuffed in her mouth, then offered a glass of water to see if she could gargle the taste away.

Soon Nurse Pat marched back into the playroom and we lifted our eyes to stare at Donna weeping as she was stood in the corner beside the gramophone.

"Face to the wall," ordered Nurse Pat. Donna turned around showing her fair-haired bob.

"No talking to Donna today! She has been sent to Coventry."

Donna stood in the corner swirling saliva around her mouth and rubbing her gums with her tongue in a vain attempt to put an end to the dry soapy sensation that dried up her lips and invaded her nose. Tears fell around her black flat-heeled lace up shoes.

A few days later, the Granvilles came to pick me up and take me to stay with them. I was happy. I knew I would get more nice presents and more nice food and be able to play with Paul.

And so each Christmas went by, pretty much like the first Christmas. School days came again but now they were dark school days when the milk in the bottles iced up and we shivered all the way back home.

As January passed to February, the first white and yellow crocuses appeared speckled around the sides of the grass banks. Then came bluebells and daffodils as the nights grew lighter and we could play out again after school. Winter melted away. Easter came and we looked forward to more treats.

A huge Easter egg as big as the television was delivered to the home. It had been sent from Monty's, a confectionery shop in the town where it had stood on display in the window for a fortnight. It was so big and thick that Matron had to give Brian Reynolds's old Mac's hammer so that he could break it up. The pieces of the fractured egg were then apportioned between us and, what with the other eggs we had been given, we had enough chocolate to last us for a month. Not that the egg donated by the confectionery shop was particularly nice. Often the chocolate was stale and sickly but it was chocolate.

Then the Granvilles came and took me to stay with them and I got more Easter eggs but Auntie would say: "Don't eat then all at once or you'll be sick." So, I would take most of them back to the home with me.

I broke my chocolate into pieces and placed it in a discarded sweet tin that I kept in my locker. For weeks after Easter, I would use my pocket money to add sweets to my supply until I got sick of them and gave the rest away.

Mary Stewart was happy with the progress of her little boy, Phillip. She certainly didn't want him to be taken out of the home to another foster home. In May, she wrote her report to Barnardo's Headquarters:

"PHILIP IS MAKING VERY GOOD GENERAL PROGRESS AND SETTLED HAPPILY WITH US FROM THE DAY HE CAME. HE IS AN INTELLIGENT, AFFECTIONATE LITTLE BOY...

"MR AND MRS GRANVILLE, HIS FOSTER PARENTS, WRITE AND VISIT FREQUENTLY AND HAVE PHILIP TO STAY FOR A FEW DAYS EVERY HOLIDAY...

"LIKES DRAWING, MUSIC AND PLAYS QUIETLY FOR HOURS WITH HIS FORT AND SOLDIERS. PHILIP IS MAKING VERY GOOD PROGRESS WITH HIS READING AND WRITING."

Miss Stewart, May, 1959

It clearly suited Mary Stewart to imply that the Granvilles were my foster parents, though she knew that they no longer had any parental rights or responsibilities with regard to myself.

The seasons passed by. Only the seagulls and us hung around. Spring passed into summer, bringing warmer weather and lighter nights when we could play out to almost our hearts' content. After returning from school we'd queue up for our tea.

"Can we take it to eat outside?" we'd plead.

Permission granted and we would rush out. I often headed for the patch of nettles that grew beneath one of the tall banks and at the back of the house. There I'd toss my fried bread, my cold sausage, and my stale bread and sour milk for the benefit of the ants, worms and maggots.

After disposing of our tea and returning our cups, plates and knives to the pantry, we would rush out to play. Our life was an endless whirl of play. There were no adults in that world, just a seemingly endless supply of other children - a constant fizz of games and dreams.

Imagine more than a dozen young waifs rushing around your house and gardens for hours on end and that's what we were.

"Let's play Kick the Can," said Mary.

"Cowboys an' Injuns," shouted Michael, dancing around and whooping and hollering like Big Chief Sitting Bull would do at the pictures.

"No let's play Commandos," argued Mickey.

"Wha' about Rounders?" asked Emily

"Hide an' Seek?" suggested Sheryll.

"Football," said Brian.

"Cricket!" shouted Tom.

"Let's get on our bikes!"

"Go to the park!"

"Jump off the swing!"

"Go to the beach!"

"Let's make tents!" Emily Brotherton would say and we'd run inside and asked Matron if we could make tents.

"All right! All right!" Matron sometimes cried, "You can take the old blankets from the laundry cupboard. But only take the old ones. Emily, how many times have I told you not to run about the house!"

As soon as Matron had turned the corner we'd scamper down the stairs and jostle for the best blankets. We'd run outside to find old sticks or pull down branches from the trees to make our tent poles. Once inside we'd play all manner of little games and then "Dare, Force, Truth or

Promise, Kiss, Command or Tell." It invariably was preceded by another game to select who ever was to be dared. What was dared in the secrecy of those tents, the nurses would never know.

"Dare you to feel me willy!"

"Force you to eat grass!"

"Promise to rob the larder before tea time!"

"Kiss Donna!"

"Command yer to show me yer fanny!"

"Tell Miss White she's an old windbag!"

And little Dick said that Nurse ________ took him to her room and played with his willy when we were at church but no one believed him. "Yer dick's too little ter do it with," said Mickey. "Little Dick! Little Dick!" sang Emily and we all laughed.

Michael said he'd seen Brian Reynolds doing "it" with Donna Brotherton behind the trees and everyone believed him. Brian Reynolds had done "it" with lots of girls.

In those hours, Neverneverland was infinite joy. It was the time when children were given seemingly endless licence to roam. The only condition was that we returned at a set time. So we went off over the road to Victoria Park, a park which then appeared to stretch forever along the edge of the beach. Sometimes we took our bikes and raced up and down. Sometimes we left them behind and went and made fun of the old ladies in their dark brown nylon stockings and sporting their blue rinses as they played croquet.

There were occasions when we sneaked around the house of the park warden, Mr Roberts, to see if we could catch and frighten his daughter, Paula. Brian Reynolds said that Mr Roberts was nice. When Brian found a rabbit with an injured leg, he took it to Mr Roberts and Mr Roberts helped it get better and let Brian and the other boys go and visit it and pick it up.

But Paula Roberts was a "snotty cow." She was all stuck-up and wouldn't speak to us. She went with the posh kids to St Wyburn's school and wouldn't speak to us even though we lived almost next door. When she rode her horse in the park she almost knocked over little Martin. We didn't like Paula Roberts. The park was ours not hers.

We ran and ran through the trees, jumped off the swings and screamed. We laughed and giggled, swore and cried until our turn came to go back home and to bed.

At weekends we'd go beyond the park and onto the beach, play Commandos like the Desert Rats, leap off the tops of the dunes into the soft sand and comb the shoreline for messages in bottles. We pulled off

Mary Ingham's shoes because she didn't like sand on her feet and we buried each other up to our necks in the soft dune sand.

If the nurses came with us, they always sat in one spot and hadn't a clue or a care what our little caravan was up to. We'd sneak up on amorous couples in the dunes and see if they were "doing it." Mickey and Mark saw a couple "doing it." They called us over and we sat peering through the reeds. Mark went right up to them with a "rubber" he had found on the shore and asked them if they wanted it. Then we all jumped up and shouted. Mark ran away and we all started laughing until we had to wipe away our tears.

Sometimes Matron would let us have a picnic on the beach and grit would get in our sandwiches and grate our teeth. The bread baked in the sun and eventually ended up in the dunes feeding the sandflies. Or we would walk to deposit our food in the sea. It was a long, long walk out to find the sea, the grey, green-brown sea that washed up life from faraway countries and lovers' "rubbers" and empty wooden crates of Outspan oranges.

August was also the time when we went along the disused railway line between the park and the beach and dived into the brambles to pick blackberries and great big loganberries that turned our fingers and our mouths a dark purple. Sometimes we picked so many that, when we took them back to Molly in the kitchen, we would be eating blackberries for a fortnight – blackberries and custard, blackberry and apple pie, blackberry crumble, blackberry jam – we must have saved a fortune on the grocery bill.

Later in August and we would stand behind the fence that surrounded the home, peering down at the flowerbeds on Rotten Row, the road that divided us from the park. In the middle of the Row, we could see the café where the people frowned at us when we went to buy iced lollies, and behind it were the tennis courts where the people frowned on us too because we were not allowed to play there. In that month, Rotten Row was the prettiest and sweetest smelling road you could imagine. Chrysanthemums, dahlias, geraniums, sunflowers, lupins and dog daisies were interspersed between the Pampas grass in the flowerbeds, which ran on both sides along the road's full length.

Whole families strolled up and down the Row, adults admiring its colours and scents, teenage couples arm-in-arm, children licking their ice cream cornets and toddlers running from the bees. When the holiday month came to an end, thousands more visitors arrived from around the world for the annual Flower Show in the park. We stood on the grass banks observing them stream in to see more chrysanthemums and dahlias and to watch the showjumping competitions. The show's loud speakers blared away from the tops of huge white marquees.

As the announcer declared: "Ladies and gentlemen! Number Five, Lightning Jack ridden by Bill Harvey!" we climbed to the very top of the fence and stood up to see if we could get a glimpse of horse and rider negotiating the course. Strain as we did, only the tallest of us could see more than a black riding hat flash by. So we amused ourselves by rolling down the grass bank and trying to stop ourselves from falling into the flowerbeds.

On the odd occasion, we were taken to the show. At other times we'd find a hole in the fencing or sneak in beneath a loose tent flap, only to be utterly bored by the whole event of massed flower, fruit and vegetable stalls. Sometimes there was some excitement in the show jumping arena, when an unfortunate horse clattered into a fence and hurled its red-coated rider to the ground. We wandered around, scruffy urchins in the Sunday best crowds, searching for things to steal or pockets to pick.

Back in the home, the summer warmth brought out the ants. They scoured through the larder, finding their way into pots of jam, eating their way through the contents of the sugar bowls and burying themselves in the margarine tubs. They turned up at dinner and turned up at tea until they drove us mad. They climbed into our shoes and pants as we sat on the grass, crawled over our legs, basked in our hair and crawled into our beds. Black and red alike, they were a menace.

We lifted up huge stones and poured hot and cold water over the invading mass. We drowned them. We stamped them to death. We dug up their nests. We burned them using our magnifying glasses. But they always came back.

Bees, hornets and wasps joined the ants in invading our world. Houseflies, horseflies, bluebottles and greenflies followed, attacking our food and our persons. Come October when the shops began to sell fireworks, we'd buy bangers and blow up the wasps' nests. But the wasps always came back.

So life went on until it was time for bed. But we were still full of energy and the long hours of daylight kept us from sleeping. We sat up in our beds in the dormitories telling each other stories, reading comics and playing games. And we dared each other over and over again to carry out various exploits until Nurse Pat came and ordered us to stop talking or she would smack the lot of us.

We raided the larder, went and kissed Mary Ingham and threw one another's clothes out of windows or into the girls' dormitory. We pissed in each other's mouth and stuck our fingers in the light socket. Dare, dare, dare. It went on and on and if Nurse Pat did not arrive to stop us, our pranks only stopped when sleep took us off to dream.

Summer was at an end and we were back to drudging our way to school, as the nights grew darker and squadrons of geese chatted merrily as they flew south in the dimming skies. The Harvest Festival was the first event on our winter calendar. The festival was celebrated in churches and schools by organisations and families donating food to the church. Their offerings of fruit and bread often found their way from the churches to our home where we were overwhelmed with over-ripe fruit and great loaves of crusty harvest bread that had gone stale as they sat through Holy Communions and vicars' sermons.

Then came the great trip to Blackpool when Southport's Yellow-Top taxi drivers clubbed together and took all the unwanted of the town in their taxis to see Blackpool's famous illuminations. The taxis arrived outside our home decorated in coloured crepe paper and tinsel with huge bunches of balloons tied to their roof racks and bonnets and fluttering in the sea breeze.

Scores of the taxis were already full. They had picked up children from the Salvation Army and National Children's homes. Once our mob were in their seats, the cavalcade drove off through the town with horns beeping and children cheering, then went off on the main road to Blackpool.

As Blackpool Tower came into view, our hearts fluttered with excitement. We knew we would be taken to the circus beneath the tower and watch the horses prance and the lions and tigers roar to the lash of the ringmaster's whip. We'd watch acrobats leap from their ladders high up in the air and wonder if they would fall to the ground. We'd eat candyfloss and go to the top of the tower and feel our feet throb with instinctive fear.

We'd be taken to the fairground and ride the merry-go-rounds and take a train through the ghost tunnel where we'd hoot and howl and frighten ourselves until we were glad to see daylight again. When night came, the taxis would parade us up and down the promenade to gaze at the lights that told the fables of our fantasy world.

"Look! There's Snow White!"

"An' Cinderella!"

"An' Jack on 'is beanstalk!"

"An' Little Red Ridin' 'ood!"

We gazed on in amazement reliving all those tales we had heard so many times. Eventually our daydreams came to an end and our silent cavalcade returned its sleeping beauties back to their world.

Our trip to Blackpool was no sooner over and we were preparing for our next big event – Bonfire Night. Of course, Halloween would come before Guy Fawke's Night but eating turnips and dressing up as ghosts and witches was much less exciting than letting off fireworks and lighting fires.

Our pocket money went into buying fireworks as soon as the shops put them on sale. We built up little collections of bangers, rip raps, rockets and air bombs, which we kept in our lockers or Matron kept for us. Sometimes we stole still more from the shops and we had to keep them secret. The penny bangers were great fun. We set them off behind the girls, blew up insect nests and toys. We grabbed the plastic ends of air bombs and shot them at each other from a distance. We let off rip raps and dared one another not to move as they hurtled this way and that around our legs.

We trawled the beach and the park for firewood as we helped assemble the monstrous bonfire that Mac would supervise in the middle of the Pitch. We built our Guy Fawkes out of our old clothes, borrowed Mac's wheelbarrow and went round begging: "Penny for the guy!" and collected more money to buy bangers and air bombs.

On Bonfire Night we put on our coats and Wellington boots and waited to be allowed outside to watch old Mac light up our bonfire, which by now was a great edifice of old chairs and tables, driftwood, sawn up trunks of trees and bundles of twigs. On top sat our Guy Fawkes with DBH on his jumper and DBH on his trousers. We were sorry to see him go. The straw man had served us so well in collecting extra pocket money.

The nurses opened up the doors to the downstairs playroom, which looked out onto The Pitch and there on tables would be sticks of red-green toffee apples, piles of hot baked potatoes and grated cheese, chunks of black treacle toffee and cups of piping hot cocoa. It wasn't all for us. Bonfire Night was another night when the worthies of the local Barnardo's committee came to see the fireworks that they had bought for the little urchins of Tudor Bank.

Dressed in their fur coats and woolly mohair jumpers, they "ha-ha'd" and "lah-di-dah'd" as they gathered around the food or stood up on the balcony watching us set off our fireworks around the intense heat of the fire. If they came too close to us, they might find themselves running from a rip rap or shrieking at the shock of a banger exploding behind them. Even when stood on the balcony, they weren't completely safe. Brian Reynolds was sent to bed early for shooting a air bomb at them. Whoosh! It went flying through the air and exploding into their midst, scorching a portly middle-aged woman's blonde beehive hairdo and an old lady's mink coat.

Bonfire Night was one night when we were allowed to stay up later than usual. Nevertheless, the next morning we were up as early as ever and out on the Pitch trying to blow the embers of the fire back into flame or searching in the grass and among the trees for fireworks that had failed to go off. Our little finds and unsupervised fire-raising were almost as much fun as the previous night's events. We stood eyes fixed on the embers and wondered what Christmas-time would bring for us.

So the seasons passed in Neverneverland. Time went by, dragging then speeding so fast that we children could not see it. The furniture in the home gradually became as tatty as in our previous residence, the walls as graffiti-ridden and the bed sheets as stained. And, if we had each other's company all through the waking hours, when peace reigned in the darkness of night, we were alone.

We still wet our beds and still were punished and shamed for it.

"I must remember not to wet my bed when I am asleep. I must remember not to wet my bed when I am asleep. I must remember..."

Then I woke up and I hadn't remembered. The back of a hairbrush came down on my bottom. I yelped but I didn't cry. My bed was stripped and the soaking mattress lay there for all to see. As it dried, a brown-yellow tidemark circled its middle, marking out the size of my pond of sin. And I came home from school and saw two white sheets billowing alone on the clothesline that hung outside the kitchen door.

"I must remember not to wet my bed when I am asleep. I must remember..."

Every school holiday, each of us would be collected for a "holiday." Some children had mothers or stepmothers, fathers or stepfathers, real uncles, real aunts and real brothers and sisters who came to see them at weekends. They had families. No real people came to see me, only the Granvilles. But I didn't care. I liked them. I liked Aunt Florence's cooking and Uncle George taking me to the zoo and I liked playing out with Paul. But they weren't my family. I didn't have a real family. That's why I was in a home being Looked After by Doctor Barnardo's.

It was the winter of 1959 that I developed a bad cough, which Matron said, was like the sound of a wounded bear. It turned out to be Whooping Cough and it stuck with me through January. It would return from time-to-time throughout my childhood. After Boxing Day, Matron called the doctor and it was decided that I was well enough to visit the Granvilles for my "holiday" in Bolton.

What stuck in my mind from that trip was returning from playing with some neighbour's children and once again hearing the man next door shouting at his big hairy black dog.

"Nigger!" he shouted. "Nigger!" he shouted again as the dog put its front legs on next door's wrought-iron gate and barked and growled at me. I was petrified and ran up the path. I glanced over and saw the Granvilles' neighbour grinning at me.

At my bedtime I went in my pyjamas to the bookshelf in Paul Granville's bedroom. There I pulled out a big book with pictures in it. It was called *Happy Valley Bedtime Stories*. I read the story about Betty's Bobtail Picnic and, since I wasn't tired and Auntie had said I could read till 7.30pm, it being holiday time, I read on:

"GOLLY RUNS AWAY"

"Golly was very sad. Little Master had called him 'stupid golliwog!' and thrown him into the dark toy-cupboard!

"The cause of all the trouble was Teddy Bear, who was a new birthday present. Now Little Master didn't want Golly any more. Golly knew it was not really Teddy Bear's fault, but that didn't make him feel any better, and at last he decided to run away... Golly stole over to the window and climbed out.

"There was a large pear-tree just outside, and he climbed down this to the ground. The garden was dark, and he took the wrong path. Suddenly - plop - there he was in the little pond where the goldfish lived."

That night I wished I was with the goldfish. I have that book to this day. It was bought for Paul as a Christmas present in 1955.

I never said anything to the Granvilles about the neighbours. I knew some people didn't like black people. At school the only black children were those from our home. Sometimes the children there called me "Nigger" or "Golliwog" and I hit them so that they cried. Mark Lancaster and Michael Ingham did too. And the children told the headmistress and we said they had called us "Nigger." Then the headmistress smacked us and told us not to hit other children. But we did because we didn't like being called "Nigger" just because we were black.

It wasn't my fault I was black and had big lips and a squashed up nose and curly hair that went into knots that hurt when the nurses combed it. It wasn't my fault that my father lived in a jungle and that he came to this country. I didn't want children and big men shouting "Nigger!" at me, or "Sambo."

"Eanie, meanie, miney, mo. Catch a Nigger by his toe..."

I hated it when they made monkey noises at me and pulled faces and said that I was from the jungle. Sometimes they asked me what it was like in the jungle and I didn't mind that. I told them that I rode tigers and played with snakes and lions and didn't have to go to school. That was fun.

But I walked past big boys in the park and they shouted: "Nigger! Nigger!" and "Go home Sambo!" and "Get back to Africa!" so I ran back home.

I didn't like having to be black.

And at night we prayed: "Lighten our darkness, we beseech thee, O Lord!" But when we woke we were still black and always would be. Mark didn't like it either and he was always in fights but he was strong – strong enough that two nurses could hardly keep him down when he got mad.

When Pamela Brotherton called me "Nigger", I hit her so hard the blow split her lip. I didn't mind that because I didn't like her. If she called Sheryll "a Nigger" I hit her too. I didn't get caned when I hit Pamela Brotherton for calling me names because Matron said that it was wrong to call people "Nigger."

Mary Stewart wasn't too sure what to do about her poor little black children. What could she do? There weren't any other black children in the town and she read in the papers of riots in London with people claiming that immigrants from the West Indies were taking their jobs and houses. As she read her Daily Telegraph, she began to believe that it was really wrong to bring all those black people into the country while people in England were still on ration books.

"Still," she pondered, "we must find a way of people living side-by-side or it will all end up going terribly wrong like in America where they lynch the Negroes and shoot them. Why can't people live together happily?"

Now she had six black children in her charge and the numbers seemed to be growing by the year. They did fight a lot but they were dear little children and she feared for them growing up: "If only their fathers had stayed in their own countries or been responsible enough to take their children back there with them!"

That January 1960, she wrote her report on Phillip Frampton:

"HAS A VERY GOOD CONTACT WITH HIS FORMER FOSTER PARENTS...PHILLIP IS A DEAR LITTLE BOY, LOVED BY EVERYONE. HE IS VERY HAPPY HERE AND ALSO FOND OF HIS 'UNCLE' AND 'AUNT' AND ENJOYS GOING TO STAY WITH THEM..

"READS WELL, HAS A FORT AND SOLDIERS WITH WHICH HE PLAYS BY THE HOUR. LIKES MUSIC, ESPECIALLY ROCK AND ROLL...MAKES FRIENDS QUICKLY AND GETS ON WELL WITH THE OTHER CHILDREN AS A RULE, BUT OCCASIONALLY LAUNCHES OUT AT ANYONE WHO ANNOYS HIM!

"AFFECTIONATE, SULKS OCCASIONALLY, OTHERWISE NEVER STOPS TALKING! RATHER SENSITIVE ABOUT HIS COLOUR."

Miss Stewart, January, 1960

It wasn't the first time that Mary Stewart felt it necessary to report that I was aware that I was black and that I didn't sit happily with facing the consequences of being black in a white world. In May 1959, the matron had reported:

"VERY SENSITIVE WITH REGARD TO HIS COLOUR, OTHERWISE A HAPPY DISPOSITION."

It upset Mary Stewart that the little coloured boys felt so hurt at being called names. After an incident in which Mark and I set upon the Brothertons injuring them quite severely, she decided to try and tackle our anxieties by talking to us all individually. I got into a fight with Tom for calling me names and Matron chose the opportunity to call me into her study.

"Sit down Phillip," she gestured to a brown leather chair and I sat down, whereupon she offered me a humbug toffee. Matron was always sucking humbugs.

"I know that you are very sensitive about the colour of your skin but you mustn't be always getting into a rage every time someone calls you names. You really are a nice boy most of the time but I do worry that you get in to these fights."

"Well," I argued, "They shouldn' call me names. Why do all the children call us 'Nigger' and 'Sambo?' It's not fair. It's just 'cos we're black. We don' call 'em names because they're white."

"Yes, but you do tease children and call them names too," replied Miss Stewart, "Lots of people get called names they don't like."

After a pause and a smile she went on: "You really shouldn't be upset about your colour. It's only because your father was from Africa. God loves children from all over the world. He loves coloured children and white children. Everybody is equal in Our Lord's eyes and I love each child in this home as much as any other.

"You don' love me as much as Pamela Brotherton," I wanted to reply, "She's always being naughty and always being let off."

I said nothing more and Matron sent me out of her office with a pat on the head.

The beatings we had handed out had an effect and the racial taunts in the home subsided. Mark Lancaster was now too big to be messed with. Matron on the other hand, concluded that her little talks to the coloured and the white children had succeeded in soothing our fears.

Soon she felt able to report of me:

"RATHER SENSITIVE WITH REGARD TO HIS COLOUR, THOUGH LESS SO THAN WHEN HE FIRST CAME."

Miss Stewart, January, 1961

"PHILLIP FRAMPTON: TALL THIN, VERY PLEASANT HALF CASTE WITH LOVELY SMILE...

"PHILLIP IS A CHARMING AND VERY INTELLIGENT LITTLE BOY. HE USED TO BE RATHER UNHAPPY ABOUT HIS COLOUR, TILL I TOLD HIM GOD MADE LOTS OF LITTLE BOYS BROWN AND LOVED THEM JUST AS MUCH AS WHITE ONES, SINCE WHEN HE SEEMS TO HAVE ACCEPTED THAT HE IS BROWN QUITE HAPPILY. WE ALL LOVE PHILLIP.

Miss Stewart, January, 1962

But the children on the outside still called us "Nigger" and "Sambo" and we still prayed: "Lighten our darkness."

"In Houston (Texas) four men kidnapped a Negro on March 7th, 1960, beat him with a chain, carved the initials K.K.K. on his chest and stomach, and left him hanging by his feet from a tree."

Mary Stewart thought the little half-caste Phillip was, apart from his occasional tantrums and reactions to racial comments, progressing well. At school, the headmistress, Miss Randall gave very good reports of his reading and writing ability.

It was coming up to Open Day in the final year of Bury Road Infants' School when all our class were told to write an essay as to what we wanted to be when we grew up. Like many children, I hadn't a clue. I was too busy living in Neverneverland to think about the world of grown ups. But I had to write something. The only man to figure even remotely in my life was Uncle George and he was a vicar. I didn't want to be a vicar. That was boring. I wanted to travel the world.

In the end I plumped for being a missionary. I'd read about missionaries in the home and at Uncle George's house. What's more, if I said that I wanted to be a missionary, then I could write down the names of a lot of places around the world and that would fill the page. I went and looked at the globe that stood on the bookcase in the upstairs playroom. I wrote:

"I WANT TO BE A MISSIONARY WHEN I GROW UP. I WANT TO TRAVEL AROUND THE WORLD TO HELP ALL THE POOR PEOPLE. I WANT TO GO TO BRAZIL AND PERU AND NIGERIA AND SOUTH AFRICA AND THE GOLD COAST AND TANGANYIKA AND EGYPT AND INDIA AND CEYLON AND HELP THE CHILDREN LEARN TO READ AND WRITE AND THAT."

To my amazement, the schoolteacher received my essay with delight. On the school Open Day, my piece of paper was posted up as the star attraction. Nurse Pat came to pick us up at the end of the day. She spoke to my teacher and was pleased as Punch to be told that little Phillip had won the hearts and affection of the staff. When she read his piece she let a little tear fall. Nurse Pat told Miss Stewart. Miss Stewart told Mr Granville and Miss Stewart told me what a good boy I had been to write such a lovely essay and how well everyone thought of what I had done.

I was rather abashed. I never told them that I didn't want to be a missionary at all. I didn't want to be anything. Neither they nor I knew that one day I would be a missionary but not for Jesus. Still, the line was a winner and it seems that I used it for some time. A few months later, Miss Wolstenholme, from Barnardo's Western Area office visited the home and asked to see me. Of her conversation with the boy, Phillip, she wrote:

"HE TOLD ME HE WANTED TO BE A MISSIONARY IN SOUTH AFRICA WHEN HE LEFT SCHOOL..."
Miss K. Wolstenholme, Barnardo's Western Area Office, March, 1961.

I suppose that must have been seen to be a pretty impressive sacrifice, a black boy wanting to be a missionary in apartheid South Africa. But then I didn't know that the whites were treating the black people of that faraway land as slaves, that I would have to become a slave too.

On March 21st in 1960, police in the South African town of Sharpeville shot dead 69 blacks who were marching against apartheid.

I might as well have asked for a crucifix and a box of nails for my birthday.

The same year, the British government conceded independence to Nigeria. Isaac Ene finally walked in a free country.

After the missionary episode, I settled down to wanting to be a tramp, wandering around Britain, being nothing and doing nothing, just like always.

My seventh birthday came along on July 18th and I got a special present – a Bible. I also got a bicycle. It was painted red. It wasn't a new bike. It had been Mickey's. Before that it was Brian's. My old bike was put away for Martin's birthday. Mary Ingham got a "new" bike for her birthday too. It was painted lime green. It had been Emily's. Before that it was Barbara's. We each got a special treat and were given two shillings and taken to the fairground to spend the money.

Being seven was special. It meant that, when I queued up on Saturday mornings outside Matron's office, I could expect to get nine pence pocket money instead of six pence. Being seven meant that I would leave the infants' school and go into the junior school. Being seven meant that I could walk home on my own from school and not have to wait around for Miss White or Nurse Pat.

Sometimes, when it was snowing or raining, we were taken on the bus to school and given money to get the bus home. I discovered that the best place to jump off the bus was as it stopped to turn right at the busy Lulworth Road. All I had to do then was run through the grounds of the dentist and I was almost home. On October 6th, I did just that, leaving Emily, Michael, Mickey, Tom and all still seated in the bus.

Back in the home, Mary Stewart was stood in the kitchen hovering over Molly Broughton as the cook sat spreading margarine from a huge tub onto that night's tea. The matron was waiting for an opportunity to question Molly as to how the whole tin of chocolate biscuits that had been ordered to entertain the local Barnardo's committee on Bonfire Night had disappeared. The first time Matron had broached the issue, Molly's reply had been rather brusque: "Ask those little wretches. I haven't got a clue."

Things were always disappearing from the kitchen and Mary Stewart suspected that Molly was helping herself and her friends to the contents of the larder. Molly was querying Matron about whether she could get a break that Christmas when the phone started ringing. Matron patiently heard Molly out then went to answer the phone. By the time she reached her office, the phone had stopped ringing. So Matron's question about the chocolate biscuits never got asked again. The children arrived from school and fried eggs and fried bread was served in the dining room after the second bell.

Emily was picking up her fried egg by its hard brown edge and wiggling it about: "I can't eat it. It's like rubber." Michael said he'd eat the middle of his eggs but not the sides and Tom had stuffed his into his mouth all in one swoop and was holding his nose to try and get the nasty egg swallowed before he could smell or taste it again.

The doorbell rang and Matron rose and left the room to answer the door. Tea-time seemed a strange hour for visitors to come calling. When she opened the door, the visitor was dressed in a black uniform. In one hand was his black police hat. In the other was a black shoe with its lace still tied.

"Excuse me calling at this time, madam. We tried to contact you earlier. Can I ask whether this is one of your children's shoes?"

Mary Stewart thought it a strange business for a policeman to be delivering lost shoes. She took the shoe in her hand to inspect it.

The policeman went on: "Only the boy whose shoe it was has been knocked down by a car on Lulworth Road and is very poorly in hospital."

"Good Lord!" exclaimed the matron, "We were just talking about little Phillip Frampton and why he was late home for his tea. The children said they last saw him when he jumped off the bus at the bottom of Aughton Road but they said he was probably in the park kicking his football around."

"The boy is coloured madam. He has curly hair and is about four feet tall."

"Oh! Dear!" It is Phillip!" cried Matron, "How on earth did it happen?"

"I can't say madam but you could come and see him. I am afraid he wasn't conscious when I last saw him."

Matron rushed inside in shock and blurted out all she had heard to the staff and children who were still seated. The children rushed out of the room to see the policeman and Phillip Frampton's shoe.

"Will Phillip die?" asked Emily.

"I bet 'e will," said Tom, looking at the shoe in the policeman's hand.

"Can we go in your car an' go an' see 'im?" asked Dick who always wanted a ride in a police car with the sirens going, and that.

"I am sorry but Phillip is very, very poorly at this moment."

"Phillip's going to die?" said Mary and she and all the other girls began to cry in little blubbers to such effect that the nurses joined in.

Molly ended up having to throw all her rubbery fried eggs (even the one that Tom had tried to swallow whole) into the bin that night. It was a night of tears. It was a night of worry too for Mary Stewart. When she rang the hospital, the sister in the intensive care ward told her the boy had still not gained consciousness.

"Will he live?" asked Miss Stewart

"The doctors say, it's 50-50," came the reply.

"What on earth do I tell the boy's uncle and aunt? And what do we tell his mother – if she really wants to know?"

Mary Stewart reminded herself that she must phone Barnardo's Western Area Office with a report. She dreaded to think that one of her children might die whilst in her care. She phoned Barnardo's Head Office in Stepney and the Barnardo's machine went into action.

"6.10.60 5.04PM. MISS SOUTHFIELD PHONED DOWN TO SAY SHE HAD JUST HAD A PHONE CALL FROM MISS STEWART TO REPORT THAT PHILLIP HAD MET WITH AN ACCIDENT ON THE WAY HOME FROM SCHOOL. HE HAD APPARENTLY GOT OFF THE BUS BEFORE IT STOPPED, FALLEN AND BEEN RUN OVER BY A FOLLOWING CAR. HIS INJURIES INCLUDE A FRACTURED SKULL AND HE WAS IN SOUTHPORT INFIRMARY...

"5.15PM. DR____ PHONED TO SAY THAT... PHILLIP HAD A FRACTURE AT THE BASE OF THE SKULL. HIS CONDITION MUST BE REGARDED AS SERIOUS. HE WAS UNCONSCIOUS...THE HOSPITAL HAD BEEN IN TOUCH WITH THE NEURO-SURGICAL UNIT AT WALTON HOSPITAL, LIVERPOOL, AND IT WAS POSSIBLE THAT PHILLIP WOULD BE MOVED THERE."

"5.18PM. I TELEPHONED TO MR. PRICE AT BIRMINGHAM. HE WAS OFF DUTY AND OUT OF THE BUILDING BUT I SPOKE TO HIS DEPUTY. I REPORTED THE FACTS AS THEY HAD BEEN GIVEN TO ME AND GAVE HIM THE MOTHER'S NAME AND ADDRESS AND ALSO THE TELEPHONE NUMBER OF THE HOSPITAL. HE SAID HE WAS EXPECTING MR. PRICE BACK IN THE EARLY EVENING BUT IF, FOR ANY REASON, HE WAS DELAYED AND DID NOT GET BACK, HE WOULD DELIVER THE MESSAGE TO THE MOTHER HIMSELF..."

Mr Freake, Barnardo's Headquarters, 10th October, 1960

Chapter 10

Into the Coffin

"I DID NOT SEE YOUR MOTHER MUCH BUT WHEN WE DID MEET SHE ALWAYS SPOKE OF YOU AND I ALWAYS REMEMBER HER SAYING THAT NOT A DAY WENT BY WITHOUT HER THINKING OF YOU."

Martha Watson, 19th August, 1968

By the autumn of 1960, six of her son's birthdays had passed by since Mavis Frampton, now Mavis Kay, had last seen her Pip.

"Not a day passes by without me thinking of him," she would tell a few of those friends she retained from her college and teaching days. Those were the only friends whom she would tell of her feelings. The rest she told nothing. To everyone else, there was no Pip, no black, bastard child.

After her marriage to PK, Mavis continued to teach music in the Birmingham schools whilst her husband continued his studies so as to qualify as an architect. She liked the house in Northfield that the couple had purchased. It was a wooden house, erected in the last war for the purpose of housing Scandinavian workers brought over to assist in the wartime production effort. Mavis decorated the house with presents from her husband's Norwegian relatives to make her PK feel at home.

Whether she wanted to think about her child or not, Mavis was forced to. Every two months or so she had to post off a slip and a cheque to Barnardo's for Pip's upkeep. On two occasions, she got around to adding a short request for information:

"DEAR SIR,
I ENCLOSE £4-0/-0d. TOWARDS THE MAINTENANCE OF PHILLIP FRAMPTON FOR 8 WEEKS FROM 11TH JAN. TO 8TH MARCH. COULD YOU LET ME KNOW IF HE IS WELL, PLEASE.
YOURS FAITHFULLY,
M. KAY (MRS)"

22nd January, 1958

I'd been at school for one year when Mavis enquired on her payment slip:

*"HAS PHILLIP STARTED SCHOOL YET?
MK."*

26th June, 1959

When Miss Merrison, M, at Barnardo's Head Office was passed Mavis's note, she was quite indignant: "I don't know what on earth this woman thinks she is doing. It has taken a year and a half for her to get around to enquiring about her child! She has the address and phone number of the boy's home but Miss Stewart says she neither writes nor phones and never sends the boy any presents."

Then Miss Merrison mused: "Perhaps she does really care for the boy and is looking for an opportunity to persuade her husband to have the boy back with her when her husband is earning and she no longer has to teach."

Miss Merrison was in two minds as to how to handle the young teacher. Nevertheless, a letter heavy with sarcasm was sent back to Mavis in reply:

"YOU ASKED WHETHER PHILIP HAS STARTED SCHOOL YET, AND I AM PLEASED TO TELL YOU THAT HE HAS NOW BEEN AT SCHOOL FOR ALMOST A YEAR, AND THAT HE ATTENDS THE BURY ROAD INFANTS SCHOOL, BIRKDALE. I UNDERSTAND THAT HE IS MAKING VERY GOOD PROGRESS WITH HIS READING AND WRITING...

"SHOULD YOU BE INTERESTED TO HAVE A PHOTOGRAPH, I WILL ASK THE SUPERINTENDENT TO LET ME HAVE ONE, OR BETTER STILL, YOU COULD WRITE TO HER YOURSELF. THE ADDRESS, IN CASE YOU HAVE LOST IT, IS TUDOR BANK, BEACH ROAD, BIRKDALE."

Chief Executive Officer, Western Area, 2nd July, 1959

Whether Mavis had it in mind to have me back with her is uncertain. But her husband had by then qualified as an architect and was about take up a post in a Birmingham firm.

"MR KAY HAS APPARENTLY BEEN WORKING SINCE JULY 1959 WHEN HE HAD COMPLETED HIS STUDIES AT THE BIRMINGHAM SCHOOL OF ARCHITECTURE AND HAS BEEN EMPLOYED AS AN ARCHITECT FOR MESRS. F.W.B. CHARLES OF BIRMINGHAM AT A SALARY OF £850 PER ANNUM..."

Miss Merrison, 23rd January, 1959

When her husband had finally taken up his post, Mavis resigned her full-time teaching job and took up a part-time teaching position at Bournville Grammar Technical School. She clearly intended to prepare the home for having a family. Was it in her mind that I was to be part of it?

If it was, Barnardo's offer, to send her a photograph of her Pip and suggestion that she write, was not taken up. Mavis contented herself with leaving her old college friend, Martha Watson, to send Pip presents on his birthday and at Christmas-time.

I sometimes wonder as to what was going in on Mavis's mind. When she told her friends: "Not a day passes by without me thinking of him," was she misleading them, attempting to maintain respect in their eyes whilst not really caring about the boy? Or was there a reason why Mavis made so few enquiries about me?

It was still October 6th and a wet, dank autumn evening. The rain patted against Mavis and PK's bedroom window. Mavis was in bed with bronchitis when she heard a knock at the door. She left PK to discover whom it might be that was calling. "Perhaps," she thought, "it's one of my girlfriends dropping round for a chat. In which case," she told herself, "PK will know not to send them upstairs."

Her husband, PK, opened the door to find a ginger-bearded man in a long grey gabardine coat and wearing a brown trilby and a soulful expression, standing before him. Whatever then passed between them, the visitor, a Mr Clements, who announced himself as being from Barnardo's, came away with a sense of having had a rather distasteful meeting.

"I CALLED AT THE HOME OF THE BOY'S MOTHER AT THE ADDRESS GIVEN.

"I SAW THE MOTHER'S HUSBAND, MR KAY, WHO SAID THAT HIS WIFE WAS AT PRESENT ILL IN BED WITH BRONCHITIS AND WAS IN NO CONDITION TO SEE ANYONE (HE ALSO ADDED THAT THE DOCTOR HAD BEEN THE DAY BEFORE BUT WAS NOT GOING TO CALL AGAIN TILL THE FOLLOWING MONDAY!).

"I EXPLAINED TO MR KAY WHAT HAD HAPPENED AND HE SAID THAT HE THOUGHT THAT IT WOULD BE BEST IF HE HIMSELF TOLD HIS WIFE OF THE ACCIDENT. I ALSO GAVE HIM THE NUMBER OF THE INFIRMARY IN CASE HE WISHED TO RING THERE HIMSELF – I MUST SAY THAT JUST AT THAT PARTICULAR MOMENT HE DID NOT APPEAR TO BE IN ANY HURRY TO DO ANYTHING CONCERNING PHILLIP – HE DID THANK ME FOR GOING HOWEVER BUT SAID THAT HE THOUGHT THERE WAS LITTLE HE COULD DO IN THE MATTER JUST AT THE MOMENT AND IT MAY BE THAT HE WILL CONTACT THE HOSPITAL TODAY..."

Mr Clements, Western Area Office, October 7th, 1960

The following morning Clements telephoned Mr Freake at the headquarters in Stepney to report on his visit. Of Clement's report, Freake recalled:

"7.10.60 9.45AM. MR CLEMENTS TELEPHONED TO SAY THAT HE VISITED THE MOTHER'S HOME LAST NIGHT... HE SPOKE TO HER HUSBAND AND FELT THAT THERE WAS NO GREAT INTEREST IN PHILLIP'S WELFARE. THE HUSBAND PROMISED TO GIVE HIS WIFE THE NEWS..."

Mr Freake, Barnardo's Headquarters, 10th October, 1960

Precisely what Mavis's husband said to her and what she said, I have no idea. What I do find hard to believe is that Mavis shared her husband's lack of concern for the child that she had nurtured – for "the only thing that I have" as she once wrote. As she received the news that the doctors were busy fighting to save my little life, it must have turned her insides out.

That her husband could be reported as showing such lack of emotion raises the question as to how much he knew of Mavis's attachment to her child. Did he really expect Mavis to receive the news with equal dispassion? Or had Mavis hidden her feelings from her husband in order to hold onto his affections?

If Mavis was being truthful when she told her close friends: "Not a day passes by without me thinking of him," then it must have been him she was misleading and not them. When I read through the files, I placed her husband's apparent indifference alongside her failure to attempt to contact the home with regard to myself, and alongside her requests for her friends such as Martha Watson to keep in contact with me.

I came to the conclusion that Mavis's actions were designed to disguise her feelings from her husband whom she once described as being jealous of her 18-month-old baby. But then there were things that did not add up. Why had she never even sent me a birthday present? Why could she not have had telephone contact with the home?

Perhaps she was being truthful on both accounts – that she wanted to forget me but couldn't and that each word that she heard or wrote about her abandoned child tore at her insides, raised The Dreads from their sleep. Each word she wrote of her son, each word she read, brought such pain, such angst that her hands ceased to scrawl and her eyes ceased to scan the pages.

She was caught between failing her child and failing her husband. A life with her child meant a life without her husband and that would be a very difficult life – no job, no income. How would she be able to bring Phillip up anyway? The same questions that had emerged when she had first been proposed to by PK still lurked and still had no solution. As she lay in her bed that night and through the next day, did she shed a tear? Did she feel any pain?

There again, perhaps she was simply embarrassed by her having nurtured her little golliwog, only then to toss him back into the cupboard. Perhaps bronchitis had not driven her to her bed, as the Barnardo visitor expected and that her husband had simply blocked Mavis's contact with the bearer of the news concerning her child.

Doubtless to say that Miss Merrison at Barnardo's Western Area Office reacted with dismay when she heard how the boy's mother had not reacted to her son's tragedy by even phoning the hospital or the home. For wasn't little Phillip such a sweet boy? Wasn't it Phillip who had taken her by the hand and led her around the home at Tudor Bank when she had visited in her new brown woollen suit?

"How in the heavens," Miss Merrison asked herself, "can a mother show such indifference to her own son as he fights for his life?"

Can a mother forget?

Miss Merrison suspected that the mother's husband stood between her and her son. She waited to see whether, after the initial shock of Phillip's accident, the mother would come round to adopting a more positive approach to her child.

The following day I regained consciousness but remained "on the death list" as it was then called. The doctors were pleased, the children in the home were happy. Mary Stewart was relieved.

It was a day later that Mavis received a letter from Barnardo's reporting that my condition had improved and that I had regained consciousness:

"OUR MEDICAL OFFICER HAS BEEN IN CONTACT WITH THE HOSPITAL AND UNDERSTANDS THAT PHILLIP IS NOW CONSCIOUS AND TALKING AND THAT HIS CONDITION IS AS SATISFACTORY AS CAN BE EXPECTED IN THE CIRCUMSTANCES...
"PHILLIP IS OF COURSE SERIOUSLY ILL BUT HIS CONDITION IS CAUSING LESS CONCERN..."

Barnardo's Western Area Office, 7th October, 1960

Perhaps a little thought flashed through Mavis's head that her life would be better and less full of angst if I were to have died. You might think that thought to have been a possibility. I do.

On the 14th of October, Miss Merrison put on her grey woollen suit and, accompanied by Mr Freake, took the train back up to Southport to discuss the boy's situation with the matron at Tudor Bank. There, the three of them shook their heads in disapproval as Mary Stewart reported that she had heard not a word from the boy's mother. It must be said that Miss Merrison was more used to hearing of the depths of apparent parental rejection of the poor little children in the homes. She detected a level of disdain in the matron's voice and counselled caution:

"We must make some attempt to draw the boy's mother into making contact with the child – even for her own benefit. It may be that her husband's indifference is holding her back but she will regret not contacting her son – whether he lives or dies."

Mr Freake turned his eyes to the floor and nodded his bald head in agreement. When he returned to his office in Stepney, Mr Freake reported on their meeting:

"WE DISCUSSED PHILLIP'S RECENT ACCIDENT AND MISS STEWART SAID THAT SHE WAS MOST SURPRISED TO LEARN THAT HE HAD GOT OFF THE BUS BY HIMSELF – THINKS HE MAY HAVE BEEN GIVEN A PENNY TO SPEND BUT NO ONE REALLY KNOWS WHAT HAPPENED. NORMALLY HE SEEMS TO BE A VERY OBEDIENT AND LAW ABIDING LITTLE BOY – ALWAYS ABLE TO AMUSE HIMSELF WITH TOYS ETC...
"IS VERY INTELLIGENT – TEACHER SAYS HE IS ONE OF THE MOST INTELLIGENT CHILDREN SHE HAS EVER TAUGHT.
"MOTHER (NOW MARRIED TO A NORWEGIAN) DOES NOT TAKE ANY INTEREST AND HAS NOT BEEN IN TOUCH SINCE PHILLIP'S ACCIDENT.
"ACTION: - MISS STEWART TO WRITE TO MOTHER AND GIVE HER SOME NEWS OF PHILLIP AND SEE WHETHER THIS WILL ENCOURAGE HER TO HAVE SOME CONTACT WITH HIM."

Mr Freake, Barnardo's Headquarters, Stepney, 14th October, 1960

Mary Stewart had already given up on the boy's mother. The matron couldn't see what her superiors considered there was to gain from further contact. "After all," she muttered to herself, "the woman has already abandoned her child. The boy has been with me for two years and she has never made an effort to contact me or him."

Mary Stewart wrote the briefest of letters to Mavis Kay and received the briefest of notes in return.

"THANK YOU FOR INFORMING OF PHILLIP'S PROGRESS IN HOSPITAL. I HAVE WRITTEN AND THANKED THE MATRON AT BIRKDALE."

Mavis signed the letter simply, "MK."

Meanwhile, in the hospital I began my fragile recovery. My waking to consciousness was something of a treat. I found myself surrounded by bowls of rosy-red apples and big Jaffa oranges, juicy black grapes, purple grapes, green grapes, flaming red peaches and brown-green pears, boxes of dates and cartons of sweets. I might as well have been in heaven.

Being in that hospital was one of the most joyful memories of my young life. I had visits from Matron and the staff, visits from the Granvilles, visits from the children in the home and so many gifts and goodies that I sent Miss Stewart home with a suitcase full of sweets, chocolates and fruit to give out to my unfortunate little friends who weren't in hospital like me.

"HE HAS A GENEROUS NATURE AND WHEN MISS STEWART VISITED HIM IN HOSPITAL RECENTLY HE ASKED HER TO TAKE SOME OF HIS SWEETS AND FRUIT TO SHARE WITH THE CHILDREN..."

Mr Freake, Barnardo's Headquarters, Stepney, 14th October, 1960

For a glorious 19 days I was kept in the hospital on the best diet I had ever known. Then it was time to return to the home for a "few days" before the Granvilles came and took me to stay with them for a "few days." It was November before I finally settled back into life in Tudor Bank.

In Birmingham, the issue of Mavis having a family was being decided. It was not for me that Mavis was now only working part-time. She and her husband were attempting to have children of their own. Barnardo's however remained more concerned about the child that Mavis Kay had already borne.

In January 1961, Miss Merrison ordered one last attempt to explore the mother's real wishes regarding her child. M was still of the inclination that the boy, Phillip, would be better off being adopted if his mother no longer wished to have any contact. Sat in her office, she re-studied the now burgeoning file on the boy. It did seem sad that he had been tossed from one home to another but it was often the case nowadays, she mused.

She noticed that Mavis Kay was two months behind on her contributions for her son's upkeep and the mother's lack of any apparent wish to have contact with the child. On the 17th of January she wrote to Bert Price, Barnardo's Welfare Officer in Birmingham, requesting that one of his staff arrange a visit to see Mavis Kay to discuss her son's future and equally her financial support for the boy.

Bert Price sent along a Mr Hector, a young Student Welfare Officer, to keep the appointment with Mavis. He was greeted courteously by Mavis's husband, and the three of them sat down in the couple's living room. Mr Hector explained Barnardo's concerns to them both.

It wasn't only the response of Mavis to her son's situation that disturbed the student. Mrs Kay concluded by stating that, since the couple were planning to have a family of their own, she could no longer afford to contribute to the boy's upkeep. The student wanted to say: "You and your husband get £1,240 a year, you have a nice house and you say you won't pay £25 of that to the child you brought into the world." But the student didn't know if it was the right thing to say in the circumstances.

He did say: "I will take your request back to Head Office but I do think that, while you yourself are working, you will be expected to contribute to Phillip's upkeep."

The young officer went away as dismayed as the previous visitor from the same office. He submitted his report, which found its way to Miss Merrison:

"MRS KAY HAS CONTINUED IN HER TEACHING POST AT THE BOURNVILLE GRAMMAR TECHNICAL SCHOOL, ON A PART-TIME BASIS, AT A SALARY OF £390PA. THEY ARE NOW VERY KEEN TO START A FAMILY AND MRS KAY INTENDS TO CONTINUE IN HER PRESENT POST UNTIL THIS WISH IS FULFILLED.

Bert Price, 23rd January, 1961

As I read the report for the very first time in April 1999, the words that followed hit me like a thunderbolt.

"MRS KAY, WHO WAS RATHER TENSE THE WHOLE TIME, BECAME INSTANTLY UPSET AS SOON AS THE QUESTION OF PHILLIP'S FUTURE WAS MENTIONED AND STATED THAT SHE WOULD RATHER FORGET ABOUT HIM ALTOGETHER."

I went into the slush and snow of that April day in Kendal and lit up a cigarette. A tear found its way to my eye. A cry wanted to leap from the depths of my stomach. The teardrop fell into a melting snowflake. The cigarette stifled my cry.

I felt lost - cheated of an explanation. I felt rejection. It was rejection I'd never allowed myself to feel before. "She would rather forget about him" – six words, nine syllables. Sixteen letters of the alphabet, on a piece of paper lighter than a feather, had just laid me low. I was not even worth an existence as a thought. She had thrown her Romulus back to the wolves.

Suddenly I was with those other unwanted children – the ones who dreamed of one day meeting their parents - the ones who as adults went in search of their parents and found them, and stood lost for words as their parents slammed the door on them. Mavis had buried her past and slammed my coffin lid shut as firmly on me as the door had been closed on them.

"Long ago," he said, "I thought like you that my mother would always keep the window open for me; so I stayed away for moons and moons and moons, and then flew back; but the window was barred, for mother had forgotten all about me, and there was another little boy sleeping in my bed."

J.M.Barrie, Peter Pan

Mavis nailed down her past. I was in the coffin.

Barnardo's Miss Merrison was angered by the news. She ordered a note to be sent to Miss Stewart in the home:

"WE HAVE NOW HAD PHILLIP'S MOTHER VISITED AND I AM ATTACHING A COPY OF MR PRICE'S REPORT... IT IS CLEAR FROM THIS REPORT THAT THE MOTHER DOES NOT WISH TO CONTINUE THE CONTACT WITH PHILLIP AND, IN THESE CIRCUMSTANCES, MISS MERRISON FEELS THAT WE SHOULD CEASE OUR EFFORTS TO KEEP HER IN TOUCH. IT WILL THEREFORE NOT BE NECESSARY FOR YOU TO WRITE TO HER AGAIN."

Chief Executive Office, Western Area, 27th January, 1961

"But at least now," M told herself, "we can go ahead with getting the boy into another foster home or adopted." Miss Merrison, you will recall, had always felt that the boy, Phillip, would be better off placed with a good family. She had been thwarted mainly because the boy was coloured and out of sensitivity for his former foster parents. She ordered a letter to be sent to the boy's mother. In it Mavis was informed:

"WE NOTE THAT YOU HAVE NO FUTURE TO OFFER TO PHILLIP AND WE SHALL, THEREFORE, ENDEAVOUR TO MAKE PLANS OF A PERMANENT NATURE FOR HIM... MEANWHILE, WE MUST CONTINUE TO LOOK TO YOU TO SEND US THE SUM OF 10/- PER WEEK, IN ACCORDANCE WITH THE PRESENT ASSESSMENT."

Chief Executive Office, Western Area, 27th January, 1961

If Mavis did wish to keep up with news about her son, she had shown so little interest herself that Barnardo's concluded that she was a thoughtless mother who didn't deserve the contact they offered. She was not aware at the time but her apparently diffident response to her son's situation, led to all avenues to news concerning her Pip being closed.

Miss Stewart, in Southport, reacted the same way as had Miss Bodell, the matron in my first Barnardo's home. When Miss Merrison's letter reached Mary Stewart, the matron was filled with utter contempt for the callous young teacher who had left her child to be loved by others, who was intent on building a fine life for herself, based on lying to her various headteachers about her situation:

"If they only knew what the young madam was like, that woman would not get into another school to parade as an example to young girls!"

In anger, Mary Stewart phoned Mavis and her friend, my godmother, Catherine Dolby. She wanted an end to the boy being a plaything for these foolish women: "It is obvious now that you have no intention for providing for Phillip or securing him a home. I do have to now request that you cease any contact with the boy. He is happy in the home where he has stable friends and any contact with you or your friends will only cause unnecessary disturbance."

Whatever Mavis's wishes, Mary Stewart severed all routes to her Pip. It was the last time Mavis would ever hear any account of his well-being.

"HIS MOTHER AND I WERE DISTRESSED WHEN WE WERE ASKED NOT TO CONTACT HIM ABOUT TEN YEARS AGO, BUT WE REALISED IT WAS FOR THE BEST WHEN MATRON SAID THAT HE WOULD BE HAPPIER AMONG THE STABLE FRIENDS HE HAD IN SOUTHPORT."

Catherine Dolby, 29th June, 1970

Besides, Mavis was quickly consumed by other considerations. At the very time when she was burying me, her white child-thought began its existence as embryo. Within a month Mavis discovered that she was pregnant. Her new life would begin. Once again, she wrote to Barnardo's requesting that she be allowed to cease her contributions for my upkeep. With it she enclosed a cheque for £8 and ten shillings. It was the first payment to my upkeep that she had made for six months and would prove to be her last:

"I NOW FIND THAT I AM EXPECTING A BABY AND SHALL HAVE TO STOP WORK IN JULY. I ENCLOSE A CHEQUE FOR THE MAINTENANCE OF PHILLIP UNTIL THAT DATE, BUT I WOULD BE VERY GRATEFUL IF YOU WOULD RECONSIDER THE CASE AS FROM JULY, AS I DO NOT FEEL THAT I CAN ASK MY HUSBAND TO CONTRIBUTE..."

Mavis Frampton, 17th May, 1961

Why she did not feel that her husband could contribute, was not questioned, but the exasperated Miss Merrison quickly acceded to the boy's mother's request. Her letter could not avoid a touch of sarcasm:

"I AM VERY PLEASED TO HEAR THE NEWS THAT YOUR LETTER CONTAINS AND I DO HOPE THAT THE FUTURE WILL HOLD MUCH HAPPINESS FOR YOUR HUSBAND AND YOURSELF.
"I CONFIRM THAT WE SHALL NOT EXPECT YOU TO CONTRIBUTE ANY FURTHER TOWARDS THE MAINTENANCE OF PHILLIP."

Chief Executive Office, Western Area, 25th May 1961

Miss Merrison informed Mary Stewart of the news, adding:

"...I THINK WE MUST REGARD THIS AS THE LAST WE SHALL HEAR FROM HER."

Chief Executive Office, Western Area, 25th May, 1961

Mary Stewart saw to that.

As to the matter of my being fostered or adopted, Mary Stewart saw to that also. Once again she resisted Miss Merrison's expressed wish to see me boarded out. Once again she argued that I was deeply attached to the Granvilles and that it was probably the case that they would have me back with them at a later date. When Barnardo's Head Office sent Miss Wolstenholme up once again to see me in Southport and assess the situation, she reported back:

"I AGREE WITH MISS STEWART THAT IF THE GRANVILLES CAN GIVE HIM A HOME THEN HE WOULD BE BEST LEFT WHERE HE IS."

Miss K Wolstenholme, 7th March, 1961

I was sentenced to remain in the home at Mary Stewart's pleasure.

In October 1961, my half-sister was born. She had blue eyes, blonde hair and a lily-white skin. Mavis later bore me a half-brother. Bringing three children into the world was enough and she started taking the birth control pill.

The pill was first put on the market in 1960. It was believed that, for the first time ever, women could safely and effectively control childbearing by simply taking a pill. With its side-effects not then fully known, the pill was greeted as a godsend by many women.

Medical anxiety grew quickly as several women suffered severe blood clotting. In time, the risk of clots was directly correlated to the amount of oestrogen in the various versions of the pill. But, in 1966 the pill killed Mavis and at least two dozen British women. Mavis died of a brain haemorrhage.

Having her first child had almost ruined Mavis's life. Her decision that she had borne her last child put an end to her life. The cause of Mavis's death gave increased cause for alarm in the medical profession. The young woman who had dreamt of fame as a young pianist finally made the national newspapers - but as victim rather than heroine.

I'll never know what Mavis thought of her actions regarding myself. Was she a product of her time? Was she a product of abuse? The old ones say: "It was understandable. That was the way it was. What else could she do?"

A victim in her childhood, she had reached out for love with a passion, but she had played light of the times. In a society that frowned upon relationships across the colour bar, that portrayed black people as little better than savages, disapproved of pre-marital sex and glorified motherhood and the family, Mavis had borne a bastard, black child then abandoned it.

Like Defoe's tragic Roxana, she would pay for her moments of bliss as she tried to hide from the condemnation of society. In vain. Try as she might, she could not escape from the consequences of her past. She was trapped between a jealous lover, social disapproval and her desire for both social respectability and self-esteem, but finally by her maternal instincts.

She cried out: "I'd rather forget about him altogether!" and gave up the struggle.

Infanticide is understandable. Is it excusable?

The old ones say: "We thought Barnardo's gave good homes to children."

Before I secured my files, my godmothers would insist that they and Mavis were blocked from having any contact with me. I was angry with Barnardo's. Barnardo's said that they had no such policy. As you will have read, I learned that the truth was much more complex.

As for Mary Stewart, her actions were those of the middle class matrons of the time. She delivered the ultimate indictment of society – "You are not worthy to be this child's mother." I find that, even given my mother's indifference, Mary Stewart's actions were cruel. Yet in the moments of writing these words, I find what the Matron did to a mother who had inquired twice about the welfare of her child in five years, to be eminently understandable.

If there is one thing I am glad of regarding these events, it is that none of this was relayed to me at the time. I was left in total ignorance, left in Neverneverland with my fantasies. I had nobody. I was alone but my father was a prince, or so I sometimes thought.

Chapter 11

An Intelligent Child

"Come on Phillip! We don't want to be late for the pictures," urged Mickey, as I crouched in the cloakroom struggling to tie my shoelace. We had just collected our pocket money from Matron. Now that I was seven, my pocket money had risen to nine pence, which meant I could even buy a bar of chocolate if I wished. I was off to town with Mickey, Michael, Mary and Emily, but that day we wouldn't buy any chocolate.

Once my shoelaces were tied and Emily had fetched her big, red, woolly, polo-neck sweater, we strolled out from Tudor Bank and, having turned the corner of Beach Road, Mickey shouted: "Race you to the dentists!"

The five of us ran all the way along Westcliffe Road till we reached the dentist's. Mickey won. He was the oldest. Mary trailed in last, huffing and puffing in her yellow dress. She was the youngest.

"Let's… Let's… " said Mickey, out of breath, "Let's go to the sweet shop first an' nick some sweets."

"Yeah," agreed Emily, "that ol' man's easy."

"Come on, Specky," Mary Ingham said, taking my hand and smiling. Just prior to my road accident, I'd been sent to an optician, diagnosed as having astigmatism and been provided with a pair of National Health issue, brown wire-rimmed spectacles.

We skipped our way onto Lord Street, Southport's main street - the prettiest street in England, everybody said. Not that I had anything to compare it with except Bolton's town centre. It was much prettier than that.

The sweet shop that was chosen for our shoplifting exercise, was one of the first shops on the west side of the street. The shop, being the nearest to the home, was a regular first stop when we ventured into town to spend our pocket money. Mickey and Emily had helped themselves to the old man's barley sugars and Mars Bars before. This trip was to be my initiation.

"You first," Mickey pointed to me as we stood outside.

"OK. I'm not scared," I replied. I was scared – scared of the old man taking me by the ear and sending me back home for a beating. Michael and his sister, Mary, stayed outside. They were scared too.

I was the first to enter the shop. The shop was small and the counter, which ran its length, left room for only a handful of customers. Rows of glass jars lined the shelves. They contained our Saturday treats – Lemon

Sherberts, penny chew Black Jack's, Lemon Barleys, penny liquorices, those bitter Pear Drops and sickly Jelly Babies. Beneath them, the counter was stacked with parades of chocolate bars – bars we would have enough pocket money to buy once we reached our eleventh birthdays.

That day I was lucky as two or three people were inside. An old woman wearing a pink woollen coat that stretched to her ankles and a hat lined with chiffon and pink paper roses asked the shopkeeper for a quarter of bonbons and, these being my favourites, I knew what the shopkeeper was about to do.

As the old man reached up for the glass jar containing the floury white sweets, I checked that his other customers weren't looking, slipped my hand over the counter and one bar of Cadbury's Dairy Milk Chocolate disappeared into my trouser pocket. My heart was racing.

"Now buy us a penny bubble gum," whispered Emily.

I didn't want to buy her a bubble gum and looked quizzically at Mickey. Mickey nodded his head and I took a penny out of my pocket and raised it in my hand. It seemed like a lifetime as I stood by the counter waiting to be served by the old man.

"Penny bubble gum, please."

The old man smiled. I grasped the white wrapper and ran out of the shop followed by Mickey and Emily.

We kept on running until we got to the Ribble Bus station close by where we stood, huffing and puffing with huge grins on our face.

"That was easy," I said triumphantly as Emily turned and stood before me, hand outstretched demanding her bubble gum.

I passed over the gum and pulled out my bar of chocolate. It was mine. I had won it.

Mickey slipped two bars of Bournville dark chocolate from beneath his sweater and gave one to Michael. Emily produced three little white Milky Bars from beneath her big, red, polo-neck jumper. Emily loved Milky Bars and could nick them all day long. She handed half a bar to Mary.

"Milky Bar Kid," said Mickey.

I took off half the silver wrapper on my bar of chocolate and bit into it. Mickey and Emily did the same and we walked off quickly passed the cafes and clothes shops and crossed another road only to see Brian Reynolds and Emily's older sister, Donna, walking ahead of us.

"Gi' us some o' yer chocolate," said Brian, as we approached them.

Mickey broke off four chunks of his bar and handed them over to the older boy. Emily did the same with Donna.

"Where yer off?" asked Brian.

"To the pictures."

"Which one?"

"The Gaumont."

"Why don't yer come wi' us ta ABC? It's better there, they 'ave better films," said Brian, pointing over the road.

"Naah," replied Emily, shaking her head, "we can't afford it, it's sixpence. The Gaumont's free."

As Barnardo kids we could get into the Gaumont for free. We could get our school friends in too, if we said that they were also from Barnardo's. Brian and Donna were older and had two shillings pocket money. Paying sixpence to get in the Odeon was not much to them.

Our troupe of five left them and walked on down the street, past Monty's, the confectionery shop that gave us our giant Easter eggs. We crossed the road that led to the Promenade. That road had lots of shops for families visiting the seaside. They sold plastic buckets and spades, plastic Union Jacks on sticks and plastic, Aussie and Canadian flags for sticking on sandcastles, shiny red and green toffee apples and postcards of fat naked ladies, and skinny naked men, who grinned and grimaced as the fat ladies smiled and squealed.

We passed by the Kardomah Café with its enticing aroma of roasted coffee beans. Matron sometimes took us there for a treat if we were very good.

"I jus' wanna go in Burton's Arcade. Won' be a minute," said Mickey.

"Come wi' yer?" I asked.

Mickey nodded and I followed him through the covered arcade of toyshops, confectionery shops and milliners until we were stood outside a stamp shop. Mickey collected stamps and put them in a big stamp album with the names of every country in the whole wide world.

He pushed open the shop door and I beheld the wonders of the world. In glass cases on the walls and glass counters around the edges I set my eye on stamps of all colours and all countries, stamps with brightly coloured birds, stamps with kings' heads on and queens' heads, stamps with tanks, stamps with soldiers. Otherwise the shop was empty, save for the thin bald-headed and bespectacled old man dressed in a tweed green suit. He was sitting behind one of the counters. The old man lifted his eyes over his spectacles and peered at us.

"Can I help you young man?" he said to Mickey who shrugged his shoulders and turned to look at a "Penny Red" hung up as the shopkeeper's prize possession. I wandered around my head transfixed on the walls of colour and adventure. I noticed that the old man's eyes darted between Mickey and me wherever we went.

Mickey turned and left the shop, so I followed.

"'E was watching us all the time. Couldn't put me 'ands on nuttin'," explained Mickey, "We'll go in Woolies later. It's easier." Like a latter day Artful Dodger, he was teaching me the trade.

We joined Michael, Emily and Mary back on Lord Street where they were staring at a dishevelled old woman across the road close to the Memorial that still marks the centre of the town. The woman wore a thick brown coat, which almost came down to her ankles. The coat left enough room to expose her once-white ankle socks now ridden with holes. The old woman's feet were clad with plimsolls, one of which was split at the toes.

A green shawl was wrapped around the woman's head, leaving little of her swarthy, grimy face and greasy, grey hair on view. When I first set eyes on her she was rummaging in a rubbish bin that was attached to a lamppost. She returned to a wooden bench to search in a black plastic bin liner. We assumed the bag contained all her belongings. From time to time she would bend over and toss crumbs of bread at a flock of pigeons that she had attracted.

"That's Necker," said Emily, "She kills pigeons."

"Grabs 'em by the neck, twists it an' strangles 'em," added Michael.

"What for?" asked Mary.

"She puts 'em in that bag an' takes 'em 'ome to eat," explained Mickey.

"Uuuh!" I stood entranced, hoping to see her strike out for pigeon. She never did but Necker was a monster, part of our Neverneverland.

"Come on," said Mickey, hurrying us up, "Let's get to the Gaumont."

He led us across the busy road to close by where Necker had sat back on her bench. Then we broke into a run, shouting: "Hey! Necker!" and racing past her.

We arrived at the Gaumont, laughing and giggling and took our place in the queue of young boys with short grey trousers and woolly jumpers and girls in dresses that reached just below their knees. The Art Nouveau building still stands but has been reduced to the status of a bingo hall.

"Cockledoodledoo!" came the cry of a great big black and grey cockerel on the black and white screen. It was time for Pathé News, the news programme that seemed to appear at every cinema sitting. We were still in an age when not all people had televisions. Pathé News was a way of the government reaching the people. But why they wanted to tell us children about the great wave of coloured people arriving on boats from the colonies to assist in building a greater Britain, I am not sure.

Pathé News was worth sitting through because a feature film followed it and we sat transfixed as Spitfires and Stukas hurtled through the air with great plumes of smoke following behind them. Aircraft carriers and submarines scythed through the seas between exploding bombs and drifting lifeboats. Rata-tat-tat! Rata-tat-tat! Men held their chests and fell to the ground; just like we did when we played out. War was exciting! And it was free to watch.

We waited for the Union Jack to unfurl and the National Anthem to end before trouping out for our next excursion. Mickey led us off down the street to Woolworth's department store – a fine place to pick up replicas of those Spitfires and Stukas, battleships and frigates that had so entertained us that morning.

We made our way around the store, peering at the mountains of sweets and toys galore on the counters before we came to the site chosen by we boys. "Airfix Kits" a small sign declared. There were small plastic kits for making up fighter planes, bombers, jet planes, cruisers, battleships, aircraft carriers, motor cars, jeeps – all that we needed to have a good war. Not a one could be bought with our pocket money. But we weren't there to spend our pennies; we were there to save them.

Michael glanced around then his hand darted over the counter and a Messerschmitt fighter plane disappeared up his woolly jumper. He winked at me and the Graf Spey slipped up mine. Mickey swallowed the Bismarck and a tube of Airfix glue and we coolly (well I was almost cool) ambled out of the shop and back into the high street. With a triumphant smile, Mickey slyly showed me a corner of a packet of stamps he'd also picked up in Woolies. Michael produced two of those small war magazines, which were a big fad with us at the time. They told tales of great heroes in the battles of the Second World War.

What, and if, Mary stole from the shops, I cannot remember but back in the cloakroom at Tudor Bank we unloaded our spoils, stashing them away in our duffel bags where they were to stay until the coast was clear. In the afternoon we returned to the cloakroom and made up our kits in conditions so secretive we might have been preparing the H-bomb.

The next week I used my pocket money to buy a small stamp book. I joined Mickey "collecting" stamps. Molly Broughton, the cook, gave me her postcards that she had sent back from her holidays and I took the stamps off them. Molly said I had a lovely stamp collection but sometimes she looked at me like she knew how I got some of my stamps.

Our little shopping trips continued for years. Sometimes we raided in packs, sometimes alone, until one day Matron called us all into the porch at Tudor Bank. There to greet us was a young policeman with a stern look on his face.

"I have something very serious to say," Matron announced, "A few children – I shan't name names – have been seen stealing in the shops in town."

She peered at us as we stood eyes fixed to the chequer-patterned stone porch floor. I felt my cheeks going red but was sure my blush wouldn't be spotted through my dark brown skin. We waited in silence, waited for her announcement to conclude with our punishment.

"Nothing more will be said this time but the next time any of you are caught, you will be severely punished. Is that understood?"

Silence.

"I said, is that understood?"

"Yes, Miss Stewart!" we chimed in relief.

Our trips stopped. For a while. We never did get caught.

When I reached eight years of age, I was able to apply to join the older children and sing in the church choir. Being paid seventeen shillings and sixpence a quarter, I would become less concerned with the shoplifting trips. Going to choir practice also meant not getting home till nine o'clock. Having already been enrolled in the Cub Scouts and doing "dib-dib-dobs" and "Ar-kay-lah! We'll do our best, to God and the Queen," for 12 months, I knew that a late night return meant being allowed to have a hot drink.

Drinking a hot cup of syrupy Camp coffee with ten teaspoonfuls of sugar sneaked in so that the teaspoon could stand up was infinitely more pleasurable than the normal compulsory cup of tepid or sour milk. Going to Cubs was good because Matron gave us each sixpence so that we could buy a bag of chips on our way home. But I left the Cubs after Akela wouldn't give me my second star for the tests I'd passed like lighting a fire and making a cup of tea. That wasn't fair.

To get into the choir and get my money and stay up until nine and get a hot drink, I first had to get through my little singing test with Mr Drayton, the organ master. Mary Stewart tried to dissuade me but I was excited at the prospect of earning so much money – just for singing.

My expectations of becoming a choirboy were low. Before I left for my audition, Matron smiled at me and said: "Make sure you sing your very best and do sing in tune, Phillip. If you sing like you do with us then they will not want you."

Miss Stewart was always telling me off when we sang around her piano in the Staff Room. As I went off to church, she pondered as to why Phillip's mother had not passed on her undoubted musical abilities.

"*LIKES MUSIC BUT HE CANNOT SING IN TUNE.*"

Miss Stewart, January, 1961

I arrived at 7 o'clock on a Tuesday night with Mark Lancaster and the other boys and girls from the home who were in the choir. Matron said Mark Lancaster could really sing. He was allowed to sing solo in some church services.

We pushed open the heavy wooden door which led up steps to the vestry at the rear of the church. There we were greeted with a frown by the bald-headed Mr Drayton sat at a piano in his tweed jacket and brown flannels.

"Phillip Frampton?" he enquired, staring at me beneath his thin grey eyebrows.

"Yes, Mr Drayton," I replied.

He motioned me to stand beside him and, on the other side, the bushy eyebrows of the head chorister, Mr Partington, appeared.

"You know 'All Things Bright and Beautiful?'"

"Yes, Mr Drayton."

"Well sing the first verse. I will start on the count of three."

I sang away and, though Mr Partington began to frown as hard as his organ master, I was considered satisfactory and enrolled in the choir. Through the rest of the choir practice I did not sing so well but I blame that on the big grin stretched across my face.

When we had left the vestry, Mr Drayton turned to his head chorister: "He's no Mark Lancaster. I thought all these blacks could sing. Don't ever suggest that he does a solo."

So each Tuesday night and Thursday night we attended choir practice in preparation for singing in the Sunday matinée and Sunday evening service. I looked forward to the end of the first three months when I would receive my first little brown packet and feel it for the ten shilling note and the silver coins which would make up my pay.

We also looked forward to weddings and funerals because we were paid extra for them – two shillings and sixpence for a wedding and two shillings for a funeral. Funerals were my favourite, for, being held on midweek mornings, they involved us having to take a half-day off school to attend.

As was usual during services we'd pass the time playing noughts and crosses or hangman or tearing out the O's on our sweet wrappers to see how many we cold amass. When we'd finally sung "*The Day Thou Gavest Lord Has Ended*," collected our florin for the funeral, and hung up our cassocks and surplices, we loped off to school for our day to begin. On the way we would use our money to stop off at the chip shop near the school to buy a packet of chips and potato fritters soaked in vinegar.

I was a member of the church choir for several years and began to believe that I could sing. When one day, my little brown pay packet appeared empty, my heart sank. Mr Partington winked at me. I opened the packet and there was one green pound note and one ten shilling note. My face beamed. I'd finally made the top grade.

Mr Partington nodded. I never was asked to sing solo.

Life at the home continued in the same routine. As we got older so children came and went. The older boys left to learn a trade at the Barnardo's Goldings apprentice centre down in Stevenage. The older girls left to become housemaids and the like. Mark Lancaster was taken away to a remand home. The nurses said it was because he had such a bad temper. We all had a bad temper, they said. We all knew that if we were really bad then we would be sent away, like Mark.
Mary Stewart commented on me:

"APART FROM THE OCCASIONAL OUTBURSTS OF TEMPER IS NO TROUBLE."

Miss Stewart, January, 1961

"VERY GOOD INDEED, APART FROM OCCASIONAL OUTBURSTS OF TEMPER."

Miss Stewart, January, 1962

We all had tempers but Mark was strong, too strong for the all women staff in the home. On a summer's day, when all the windows in Tudor Bank were open, you could sometimes hear his screams and shouts if you came within a hundred yards of the home. When Mark was angry he went wild, kicking and punching. Each year, Mark got angry more and more frequently. Matron had him taken to a remand home. He never came back.

Jenny Thompson came back. Jenny had left to go into digs and study at the local art school. Jenny was good at art. When Jenny came back Matron put her in the girls' dormitory. Matron said Jenny could paint Mary Ingham, Barbara Carson and Emily Brotherton in the nude. Matron told them they could take all their clothes off and Jenny sketched away while the girls were told to sit naked on the chairs, shelves and windowsills, for the sake of art. Mary wondered what her stepdad would think.

Barbara Carson got too old and she left too but she often came back. Most of the older children came back to visit from time to time. Some had brothers or sisters in the home. Some just liked returning to our Neverneverland. Tom Chorley was fostered out but he was sent back. Tom was fostered out again but he was sent back. Nobody thought Tom cared. Tom just loved trains and cricket.

New faces always replaced those who left. In came three more black children, all six years old. Colin Smith and his twin sister, Carmen Smith, were both very black with tight curly hair. Valerie Lomas was a lighter shade – brown, as Matron would say - and had light fluffy curls. All three were the same age as Sheryll and they played and played with each other. Shania came too but she was white.

Those who have never been in children's homes think that we never had love and never knew it. They are wrong, I loved Shania, Sheryll, Colin, Carmen and Valerie, but like a caring elder brother. I organised little tea parties for them on Saturdays, taught them to look after the pets, which we were sometimes allowed to keep in the two huts behind the home. I taught them to clean out the mouse cage and the guinea pig and rabbit hutch. I went searching with them when our pets went missing and dug the little graves beside the sandpit where they were buried.

We rose early on summer and spring days and I took the "little ones" for walks along the beach and down the railway line, searching for treasure and searching for war secrets. I read books to them and I told them stories of monsters and giants.

I liked Valerie with her mop of short curly hair and her pretty face and her tempers. Then Valerie was fostered out. But she was sent back. Then she was fostered out again. But she was sent back.

Carmen and Colin had really bad tempers, as bad as Mark Lancaster's, they said. I often heard Carmen's screams as I turned into Beach Road. I knew the nurses were trying to pin her down. Carmen got angry and kicked me once, but I loved Carmen. We all were a problem when we were in a temper and I had my fair share.

Sometimes we would go to bed crying, wait until night-time and run away. Once I ran away. I slipped my long black gabardine coat over my trousers, sneaked out of the house and took a bus into town. I got off the bus after two stops because that was all I could afford. I was cold and had nowhere to go.

I walked back to the home. I sneaked through a window that I'd left open – just in case – and hid behind a cupboard. I sneaked back upstairs before the police had arrived. I never tried to run away again. What was the point of running away if you had nowhere to run to?

Pamela Brotherton got into tempers a lot. She was always running away. She stole from us and I was jealous of her and I wished she would never come back. She always did. Everyone who ran away always came back in a police car or on their own.

Mary Ingham was also the same age as me but I came to love Mary Ingham. I loved Mary in a different way. Mary's father was from India and her skin and hair said so. That much she knew but, as with myself, she had no recollection of her natural parents. Like most of us, she threw lots of her meals away, so she grew to be pretty skinny. Being as she was born three months later than I, she was put in the school year below mine.

Mary had big brown sparkling eyes, the prettiest face, perfect white teeth and the sweetest smile. Her thick, dark brown hair would grow waves when it grew long but it was rarely allowed to. It was almost always cut in a bob, which just covered her ears and left her perfectly formed face peaking out from beneath.

When Mary was allowed to walk home from school on her own, I said she could walk home with me and I was happy skipping and walking with Mary. I looked after Mary in those days. I wanted to. If we played games together. I was happy. If we took our bikes down to the beach. I was happy. If we sat together at dinner time, I was happy.

Was she sweet natured? She was to me. What is more, I trusted her; trusted her with my secrets; trusted her with my promises and never set out to hurt her. I cared for her. I basked in her company, never fearing hurt or betrayal.

So is not all this love? Is not love caring, trusting, sharing and respecting? And who taught us this? Certainly not absent parents or itinerant adults and staff – unless one dares to argue that love is taught by adults in a few days or months and children catch it from a splattering of words buried in pain and anxiety.

Children are young adults and as much social beings as those who combined to bring them into existence. Caring and trusting are part of social existence. We had to exist and seek what stability and pleasure we could in each other. With some we achieved it. With others we achieved even more and learned to care for one another, to love and to cherish, in sickness and in pain.

I was her Pip and she was my Estella. I was a prince and she was my princess. Asked if I loved her then, I would blush and deny it, for loving was an unboyish thing to do. Love was soppy and for grown-ups we saw in films. Nevertheless, one day we would be proclaimed as Prince 2Ls Phillip of Africa and Princess Mary of India.

"I DO ALWAYS REMEMBER YOU HAVING TIME FOR ME, I ALWAYS FELT QUITE SPECIAL! I STILL REMEMBER TOO YOUR ALWAYS LETTING ME WALK HOME WITH YOU FROM SCHOOL, HOWEVER, I DO REMEMBER YOU ALWAYS MADE ME WALK ONE LAMPPOST AND RUN ONE LAMPPOST - IT USED TO JUST ABOUT KILL ME!!"

Mary Ingham, 1999

I loved Mickey and Michael too, but like brothers, elder brothers, and we laughed and fought together. Mickey took me to my first real football match when I was nine. I went to watch Southport Reserves play Chorley Reserves at the local ground on Haig Avenue. Then, on my tenth birthday, he was allowed to take me on a train to Bolton to watch Bolton Wanderers play Norwich. Both matches were boring but going was exciting. Mickey had a wooden rattle painted black and yellow in the colours of the Southport team. One day I got myself a rattle in the same colours and Mickey and I went off to watch Southport's football team on the following Saturday. After that, we went every fortnight to watch the "Sandgrounders," as they were called, play in the Fourth Division of the Football League.

As Mickey introduced me to "top class" football, like many young boys I came to love the sport and dream of one day being a Pele or a Puskas. When I returned from school I would search out Matron's copies of the Daily Express and Daily Telegraph and read the sports' pages thoroughly. If I saw anything else of interest, I read that as well.

I soon started to use my pocket money and choir money to buy the *Daily Mirror* to catch up on the previous night's matches. I read and read every book and magazine about football that I could get hold of. I was in love with football. I only ever made the school B team but I always believed that I was better than that.

From wanting to be a tramp, my ambition turned to becoming a football player. Mary Stewart's ambition was for me to become the missionary, I'd spoken of, or a doctor or lawyer. She caught me reading, morning, noon and night. Each time she heard reports from the school, she was convinced that she had a special little boy:

"IS A GREAT READER"

Miss Stewart, January, 1961

"PHILIP IS VERY INTELLIGENT – WAS TOP IN ENGLISH, AND SHOULD DO WELL."

Barnardo's Educational Advisor, June 1961

"VERY FOND OF READING AND DOING PUZZLES. COLLECTS STAMPS...PHILLIP IS A CHARMING AND VERY INTELLIGENT LITTLE BOY."

Miss Stewart, January, 1962

"TRUTHFUL AND HONEST, OCCASIONALLY LOSES HIS TEMPER, OTHERWISE IS AN EASY CHILD... INTELLIGENT AND WORKS WELL... NEVER HEARS FROM HIS MOTHER."

Miss Stewart, January, 1963

I found myself at ease in the junior school. I coped with the lessons adequately and was always pleased to find myself among the top ten in the class when we sat our little tests and exams. I didn't bother with homework and the staff at the home never bothered us about our schooling, unless, that is, we were caught skiving off school. I was happy being left to my own devices as far as school was concerned.

In the final year of the juniors, I was ten when our class teacher informed us that we would have to fill out a form as to which schools we preferred to attend if we passed the eleven-plus exam, and which we wanted to attend if we failed to pass.

"Put King George V Grammar School first in case you pass the eleven plus and put your chosen Secondary Modern school second, in case you fail," our teacher instructed.

I had heard about the grammar school. They played rugby union there. I didn't want to play rugby. I wanted to play football. I wrote down: "First Choice – Birkdale Secondary Modern. Second Choice – Birkdale Secondary Modern."

That was it! I would join my friends, Mickey and Michael and Tom and play football with them at the secondary modern.

Nothing more was said until after I had sat the eleven-plus exam with the rest of our school year. Then, one afternoon, I was told to leave the class and report to Mr Johns, the headmaster, in his office.

I knocked on the door and pushed it open as a deep officious voice called: "Come in."

Mr Johns swivelled round on his leather chair and put his hands on the desk before him. Mr Johns was a short rotund man, in his mid-fifties, very stern but able to smile now and then. He was peering down through his brown bifocals at a form on the desk.

"Sit down Phillip," he instructed and, as I took a seat before the desk wondering what news he had for me, he continued, "It seems you have been rather a silly boy, Phillip. When you were told to complete your form concerning your education you were told to put the grammar school first. I see you didn't. Why?"

"I want to go to the secondary modern and play football, Mr Johns."

The headmaster smiled: "That's all very well but you have bright prospects ahead of you and I don't want any more of your nonsense. They say that you have one of the best results in the school and you are very likely to be accepted at King George V."

He slid the form across his wooden desk and with almost a growl ordered: "Now change it this minute."

My football career melted away in my first tear.

"Yes, Mr Johns."

"Thank you," said Mr Johns, shaking his head slowly from side to side as he rose and opened the door to indicate my exit.

As soon as I was outside the head's office, I began to weep little tears, little tears that formed a track back to my classroom and a small pool on the tiled floor outside the classroom door. I was condemned to a life of rugby.

I didn't know then that I was crying for something of much more impact on my life. I had been sentenced to leave Neverneverland. Sentenced to grow up and leave my childhood behind.

I rubbed my tears away and told my classmate and school friend, John Barstow, what a calamity had befallen me. When I got home I told Matron what had happened.

"I'm so pleased that you have changed your mind," Matron said to me, "You will be the first of my children to go to King George V, if you pass. And if you do I will buy you a present and hold a big party for you."

I hadn't changed my mind. I had been bullied into signing away my life in Neverneverland.

On March 6th 1963, Mary Stewart opened the front door of Tudor Bank to greet a beaming Mr Johns. That night Mary Stewart positively glowed in triumph. She wrote to the regional Barnardo's Welfare Officer:

"I AM SURE YOU WILL BE AS DELIGHTED, AS WE ARE, TO KNOW THAT PHILLIP HAS PASSED HIS ELEVEN PLUS WITH VERY GOOD MARKS. HIS HEADMASTER CAME TO TELL ME, AND SAID THAT HE WILL GO STRAIGHT INTO AN 'A' CLASS AT THE GRAMMAR SCHOOL.

"ALL THE OTHER CHILDREN ARE SO PROUD OF HIM, IT WAS REALLY LOVELY TO SEE THEIR EXCITEMENT WHEN THE NEWS CAME."

Mary Stewart, March 6th, 1963

March 6th was my Ides of March. It would prove the most auspicious and inauspicious date in my calendar for many a year to come (but that's another story).

As for myself, I soon grew accustomed to my fate and was pleased that everyone else seemed so pleased.

"Yer a right little brainbox," said Mickey, "You'll become a right posh 'un before we know it."

Miss Stewart bought me a big bar of Cadbury's Dairy Milk chocolate, of a size that we were always too scared to stick up our jumpers when we were at the shops. That was to be my reward. The party, that Matron had promised, never came. For me the party was already over.

When Miss Merrison heard the news at the Barnardo's headquarters in Stepney, she too was delighted for the little boy who had so nearly died. She wrote to congratulate me:

"I AM ABSOLUTELY DELIGHTED THAT YOU HAVE PASSED YOUR 11 PLUS, AND THAT YOU ARE GOING TO A GRAMMAR SCHOOL. WELL DONE... WHEN I COME TO SEE YOU NEXT I SHALL MAKE A SPECIAL POINT OF GIVING YOU A HEARTY SLAP ON THE BACK."

Miss Merrison, March 9th, 1963.

Meanwhile, I had learned that my school pal, John Barstow, had also passed his eleven plus and would be there with me at the grammar school. That lightened the blow and I wrote back to Miss Merrison a letter in the scrawniest of handwriting:

"THANK YOU VERY MUCH FOR YOUR LETTER. MY BEST FRIEND IS GOING TO THE GRAMMAR SCHOOL, SO I AM GLAD I HAVE PASSED TOO."

Phillip Frampton, 13th March, 1963

What Mary Stewart had not taken into account in her fulsome praise for her ward was the rest of Miss Merrison's response.

Miss Merrison had followed the turbulent history of the boy for some time. Once again, she was spurred to contemplate the young boy being pushed in his education and, if that meant leaving Mary Stewart's' care in Southport, then so be it. Phillip would get a far better education if he had a supportive background and that meant going to public school and being fostered out. She wrote to Miss Bailey the regional Welfare Officer for Barnardo's:

"WOULD YOU BE KIND ENOUGH TO DISCUSS WITH MISS STEWART THE POSSIBILITY OF ABBOTSHOLME AND SEE WHAT SHE THINKS ABOUT THE IDEA OF A BOARDING SCHOOL FOR HIM... "

Miss Merrison, March 11th, 1963

I have no record of the discussion that took place regarding the Chief Executive Officer's proposal but whatever was said, I expect that Miss Stewart once again gave the Granvilles as the excuse for my not being moved. I was once again kept in the home. Once again, the choice was taken by others without me ever becoming aware of what had transpired.

Chapter 12

On the Outside Looking In

In the summer of 1964, when America's blacks were rioting, when the British Conservative government was in free-fall and the Beatles were storming the music world, I was being prepared for my new life as the Grammar School Boy.

Matron took me around the clothes shops in town where I was fitted out with my school clothes. She smiled as I donned my new maroon and black striped blazer over my white shirt and maroon and black striped school tie. I was bought a new pair of grey short pants and three white shirts – three, so that I could wear one each week. She bought my rugby kit and I received a new pair of football boots. "Those will have to do you for both your football and rugby," Matron said.

On a warm September day, I went off on my own to my new school. The school was two miles away, so I walked into the town and then took a bus. Every child who attended those large boys' schools, where the ages of the children ranged from eleven to sometimes nineteen, will know of that enormous sense of intimidation on one's first day.

Boys much taller than my friends and I strolled this way and that in their maroon and black striped jackets. Some boys were different. They wore black jackets or brighter maroon jackets with fewer black stripes. Some wore black ties sporting the county's red rose. Others wore badges, different coloured badges, announcing that they were Senior Prefects or Junior Prefects.

We watched as a very tall, well-built boy with a black jacket, blond hair and a totally superior air, walked past chatting to two cronies. He was Molyneux, the Head Boy. He would go to Cambridge.

"What's Cambridge?" I asked my friend, John Barstow.

"It's the best university in the country," he replied.

I thought that one day I might have to go to Cambridge.

"Hey, Barstow! Hey Frampton! Hey Jones!" he shouted. Everyone at the school seemed to call each other by their surnames. We'd left behind the junior schooldays of being John and Phillip and Ken.

Our new teachers emanated a different aura to those in our junior school. These teachers were aloof and barked. They made fun of you. They ordered you about as if you were a soldier cadet and expected you to understand every instruction they gave out. In lessons they spent most of their time displaying the backs of their heads as they furiously wore down their chalk crayons on the blackboards.

My form master was a Mr Tony "Jim" Honeybone. He had a history degree from Cambridge University. I liked him. Teaching us the history of Roman rule, he took the opportunity to call me "Frampus." From then on my classmates always called me "Frampus." Then, some called me "Pussy."

Honeybone kept firm control but he was sometimes very funny. He kept control by meting out punishment using "Jankers." That meant detention – being kept behind after school and writing silly things, like: "I must not talk in class," over and over again.

Our mathematics teacher was Eddie "Ted" Johnson. Johnson's displeasure at us was expressed via one of the loose, wooden floor tiles that had tar on the reverse side. He, humorously, called it Willie.

"Bend over Frampus," Johnson would say, "Time for Willie." The tile crashed down on the cheeks of my backside.

Willie hurt.

Then there was the biology teacher, "Ding-dong" Bell, whose teaching consisted of him taking the neatest exercise book from his last year's class and dictating the contents to us verbatim, lesson after lesson. His black gown made him look tall and hid the thinness of his frame. For our weekend homework, we had to read and learn what we had spent the lesson copying down. Then, first thing Monday morning, we had a test. If we scored less than 15 out of 20, we were hit by a metre rule. On one occasion virtually the whole class lined up to get hit.

Once, Tony Moreton unintentionally emitted a loud burp. "Ding-dong" grabbed him, and took him and the rule to the back of the lab where he knocked seven bells out of him. Morty screamed and yelled out: "No more, sir! Please, no more!"

We sat and watched in horror as Bell turned Brutus, his cloak fluttering and dagger lunging at the poor boy's head and legs. The slings and arrows of outrage left Morty crumpled in an amoebic mass. "Not to be," was the answer.

What a different world. It was a world of men, aloof and macho – except for the religious instruction teacher, "Batty" Batson, who wore a dog-collar and spoke softly. Everybody said he was "one of them." I had entered a middle class world. Here were 800 sons of the town's managers, businessmen and teachers. They were at the grammar school to be moulded into managers, businessmen and teachers, as their parents had been. These boys woke up in their own bedrooms and wore clean white shirts and clean white faces everyday. They had parents who sometimes drove them to school. Some boys who were older turned up in their own sports cars.

These boys went on proper holidays. When they were older, some would go skiing abroad or return back to school in September with a tan picked up in Greece or Spain. They would meet up with girls from the local high school who went horse riding at weekends and also had sports cars.

I found myself on the outside of this world looking in. I wanted to be part of it.

There were a very few of us from the other side of the track. But we were tough. We could fight. We survived.

Of those 800 boys, I was the only black. I was the only Barnardo's boy. I was left-handed, bespectacled and as skinny as a rake. I didn't need to be called Nigger. I knew I was different. If they called me "Nigger" or "Jungle Bunny," I had to fight them, and I could fight.

Not that I was called "Nigger" often. We kids from the home were virtually the only blacks to be seen in the whole town. In the school I was a novelty. I was a novelty, so they mainly left my colour alone.

The one advantage I had on my classmates in that first school term was that I was already institutionalised, already used to fitting my individualism into the needs of an authoritarian system. I knew a few boys in my year. They had been at my junior school. I fitted in well enough to be able to speak out confidently in class.

When the Conservative government called a General Election for October 1964, the teachers arranged mock elections throughout the school. I was confident enough to stand as a candidate in the mock election held in my class. I stood as a Buddhist Communist promising an end to government, a free tuck shop, and no more Prefects' privileges. I didn't know what either communism or Buddhism was but I won. In the cross-school mock election, I voted Tory. I blame reading Matron's Daily Telegraph for that. The school voted Tory en masse. The country voted Labour.

As for having to play rugby, I loathed it. I hated going into the school Games Room on a Wednesday afternoon and running out into the cold autumn and winter days to stand about shivering, waiting for a teacher to order my skinny frame around. It didn't stop me running in six tries in our first match but hanging around on the wing was a finger numbing business. I did make the school cross-country team that first winter but there wasn't much glamour in running through mud and snow on your own.

I remained football crazy. I still walked to school to save my bus fare and buy the Daily Mirror newspaper so that I could read its sports pages. Fortunately the school had large grounds and rugby pitches where we played football in huge teams of up to twenty boys at every possible break time. Then I went home and practised on the Pitch or by kicking a ball against the garage door.

In my studies I returned reasonable reports, though I was nowhere near top of the class. In fact, when I arrived at the school, I was disappointed to learn that the A-stream class that I had been placed in was not the highest stream. The brightest pupils were put in a stream called Trans X. I wasn't that brilliant after all. I would have to work hard.

For the first two years my academic work was pretty mediocre. Then my friend, John Barstow, and his stepbrother, Steve Moore, showed me how they and some of the other boys cheated in Latin tests. John and Steve were usually ahead of me in their class results. Now that I knew how to cheat, that changed.

Amo, amas, amat.

Amabo, amabis, amabit.

Amabor

I will be loved.

Once I had confidence in returning acceptable Latin work, my self-esteem increased. It increased to such an extent that I began to feel able to cope with my Latin studies and didn't have to cheat anymore.

"HE READS A GREAT DEAL AND IS FOND OF LATIN."

Miss Bailey, Executive Officer, 24th August, 1967

In the home, the effect of my being sent to the grammar school began to tell almost immediately. While the other older children went off to Birkdale Secondary Modern and became a part of that life, I went off to school on my own and to a different world. They came home and chatted about their world to each other, and I was left alone with my thoughts. I still went to watch football with Mickey but then he was sent away.

Michael Ingham found himself in a different world too. He was 14 when he would slip out of the big boys' bedroom at night and sneak down the corridor. And who was that member of the staff who took him into her room and put her hand in his pyjamas and played with him? Who was that "aunt" that took him to her house and taught him a little more? They taught him what was wrong was right.

The Beatles' *Sergeant Pepper* album was at number one. Remember that song that went: "It really doesn't matter if I'm wrong, I'm right. Where I belong I'm right, where I belong"?

Yes, there were those women members of staff who sexually abused boys, and girls too. You might ask why these grown-up women sought gratification in pulling a young boy's lips onto their bare nipples, in feeling an immature penis with not a trace of pubic hair, in placing a young soft hand on their breast. But these were unwanted women in an unwanted place and, as we were the playthings of parents and society, so, in those secret moments, we were the playthings of our carers. For the boys, at least, it was not harsh – not when they were boys. But children become adults. Not all of them then learn that the way they were treated was wrong.

The floorboards creaked and doors clicked shut and Michael was happy – until he was sent away from Neverneverland and became a man. I don't know what happened to Mickey but Michael was sent down south to the Barnardo's training school. He left behind his younger brother and sister. He was 14 years of age.

Those boys who were still left in the home were just myself, Tom Chorley, Martin, Dick, Colin Smith and a new black arrival, Alan Maddox. We all slept in the boys' dormitory. Tom had become very withdrawn, rarely washed, got terrible acne and left his hair forever greasy and falling down over his eyes.

At first, when Tom was due to be fostered out, there had been a glint in his eye. He was wanted. Then he was sent back. Then he was fostered again. By now he had been fostered out and sent back too many times. Fostered out, sent back. Fostered out, sent back. Fostered out, sent back. Wanted, unwanted. Wanted, unwanted. Just like his trains. Shunted out, shunted back. Shunted out, shunted back. Shunted out, shunted back. One day a train didn't come back. Nor did that gleam in Tom's eyes. We all peered inside but the watchman's lamp had gone out.

So, though Tom was older than I was, I was considered the senior. I told the monster stories.

As for my affections for Mary Ingham, we stopped talking after an incident on the Pitch in front of the house. Martin and Dick were squabbling over something. Martin, who was slightly the older of the two, started hitting Dick. Dick yelped. I liked Dick and told Martin to stop. Martin didn't, so I punched him hard and he started crying. Dick was so angry that I had hit his best friend that he challenged me to a fight there and then.

Dick had more flesh on him than I did but I was easily the taller boy – and the wiser. I "gave him the nod" – I head-butted him so hard that he fell to the ground clutching his forehead and sobbing. "That was not fair," he cried, "I'll tell my brother."

But Dick's brother wasn't in the home any longer. He had been sent down south. His sister, Mary Ingham, was there. She stopped talking to me. I stopped talking to her. Besides, she was a girl and I now wanted to be in the boys' world that I'd found at school. That was my rationalisation but there was much more to my abandoned love.

My forced removal to the grammar school had split us apart. Now there was no sharing time at school, no walking her home. My nights were homework, so we saw each other much less frequently. As I began to feel myself as apart and different from the other children, I also increasingly resented being in the home. Not that I had anywhere to go or any wish to be fostered out. I simply felt embarrassed and self-pitying at my circumstances.

Mary was no longer my Estella. For if Pip looked up to Estella and her social circumstance, I now looked down and deplored all that Mary appeared so happy in. She remained as sweet-natured as ever, as slim and, if anything, had grown even prettier. But I was now the social snob.

As much as I had loved Mary as a young boy, I had never needed her, and now I had more pressing needs – to succeed at my schoolwork, at football, at rugby and all those competitive issues that are part of a middle class boys' school.

If adults teach children love, they teach them the need to be loved; the need to be picked up and comforted, the need to be sustained, the need to be cared for. And those children grow up to feel that they need the one they love.

I, on the contrary had, quite unconsciously, been on a long road learning not to need anybody – in the sense that I had no option but to learn emotional self-sufficiency. I didn't need a kiss. I didn't need a hug. I didn't need to be cuddled and comforted. And after all, wasn't that the same as the heroes I read about in my boy comics and war magazines? Didn't that make me a brave young man?

It was easy for me to abandon her whom I cared for and chase after my dreams, my needs. I placed a mist around her presence and fixed my eyes on my future, or so it might have seemed.

We drifted apart. I drifted apart from the other children too. Pretty quickly, in the home I also began to feel like I was on the outside looking in.

A new girl, Annabelle Leyland, arrived. She was about 14 years old and around the same age as I. She was white, pretty but less slim than Mary. She arrived well-dressed and well-spoken, almost insisting that she should not be in the home and that her family would soon have her released from what she allowed everyone to know was a situation very much beneath her.

The other children considered her to be a snob. I did not see it, for wasn't I becoming as much of a snob as her? Instead I admired her spirit and her looks.

Within a few months, the love I had packed away returned. Only this time it was reserved for Annabelle. I wanted her to reciprocate my affection. I respected her and enjoyed her company and her rebellion and her contempt for the wolves. But it was a different kind of love, a pining, and yearning, teenage love, more about having her than the free feelings of total care and respect that myself and Mary had shared.

So I progressed from the childhood sweetheart stage to the teenage crush, a process that engulfs so many young people without an ounce of assistance from their parents. On the contrary, the crush, with its blushes and harsh words of disguise, is so private and confusing to us that we attempt to hide it from all, even the target of our new affections.

We shared our world with our child sweetheart but now move on. We want to become a part of the world of our crush and recreate the sweetheart. But the sweetheart appeared without intention, without desire and the crush is the torture of want over caring, of desire over love. We move into adolescence where society ordains that we can now possess a lover and make the transition from freedom to ownership. The target for the crush is ill defined, its direction as untutored and wild as the aim of a little boy's penis. Who knows where the crush might first land – on the girl next door, the girl on the bus or on the beach, the schoolmistress, the waitress, the cousin, the aunt or a male?

We snatch Cupid's bow but, drunk with this strange emotion, we misfire the arrow, which, instead of falling on our intended target pierces the hapless archer's heart, for a double dose of the toxin that drives us crazier still. We're driven mad to the point where we do or say the least appropriate thing; a mistimed invitation, a scrawled declaration, a snatched kiss, reaching for a hand, a mumbled phone call. And we receive for our efforts merely another blush.

We study Chemistry at school but no amount of laboratory experiments, only years of love can teach us the importance of Chemistry to the compound molecule of love as mutual desire, and no parent can show us that!

I took long lonely walks through the park and out onto the beach, contemplating her only. I composed songs about her and sang them across the deserted shore. I wrote her name down a thousand times in a secret notepad that I kept in my bedroom, scratched her initials on trees in the park, anything to caress this new so tender but cruel emotion. So I learned a new form of love. No, you say, infatuation is not love, true love is infinite forgiveness. But then does not infatuation carry infinite forgiveness? For in our smitten state we blind ourselves to another's faults and crimes and forgive them every hurt. The only difference is that "true love" is based on knowledge whereas infatuation is bolstered by ignorance. Both become a dangerous insanity along the road to that infinity of forgiving.

One day, Annabelle came to my room as I lay on my bed. I asked her to come closer as I wanted to tell her a secret. She bent down and placed her head close to mine. I kissed her on her cheek. Suddenly made aware that the crush had landed on her, she had two options to grasp or repel. She bolted herself upright and her face went so red that for a moment she could have been a cherry penny-lollypop. She darted out of my den and whatever we had was over.

Had I conquered her whom I desired, would I have grown to need her, to be "in love" with her? I doubt it very much. For as much as she rejected me because I represented part of her miserable incarceration, so she would in time have become part of the ball chained to my foot. She had no key to set me free. I did not need her to comfort me, to cuddle me, to pick me up and sit me on her knee and tell me everything would be all right. I was a young man. I had learned to want but not to need or be wanted.

What I desired was that which I felt I needed, but as soon as I had achieved my goal, I was impelled to strive to be free of that very need. Besides, if I was a child of love and child of pain, I had not learned that being loved could involve those one is loved by delivering pain and demanding sacrifice. I did not learn that love was a compromise.

When our goals are great, it is so easy to devalue that which we already possess and, once we have devalued our possessions, then to abandon them.

In love as in life. It was a pattern, which would follow me for decades.

Emily, Mary and Annabelle, danced in the upstairs playroom to Elvis and Cliff, to Roy Orbison and the Beatles. They danced the Hippy, Hippy, Shake and the Locomotion. They did the rock 'n' roll to Elvis Presley and twirled so fast that the boys could see the DBH tags on their navy blue knickers.

Emily and Mary were growing up. When they reached the stage of demanding a bra to wear, Matron slipped her cold hands under their school blouse and wrapped them round the girls' pert breasts. "Not big enough yet," said Miss Stewart. The nipples went stiff and the girls went away disappointed until Matron finally conceded that they were young women.

Mr Burt, the dentist in Drayton House, noticed the girls growing up. The girls began to feel uncomfortable with him. They told Matron that they didn't want to go the dentist's because Mr Burt was a dirty old man who touched them up. Matron told them not to talk nonsense as she was there with them. "It's utter rubbish!" she had declared to Mary Ingham as she ordered the girl to go brush her teeth and fetch her coat. But when Matron accompanied Mary to see the dentist and Mr Burt sat her in a chair to be treated, the dirty old man turned the chair so Mary had her back to Miss Stewart. Then he rubbed his hands across her breasts as he made to reach over for his utensils.

When the girls went for treatment that Mr Burt said required gas, Matron did not accompany them. If the girls went together as a pair because they didn't trust the dirty old man, the other girl was told to sit outside in the waiting room. What happened when they were gassed and unconscious, they will never know.

The girls began to change. They sneaked out of the home at night to watch Gerry and the Pacemakers make their entrance for a performance at the Floral Hall. It was the era of the mini-skirt. They hitched their navy blue pleated school skirts to halfway up their thighs. Then, before they went off to school, Matron would say: "Pull your skirts down. I don't want people thinking that you are badly brought up." But when the girls got out onto Beach Road, they hitched their skirts back up. And they hitched up their school skirts when they went to the fairground to flirt with young men and hung round the Lido chatting to the boys.

I felt too skinny to go to the Lido. I sat in the dining room doing my homework while the others watched the television. I was just the speccy four-eyed, National Health-rimmed glasses, brainbox who sometimes helped them with their homework and the one who wrote letters for us kids, like when we requested a television of our own to watch.

"TALL, THIN HALF CASTE, WEARS GLASSES…APART FROM ARGUING TOO MUCH, PHILIP IS WELL BEHAVED AND HAS CHARMING MANNERS BUT A QUICK TEMPER…PHILLIP IS A VERY INTELLIGENT BOY, WHO READS A LOT, AND IS INTERESTED IN EVERYTHING."

Miss Stewart, June, 1965

I went off on my own to see my grammar school mates on Saturdays and played football with them through the holidays.

The more I strove to do well and be accepted amongst my peers at school, the more aware of my handicaps I became. John Barstow would invite me round for tea at his house but I didn't dare to invite him to the home, my *Strawberry Fields*. There seemed no point in inviting my friends to eat what we wouldn't, to see the urine pools and screaming kids. I had nothing to offer my friends but my friendship. I became ashamed. I became angry. When Pamela Brotherton annoyed me, I hit her even harder.

In school I was happy. The school bell rang and school time was over. I dragged myself back to the home, walking past the houses and mansions of the well-to-do and feeling poor, and feeling like I was going home to survive till the next morning or next term when I could return to school.

The Granvilles had moved to the Rockferry district in Birkenhead and they continued to have me to stay for a few days of each school holiday. How my school friends mocked when I said that I was going to the dire, industrial town of Birkenhead for my holidays. Still, it was a respite from the home and Mr Granville took me to watch Tranmere Rovers play football sometimes and took me around Cammell Laird's shipyards and the dockyards where I enjoyed seeing ships from every part of the globe.

Their son, Paul, who I had so often enjoyed playing with, seemed to be out most of the time and I spent many a boring hour sat on my own, trying to read a book to the tick, tick, tick of the cuckoo clock in their dining room.

"APPARENTLY HE JUST GOES TO THESE PEOPLE AS A SENSE OF DUTY SINCE HE WAS FOSTERED THERE AND THEY INVITE HIM EVERY HOLIDAY – BUT I DO NOT THINK THAT HE REALLY ENJOYS IT."

Miss Bailey, Executive Officer, 30th August, 1967

Of more impact was my beginning to read the newspapers from the sports pages at the back to the political news at the front. I began to learn about blacks fighting for equality in the United States and being hung up and shot down. Ian Smith established white minority rule in Rhodesia and the world did nothing. Students protested against apartheid in South Africa and whites marched against blacks in English cities.

A man came to the home, asking us if we wanted to learn about our family background. He wrote back about my father and I was told that my father was from the Calabar region of southern Nigeria. He also sent me a big photograph showing an aerial view of the Calabar area. The picture showed a wide river passing through miles and miles of dense jungle. So I really was from the jungle after all.

"Were my people cannibals then?" I asked.

"They could well have been. We don't know, but probably."

I wrote a little poem on the home's letter headed paper:

"I THANK YOU PEOPLE OF DAYS GONE BY
WHO IN POOR LIVING THEN
FOUND THE STARS IN THE SKY,
MADE EASY LIVES FOR MEN.
BUT I HATE YOU PEOPLE OF DAYS GONE BY.
INFERIOR NOW I FEEL.
YOU'VE MADE ME FEEL AN OUTCAST
TO ALL THAT'S WHITE I KNEEL."

Phillip Frampton, 1965

I would have felt even more of an outcast if I had been aware of who and what was visiting the annual Southport Flower Show, which took place in the park opposite Tudor Bank. Now, whenever I snuck into the event, my interest was taken by the magnificent horses on parade and the huge exotic cacti displayed under canvas. If I had spent more time examining the rows and rows of carnations and chrysanthemums, I might have noticed the stands of Frampton's Nurseries. I might have talked to the men in their forties who had hired the space and proudly announced that their business had been first established back in 1887 by their grandfather, Joseph Frampton – my grandfather, Clyde Frampton's uncle.

At the stand would have been Mr Donald Frampton, whose successful nurseries would later lead to him being made a Commander of the British Empire. I might have heard Donald speaking of his cousin, Clyde, who lived just 100 yards away from him in East Preston, Sussex, with his second wife, Gladys Emily. They might have commented on how keen Gladys was to play bowls and that Clyde could have brought her along to enjoy the bowling greens in the park. They might have mentioned Clyde's daughter, Mavis and her new child. But they would not have mentioned me. Clyde never told another soul about his discarded black bastard grandchild.

If there was a god then he had failed us blacks and he had failed me and left me with nobody and stuck in a home. I became estranged from religion and George Granville's god and his biblical heroes. My days of slipping into the back of the church to sit through the morning or evening service on my own came to an end. One Sunday, I knelt and prayed: "Dear God, I'm bored of church. I'm not going to come anymore. If you want me you'll call me back."

No one ever called.

I still went to church when the Granvilles took me to stay with them. I didn't discuss religion with them because I didn't want to upset them. I just went along with my chore. All that was left of my religious upbringing was a strong sense of right and wrong. The world was wrong and I was being wronged. But there were still good people, like Uncle George and Paul Granville and Michael and Mickey. There were still new heroes emerging, like Martin Luther King and the people I had read about in books.

I searched for truth and demanded truth. I wanted to be a lawyer but when I found out that lawyers had to sometimes tell lies or bend the truth, I stopped wanting to be a lawyer. In my growing sensitivity, I wanted what I saw in the world to be fixed, to be the truth. I took the search to extremes. If friends told me that they didn't like me for this or that reason, then I concluded that they hadn't been telling the truth before, and I cut myself off from them.

I didn't understand that truths and feelings were flexible and transient. Had I grown up in a family I might have understood that feelings expressed were not feelings complete. I stumbled around without a mentor, trying to find the basis for my relationship with others and the world at large.

"HAS A VERY REAL SENSE OF RIGHT AND WRONG. ON HAVING TO GO TO SCHOOL FOR DETENTION ONE SATURDAY, HE SAID, 'I'M NOT ASHAMED, IT WAS ONLY A LARK (I'd let off a stink bomb in a class we were warring with-PF) AND I OWNED UP, BUT I SHOULD HAVE BEEN ASHAMED IF I HAD LIED AND GOT AWAY WITH IT.'"

Miss Stewart, January, 1967

I was more righteous than the religious. "I will not tell lies," I told myself, "and I will not accept others lying to me."

Similarly, if I felt that any staff or children had wronged me, I cut myself off from them. Even the matron and the staff would then get no more than a few syllables from me for months at a time. But when I lost my temper, my righteousness did not extend to being non-violent. On one of the days that I hit Pamela Brotherton and she went crying to Matron, Matron came storming over to me in the hall. "You are a savage!" she shouted.

I glared at her for a moment, then said: "Like my father I suppose."

"Yes!" she shouted back.

I said nothing to her for weeks. Mary Stewart's words put an end to any respect I had for her. There again, Mary Stewart didn't quite want to understand what was happening to her lovely little boy.

"FROM TIME TO TIME PHILLIP GETS OVERTIRED AND IRRITABLE, WITH AN OCCASIONAL DISPLAY OF FURIOUS TEMPER, OTHERWISE HE IS NO TROUBLE AT ALL."

Miss Stewart, January, 1967

"HE IS VERY HAPPY AT BIRKDALE."

Miss Bailey, Executive Officer, August, 1967

Eventually, I even cut myself off from my old school friends, John Barstow and Steve Moore, and left them for my new footballing friends. In the home I grew more and more alone. Even Christmas time ceased to be fun anymore. Every card and every gift from Auntie This and Auntie That said: "You are alone."

The only friend I could find in the home at that time was a pretty new blonde member of staff. Her name was Ann. She had a little turned up nose. The Chinese pandas, An-An and Chi-Chi, having reached the news, we nicknamed her Chi-Chi. Chi-Chi was kind and considerate and talked to me with respect, like I was a young man. I loved talking with Chi-Chi, as did virtually all of the children. It was as if she was with us. If ever I upset her I tried to make amends. But she only stayed for a short while. When she announced that she was leaving, I felt heartbroken.

The only things I had were my school life and football. I buried myself in my school life. By my third year at school, I was already secretary of the Junior Debating Society and of the Middle School French Society. I got involved in rugby eventually and played for my house team in school competitions. I had developed a reputation as someone who could handle himself. I had knocked out one boy in my year with a single blow to his chin. When he came round I was relieved he was still alive. Sometime later I had won a fight against McNally, a hefty lad who arrived from a Salvation Army home. I didn't like the Sally Army kids. He didn't like being in a home. Unlike me, he told everybody so. We were different but the same. Perhaps that's why we clashed. He scratched my hand but I won, then felt sorry for him.

There was another boy in my year, Bainsberger, who was considered to be tough. He challenged me to a fight for top dog of the year, calling me "Nigger." Out we went onto one of the school's rugby pitches by the roadside. The other boys stood around forming our arena. School blazers off and we set to. We ended up grappling on the ground in arm locks and headlocks and the things that boys do. Then he rose first and as I looked up, his boot landed right on my jaw. I had lost. I was not so tough after all.

I joined a football team, Royal Albion, which was run by some school friends. The team got into the local junior league. The team broke up when a group of us from less well off backgrounds decided that those boys running our team were snobs and only picked their well-to-do friends for the team. I organised the breakaway Corinthians team and we took in lads for our team from secondary modern schools.

We had a great laugh then. We never beat the snobs' team. Our side had players who were too good. They were always being sent off for trials with professional clubs or being hauled off to play for their school football or rugby teams. The last time we played the snobs, we played on our pitch in a park covered with snow. They were late and we were left to dig the snow off the pitch by ourselves.

When the match started, I headed in our first goal, then the crossbar on our goal fell on our goalkeeper, Edgey's, head. In the frantic game, nobody noticed for a while. When we finally looked to our goal, there was Edgey, flat out, unconscious on his line. When he had recovered we laughed ourselves silly. Edgey was crazy. It could only happen to him. We lost the match 5-1.

I returned alone as on every Saturday and each evening to the home. One evening, Matron requested that I see her in her office.

"Sit down, Phillip," said Matron in a firm tone. It was one of those times when I had not spoken more than a sulking word or two to her for weeks.

"I am very sorry," Matron continued, "but I have some bad news for you."

I expected to be told that I was being sent away to a remand home like Mark Lancaster but she said: "I have had a letter from your godmother saying that your mother died last year."

I asked her several questions, like: "If I had a mother then why was I put in the home?"

"I don't know but perhaps you should write to your godmother. She might be able to tell you more," she replied.

Mary Stewart said she had no answers. She knew very well that she had answers but she wasn't about to tell me for fear of making me an even angrier 14-year-old boy than I was at the time.

For I, who thought I never had a living mother, it was a shock. That very same moment that I was told that I had a living mother, she was dead. In the same moment that I could have hoped that she might take me out of my living misery, she had finally left me alone.

I didn't cry. I didn't grieve. It's hard to grieve a loss for what you never had, to grieve for the loss of someone you never knew. My life was not affected in any way. At least one hole in my identity was plugged.

For a while, Matron's attempts to limit my anger were successful. I wrote off in curiosity for information to my godmother, Aunt Martha. Her reply arrived one year later.

Martha sent me pictures of Mavis and kind words of solace. But the pictures were of no solace to me. I tore them up. I was a Prince but she did not look like a Princess to me. I wanted her to be another woman in one of the photos. This other woman was pretty and appeared confident and strong. That was not to be. Mavis was the gangly, thin woman that I had to gaze at who appeared to be weak and mentally fragile. There was nothing in her pictures that I wanted, not an ounce of hope. I had to be strong. I needed an image of a mother who was strong and able to be a receptacle for my love, a mother that would carry me, not a burden for my own back. I was not ready to carry the weight and suffering in the picture. As much as she could not carry me beyond birth, now I could not carry her beyond death.

Nothing her friends would later write would console my disappointment and prevent my memory of those pictures from refreshing my loneliness.

Meanwhile, Matron's mother, whom we all called "Granny," had stopped tending to her rockery in the home for some time when Mary Stewart heard the news that her mother was dead. The announcement caused a stir in the home. We children had never experienced death in the home before and we scared ourselves silly with ghost stories and howls and screams that would have woken the dead themselves.

That night we lay awake afraid of the dark and its secrets. Some children said that in the darkness they heard noises. Sounds of moaning, sounds of creaking floorboards like someone was walking around. They said that was Granny walking up and down the stairs. Mary Ingham lay awake, waiting for her but Granny never arrived. The girls said they heard banging windows and whispers. Granny's ghost was about. In the boys' dormitory we all swore that we weren't scared but we all dived under our sheets and hoped the darkness would hide us from the evil spirits.

From that night on, I remember a feeling of apprehension whenever I reached the home in darkness. I entered by the small gate at the rear of the house and walked down the back path we called the Backway. The leaves of the sycamore trees rustled in the night breeze and the streetlights cast shadows across the grounds. The route to the kitchen door was a forty-yard-long walk through the trees in the almost still and black night. There was plenty of time to be scared. I was 14 and it was as if I had become aware of an evil presence in the home.

Mary Stewart retired from her post as Superintendent and Matron of Tudor Bank in 1967. She was the last to be called "Matron." In the year before she went, she tried her utmost to get the older children out of the home. Did Mary Stewart have an inkling of what was to come?

We had no idea. In the summer of '67, we were taken up by the era of Flower Power. Scott McKenzie sang: "There's a whole generation with a new explanation," and we wanted to be part of that. The girls made daisy chains and Michael Ingham came back to visit his brother and sister in the home, wearing flowers in his hair and a floral chain around his neck. But on lonely nights, I sang the words of the B-side of McKenzie's hit record over and over again:

"Hey friend, wake up. I'm throwing rocks at your window pane.
Get out of bed. I've got something to say.
Pick up a toothbrush.
Sneak down the stairway.
You got no reason to stay.
Hey! What's the difference if we don't come back?
Who's gonna miss us in a year or so?
Nobody knows us or the games we've been playing in.
So what's the difference if we go?"

Within twelve months of Matron leaving, Mary Ingham was boarded out. Barnardo's offered Mary adoption but she turned it down, fearing that she would never be permitted to see her two brothers again. Emily Brotherton was also boarded out. Tom Chorley went into digs and Alan Maddox left as well. The remnants of childhood friendships had finally gone. I was offered fostering with a family in Derby but I turned it down. I wasn't much interested in going to another family again, least of all a family in a town with such an unfashionable football team as Derby County.

I was not unhappy to see Matron go. Indeed, when the new Superintendent and her husband came, I was pleased to see that they were much younger, probably in their mid-thirties, and brought changes. With them came a new nurse, Miss Davis, from South Wales.

The new couple set about improving the food. They dispensed with using the local deliveryman, whom Molly Broughton had swooned over, and began bulk-buying the groceries. Cheaper groceries meant more variety. They even gave us cereal and toast for breakfast and we occasionally had the toast with real butter. But I fell out with them fairly soon and stopped talking to them too. I found them to be a very strange couple. The woman had a pudding basin haircut like those old pictures of Joan of Arc and an extremely puritan and correct manner. The man hardly said a word – even to his wife. They didn't last long. In their place came the Norrises, a couple in their fifties with their chubby, buck-toothed son, Geoffrey, who must have been thirteen. He joined me at the grammar school.

Mr Norris arrived with a full mop of grey hair and a grey beard. He was slim but strong, as a result, I believe, of time he had spent in the army. His wife was short and plump with the same buckteeth she had bequeathed to her son. They arrived to a home with none of the discipline they had been used to when they ran another Barnardo's home in Cardiff. We were pretty unruly and the nurses sometimes said that when new staff arrived, they were terrified. Weren't we the worst children in the world?

Norris arrived and read the riot act. If I had left the other children in their Neverneverland, then Captain Hook Norris had arrived in their world and pinned his cutlass to the mast. We would not do this and not do that or we would be punished but he would be fair.

The old hut at the back of the home had been knocked down and a bungalow built in its place to house whoever was Superintendent in the home. I was now separated from the younger boys and placed in my own room so that I could study. My new room was once the "Sick Room" where any of us who had caught infections were isolated. The room was above the kitchen on the back corridor, in the quiet, and close to Matron's old bedroom.

I was pleased with having my own little room where I could lie on my bed and read and do my homework. But there once more, I heard the creaking floorboards, the clicking of doors as they were opened and closed and the moans of the night. Eventually I wrote of the sounds in the night to my Welfare Officer, Miss Bailey. For this I was called to see her and Norris in his office. I received no sympathy off the bearded woman whose pendulous breasts rested on her stomach. As she gave me a dressing down, I followed her beard as it shifted from side to side between the swaying of her huge jowls.

"I TOLD PHILIP THAT I WAS SURPRISED THAT HE HAD WRITTEN TO ME ABOUT THE NOISES HEARD IN THE HOME AND HE REGRETS WRITING IT. HE TOLD US THAT REALLY THEY COULD BE ANYTHING, I.E. IN AN OLD HOUSE STAIRS CREAK AND DOORS BANG, BUT HE WROTE IT ON IMPULSE, OR RATHER HE DICTATED IT ON IMPULSE, AND I THINK HAS REGRETTED IT. HE TOLD ME THAT NOISES HAD BEEN HEARD THE NIGHT BEFORE MATRON'S MOTHER DIED AND PEOPLE HAD MADE A FUSS ABOUT THIS."

Miss Bailey, Executive Officer, 30th August, 1967

Of course, to her there was no evil in Barnardo's then. But Barnardo's would insist that, for us urchins, everything was for the best in the best of all possible worlds.

The same was the case regarding the arrival of Gilbert Norris:

"I THINK THAT WHEN MR AND MRS NORRIS COME PHILLIP WILL WELCOME THE OPPORTUNITY OF TALKING TO A MAN."
Miss Bailey, Executive Officer, August, 1967

Barnardo's were wrong. By then all I wanted to do was leave the home, even if it meant being fostered. I requested to leave but nothing happened. Then one night I returned home late from participating in a school debating society competition. I had spent my bus money earlier in the day on iced buns from the school tuck shop.

"Why are you late?" said Norris, looking angry.

"Because I walked home," I replied.

"Walking home wouldn't make you that late," he insisted, "What have you been doing?"

"Nothing. I walked home."

An angry vein swelled up on Norris's forehead: "You are lying."

"No I am not."

"Come to my office now," he demanded.

He took out his cane, ordered me to hold out my hand and whacked it.

I grinned defiantly at him and he whacked me again. I continued to grin. This time he gave me a vicious slap across my head. That wiped the grin off my face.

"You're too big for your boots, lad," he concluded, "Don't ever do that again. Now go to your room."

So Captain Hook began his bid to rule the unruly roost. He hadn't started well. I disliked his son for his arrogance and his "I've got this" and "My dad that." And I refused to co-operate with any of them.

"MR AND MRS NORRIS REPORTED THAT PHILIP IS BEING EXTREMELY DIFFICULT AT THE MOMENT. HE IS VERY RUDE INDEED TO MISS DAVIS, A WELSH MEMBER OF STAFF, AND HE CALLS HER A WELSH COW. HE WILL NOT TAKE ANY MEALS FROM HER AND HE IS INCITING THE OTHERS TO BEHAVE BADLY AND HE WOULD LIKE TO GO TO A FOSTER HOME."
Miss Bailey, Executive Officer, August, 1967

Norris wanted me out. I wanted out. But I had nowhere to go. Despite his pressing, Barnardo's could find no place to send me and would not put me in digs unless they could secure a maintenance allowance for me from the government. On that score they failed. Once again I made the newspapers.

"MR NORRIS REPORTS THAT PHILLIP IS AGAIN ASKING FOR A FOSTER HOME. I AM GOING TO PUT AN ADVERTISEMENT IN THE SOUTHPORT NEWSPAPERS."

Miss Bailey, Executive Officer, 7th December, 1967

Mrs Norris appeared to be reasonable and I did begin to accept Norris's rule for a while. I showed his son that he wasn't so clever and began to get on tolerably well with the boy. For a time we even walked to school together before "daddy" began taking his son to school by car. His father changed tack for a few months and humoured me while he pressed for me to be boarded out. In the meantime he began setting about the other older boys.

Dick was 12 now and growing into a strong young boy able to hold his own with any lad of his age in the secondary modern school. His sister had just left when Norris decided to teach him a lesson. It was one mealtime. Dick gave Norris a bit of cheek and suddenly found himself sprawled across the floor. Norris was showing that he could be brutal. This was a different regime to anything we had witnessed before. I wanted out even more.

At school I remained happy and began to finish in the top ten of the class. I could see that a university place was a possibility for me and was a ticket for my future. I scoured the school library for books to take home to read in my room. I raced through all Hemingway's works. I was there in *For Whom the Bell Tolls*, there in *Death in the Afternoon*, there in *The Old Man and the Sea*, there in my world of heroes.

At that stage most of my heroes were white despite the fact that I was black. Apart from my limited knowledge of or access to black writers, in those days to me the black skin simply meant pain and I carried that pain. Some might think that I was not black but "mixed race" or "half caste" or "coffee coloured," but I was black. In art, we are commonly taught that black and white are not colours. So too with peoples. Our skin may change colour with its exposure or otherwise to the sun's rays but our being black or white is a social construct imposed upon us and then absorbed.

I was black because society made me black with its taunts of "wog" and "nigger," and the stares, and the news of lynchings in The States and massacres in South Africa.

It is true that I had no black cultural heritage. From birth I had been in the care of white people. If anything, my "ethnicity" and cultural heritage were my institutional world of orphans and abandoned and rescued children, where one might find Romulus, Pip, Oliver, Peter Pan and Wendy and the Lost Boys. Our parents might have originated in Africa, Asia, Caribbean islands or the British Isles, but, whatever that parentage, we shared the same fate and the same life. I read on with my dreams to escape that life and survive in the white world.

When I was not out at football or at school, I studied and studied in my room. In the school holidays, when there were no school pals to mess around with, I stayed in my room and read. Otherwise, I went for long lonely walks on the beach, peering out at the sea and listening to the seagulls' cries; wishing I had money like the other boys and the people in the rich houses of the neighbourhood; wishing I had someone, like the other boys and the people in the rich houses of the neighbourhood.

Once the ocean's waves had been my light, the chorus to my childish laughter. Now the sea drowned my cries. When the wind blew and I was alone, I would sing my songs, songs of loneliness, and ache for a youthful romance.

Yet the very immensity of that liquid mass before me placed my self-pity into perspective. That sea had always been my friend and we had shared our dreams. I knew it was as lonesome as I, and returned its love. In turn, through all its twists of temperament, the ocean never beat me, never threatened me, never mocked my colour or my condition, never shackled me.

In its happiest times, when the sun shone, the ocean caressed the sand, its waves gently rolling to shore. But there were times when the howling of the wind whipped the sea to fury, hurling wave after wave at the shore, grabbing at the sand and flotsam, and tossing them in frenzied, dizzy whirls. Waves crashed down transforming into billowing, white clouds, then effervescent, drifting snow, before, the sea's anger exhausted, and tired surf appeared like breaking ice floating to rest on the beach.

This awesome power calmed me, instilled into me a sense of the vastness of the world awaiting me once I had unlocked the chains of childhood. Often I faced into breezes strong enough to bring tears to my eyes and sang that sixties pop song by The Monkees:

"I want to be free,
Like the bluebirds flying by me,
Like the waves down on the blue sea.
If your love has to tie me,
Don't try me, say goodbye..."

What I did not appreciate was the value of my loneliness. You may find such a statement to be strange. However, I am convinced that being alone from birth helped me to survive. Never having anybody to turn to for comfort and protection left me without the hope of a Peter Pan or a Wendy, who might rescue me from my world. I had no big brother behind which to shelter, no others' skirts beneath which to hide.

Most unwanted children grew up with the knowledge of their mother or father or with the presence or knowledge of brothers or sisters. Some were still visited from time to time by a mother or stepfather. Rejected as these children might have been, their awareness of being parented, of being owned, often nurtured the hope that their parents or siblings would rescue them. Their knowledge, of having brothers or sisters present or elsewhere, still left them with the hope of being comforted. In contrast, to all intents and purposes, I had grown up as a lonely orphan. I was left with no illusion of being rescued from my situation.

I was alone with my instincts – those undeveloped, primordial instincts that each one of us possesses but often dismisses in the complex, word-driven, family-protected world. Long ago, these instincts would have been essential tools for mankind's survival. Yet in today's world we are only encouraged to trust that which our eyes can see, those words our eyes can read and our ears can hear. And doesn't a parent try, with hugs and cuddles, to soothe their child's fears, to reassure, to kiss away those dark, instinctive, infantile forebodings?

I was left to guide myself through the jungle of adolescence. It's not that I learned to trust my fears. I unconsciously but stubbornly followed my instincts, side-stepping danger, drawing back from cliff edges, unsafe situations and unsafe people. My reasoning for each survival manoeuvre was often flawed. If I believed, in my headstrong state, that I shunned wrongdoing, I did not recognise that I operated my moral code quite selectively – when it suited. I didn't understand, and still don't, all the reasons why I chose the paths I took, but each one led me to a safe, if lonely, haven.

I was coming up to my 15th birthday and I was still in the home. But being 15 meant I could be moved out into lodgings or digs as we called them, and live on my own. Barnardo's said that it would be difficult to find me any place to stay. So, I tried myself. I went round the seedy areas on the edge of the town centre. Where any house had a notice, "Board & Lodgings," I enquired of the landladies as to whether they would take me. The answer was always the same: "You seem like a nice, coloured man and I'd like to take you but what would the neighbours say?"

I gave up. In anger I wrote a complaint to the Race Relations Board. The Board sent me a huge wad of forms to fill in. Filling the forms in seemed a complete waste of time. I wanted somewhere to live. I threw the forms in the dustbin and accepted that fostering might be my only way out.

"You better get that great big chip off your shoulder about being in care or nobody will want you," Norris would say.

I was aching to leave that home with its poverty and neglect. Each dark night I returned, reached the Backway and sensed an evil presence. I thought this presence was my hatred of Norris but you will see that it was much more than that.

I made it clear to Barnardo's that I did not want a foster family. All I wanted was a family who would take me away from that home and give me lodgings that Barnardo's would be obliged to pay for.

"HE HAS A CHIP ON HIS SHOULDER ABOUT BEING IN CARE, AND ASKS AT LEAST ONCE A WEEK IF AN ALTERNATIVE HAS BEEN FOUND FOR HIM E.G. FOSTER HOME OR LODGINGS. HE RESENTS HAVING TO ACCEPT ANYTHING AT ALL FROM BARNARDO'S BUT HAS IMPROVED IN AS MUCH AS HE IS ACCEPTING THAT HE MUST FOR THE TIME BEING...HE IS AT THE STAGE OF REJECTING RELIGION AND GOES TO CHURCH ONLY BECAUSE WE ASK HIM TO."

Annual Review, 24th July, 1968

With the occasional beating, I survived until the autumn when Barnardo's said that they had found a potential foster couple for me to stay with. I went to see the Jamesons' house and was glad to accept any chance to get out of the home.

"I HAVE ARRANGED FOR THIS LAD TO MOVE FROM THE BRANCH HOME TO LIVE WITH MR AND MRS JAMESON ON SUNDAY 10TH NOVEMBER.

Mr Makin, Welfare Officer, 28th October, 1968.

With one leap I was free. I was 15 years and three months old. I knew that I had escaped from Norris, who would clean his ears out with cotton bud sticks whilst he ate with us in the dining room. I knew that I was free of this man who, whenever he displayed his Gurkha knife to us, would cut himself with it, declaring: "Whenever this knife is unsheathed it must draw blood."

I didn't know all that I was leaving behind.

Chapter 13

Captain Hook

"It was his hour of triumph. Peter had been removed for ever from his path, and all the boys were about to walk the plank."

J.M.Barrie, Peter Pan

When and how it first started no one will ever know. Nor will I know whether it began while I was there. Perhaps those floorboards I heard creaking and doors shutting and closing in the dead of night were not simply the groans of an old house. Perhaps Mary Stewart knew of why Gilbert Norris had been transferred from the home he ran in Cardiff and that may be why she tried to get so many of us children moved before he arrived. Perhaps she had her own reasons. It's for Barnardo's to say whether they have files on what happened and to explain why they turned a blind eye for so long.

For sure, I did not realise that the rows and beatings I suffered were designed to make sure that I would remain keen to leave the home. Norris wanted the older children out of the way and, unwittingly, Mary Stewart also played into his hands. Michael Ingham, who had been sent down south to the Barnardo's training centre, found the centre closed down on him. He was sixteen. He returned to live in Southport and applied to live in the home with his brother, Dick. He was told that he was too old to stay at Tudor Bank and would have to find his own digs.

Left alone with the younger children, Captain Hook had almost absolute power to do as he pleased. He did. With the older children out of the way, Norris began sexually abusing those that remained. Carmen, whom I had taken for walks, taken blackberry picking and organised little tea parties for, was one of his victims. Perhaps it started when he found her crying alone in the bedroom and went in to comfort her. Perhaps he put his arms around the young girl and felt her breasts then felt her vagina and slipped his finger inside. We don't know and never will.

He abused little Shania too. Shania was a sweet and shy girl whom I'd also spent a few years with in the home. Shania didn't like Norris turning up in her bedroom after lights out. She didn't like what he did to her either.

Shania was old enough to know what Norris did to her was wrong. She'd spent enough time playing Dare, Force, Truth or Promise in our summertime tents to know that. She knew about Victor, the wanker, and she knew that was wrong too. There came the day when Shania collected every bit of courage that she could gather and complained to Norris's wife. "And I know he does it to the other girls too!" Shania added.

Norris's wife must have been mortified. Whether there were past acts of abuse by her husband, we do not know, but if news got out of this, not only her Gilbert, but also herself and her son would face a calamity. The family would lose their jobs and their house. No doubt Geoffrey would have to move school again. She faced a calamity.

We do not know whether she questioned her husband about Shania's accusations but he would have been relatively confident. He would have said that the nurse who had arrived from Wales had followed him up there and for her own reasons had put the children up to it. Then who would believe the words of these little urchins? Who indeed?

Did Mrs Norris know what her husband was like? Rather than dismiss Shania's claims out of hand, she called all the girls together in the office where the sun shone through the stained glass window, lighting up the words: "The Lord is my shepherd I shall not want. He leadeth me to lie down in green pastures."

As for Shania, she was relieved. She felt that at last Norris would stay out of her room at night. She entered the office in a tense, expectant mood. There, the eight girls aged six to twelve stood where they could amongst the chairs. Shania being the last to arrive, Mrs Norris closed the door and began: "Shania says that Mr Norris is being too affectionate to the girls. Has anyone anything else to say?"

The little, mixed race girl, Marjorie, looked up at her elder, white half-sister, Susan, who stood beside her, holding her hand. Marjorie could see Hook's willy, could feel Hook's hand on her breast. Susan could hear the click of the door and flesh entering her flesh and making her cunt moist. Susan squeezed her younger sister's hand hard. The room was silent. Shania looked over at them, her eyes appealing to the elder sister: "Please Susan, say somethin'. You know what 'e does to yer and yer sister. I've seen 'im in our bedroom with yer. I've heard you cry. Tell her! Tell her!" But Shania's eyes were appealing to the top of Susan's mop of black, wavy hair.

Susan had her eyes fixed on Marjorie's shoes: "Don' say anythin' Marjy. Don' say anythin'. Keep yer mouth shut. He'll split us up again. He'll send you away."

Sheryll shrugged her shoulders but said nothing. Shania turned to Carmen but couldn't find her eyes either. Carmen was staring at the wooden desk that Captain Hook made her sit on when he wanted to find his way inside her: "'E said he'd send me to a remand 'ome if I said anythin'."

Nobody said a word. Shania felt her face blush. She was on her own. Mrs Norris would call her a liar. "That will be all then," said Captain Hook's wife. Susan released her grip on her sister's hand and the girls shuffled out of the office. Captain Hook had won the day.

When Marjorie and Susan and their brother had arrived at the home, it was the first time that they had been together in their lives. The little family had sworn that they never wanted to be parted again. They would do anything to stay together. This Norris knew.

Had the other girls backed up Shania's accusations, what could Mrs Norris have done? She could tell her husband that he was in deep trouble if he continued with his activities. She could have asked her husband to stop, but it is likely that he would then cover his tracks by having most of those he had already abused removed from the home. Alternatively, she could have packed her bags, gone to the police and had him charged.

After the meeting, Shania went up to the sisters and asked them why they had said nothing and left her on her own.

"We were frightened. Norris 'as told us that if ever we breathe one word about what 'e was doing to us, that 'e would 'ave us split up again."

Norris was free to carry on with his destruction. Perhaps he was a victim of his army life. Perhaps he got his sexual excitement from having absolute power over children, and abusing them sexually was a way to that power. And how Hook did like to walk around with no shirt on showing that he still had powerful muscles beneath his wrinkling skin - muscles powerful enough to hold down his little victims and a mind cruel enough to rip out their insides. Whichever way, after the girls' meeting with his wife, he continued to appear in the girls' rooms late at night. He abused Shania and the other girls even more.

It was Shania who finally told one of the nurses about Norris: "If you don't believe me, you can see for yourself. Come up to our bedroom after lights out."

After lights out at nine o'clock, the nurse from Wales tiptoed down the corridor as quietly as the creaking floorboards would allow. She swiftly opened the door and to her horror, there he was on the bed with Shania. Norris turned round, zipping up his trousers and hissed at the nurse: "Get out!"

The nurse, Gwendolyn Davis, fled back to her bedroom: "That horrible man has done it again. I knew all along that he would. But what do I do now?" She lay on her bed, sliding her long fingers through her permed, ginger hair. She racked her brains as to what to do next. She could go to the police. She could make a report to Barnardo's. She could confront Norris. She decided on the latter course. She believed that he could be stopped. Did she go to bed also believing that now she had more power over Norris, more chance of being given better holiday dates, more chance of receiving that pay rise?

Shania hoped that, at last, she and her friends would be saved from Hook. She cried herself to sleep. Norris had a sleepless night. He was terrified that he would be reported. He spent the night sat in a chair in the bungalow staring at the dark night. Doubtless that was where he hatched his plan of action:

"I'll tell Gwendolyn Davis that I will deny it all. I'll tell her that she was imagining things, that I was calming Shania who was having one of her nightmares again. I'll say that she has put Shania and the other girls up to making allegations against me. That's what I'll say to Barnardo's too and I'll warn the woman that she will never work in a children's home again."

Morning came and after breakfast, Norris ordered Nurse Gwendolyn into his office. Gwendolyn tried to steady her nerves for the confrontation. Sweat seeped out of her hands. She wiped it off on her green nylon overall. When she arrived at the office door, she could see Norris standing peering at the stained glass window: "He maketh me lie down in green pastures." Norris turned to face her: "I think we better talk in my bungalow, don't you?" Gwendolyn nodded and together, in silence they walked off.

All that transpired in Captain Hook's bungalow is not certain. However, the ginger-haired nurse managed to almost burst that angry vein on the man's forehead. One hour later, Shania and Carmen saw Nurse Gwendolyn coming into the hall with her bags. The nurse went over to Shania, put a small piece of paper in her hands and whispered: "He's told me to leave."

She took her bags and left with Shania's hopes. Shania went into the upstairs playroom and unfurled the scrap of paper that had been the nurse's parting gift. On it the nurse had written: "If ever this goes to court, here's my number." She passed a note, which told Shania that she couldn't protect the girl from danger, that only Shania could protect herself. But Shania was 12 and didn't know anything about courts.

The nurse heaved her bags down the drive. Tears streaked down her face. She took one look back and saw Norris watching her from the playroom window.

Shania and her friends were left to the mercy of Captain Hook. It hurts to think how that order to bed must have been feared. How those pillows stifled the sobs and became sodden with tears. How those little girls must have dreamed that Peter Pan and Wendy would fly through the window, chop off Norris's claw and take them home. But there was no relief. Hook tore his claw across their guts and left them whimpering in the dark: "Mummy! Mummy!"

Only their friends lay in the beds beside them were relieved. It was not their turn that night. They had heard the door click open. They had shut their eyes and pretended to be asleep. The sweat had amassed on their brow. Each had clutched their sheet and prayed they would not feel his cold hand on their neck. Then they had heard a creak of another girl's bed and they kept silent. Carmen kept as still as she could, hoping that she wouldn't pee herself. When she did, she knew that the Captain would punish her. And she knew how.

The other girls knew that their time would come round again to wake up from a nightmare in a sweat, the time when they would wake with a pain on their insides or a sweet, sickly taste in their mouths.

It wasn't once. It was week after week, month after month, Christmas after Christmas.

As each Christmas arrived, Captain Hook smiled as he stood before the town's worthies presenting his victims. He had them dressed up as rescued fallen angels. And the worthies saw St Michael with his wards.

Shania saw hell, and the rich and the good were all in there, dancing with Hook.

Some time later, Shania had the courage to complain about Norris to Barnardo's officials. Now it was Shania's turn to be told to leave. Barnardo's sent her to another home 20 miles away.

"Don't bring this up again or you will be branded as a troublemaker," they told Shania. "What is wrong is right," Barnardo's said.

Barnardo's did nothing about Norris. Norris was left to continue destroying Carmen and her friends. Not content with abusing the girls, Captain Hook announced lessons on "the facts of life" for the boys. Lenny was all of 13. He was a pasty-faced, quiet boy. His greasy dark brown fringe forever fell over his eyes – the startled rabbit eyes of a shy young man. He'd been moved from a home in Liverpool. Norris announced that Lenny would be the first to enter his office and learn "the facts of life."

None of the boys saw the point in going to learn "the facts of life". We'd learned about the birds and bees long before the Captain had arrived. Lenny knocked on the door ready to learn that which he already knew. Norris called him in. To Lenny's surprise, the office light was on and the curtain drawn.

Let's leave Norris's pre-amble.

"Now unbutton your trousers and show me your manhood," declared Norris.

Lenny hesitated, then "Thwack!" Norris brought his cane down on the desk. Lenny did as he was told.

"Good lad," said Norris, "Now I'm going to show you how men make sperm. But you can't do it with that pathetic, little white thing. Rub it and make it harder and bigger."

Lenny gingerly put his hand on his penis. He didn't want to have a wank. He thought that it was wrong: "Real men don't wank. They stick their dicks in women and shag."

"Look man, hurry up," said Norris, and he moved towards Lenny, grabbing hold of his penis.

Lenny couldn't get an erection in front of Captain Hook. But Captain Hook could.

"Right, I'll show you lad," declared Norris, unzipping his trousers. Sure enough, stood before Lenny was a white cock, pink at the top and crowing like the king of the coop.

"Now lad, grab hold of this and rub it like it was Aladdin's Lamp."

Captain Hook took Lenny by the shoulders and pulled him towards him. Lenny was frightened and took hold of the warm, soft lamp. He knew how to wank and he knew the Captain expected him to wank him off. The boy felt the Captain's cold hand slide down the back of his shirt and press him further towards the man. It seemed like forever then the Captain shuddered, hissed: "You bastard," and pushed Lenny away.

Lenny recoiled to the edge of the room but the Captain came towards him, patting his head: "Now lad that's what you have to do. There's another way of having babies and I want to show you. Women like it this way. Pull down your trousers."

Lenny stared at the Captain. He had never heard of this one before.

Thwack! The Captain's cane came down on the mantelpiece this time. "Pull down your trousers!"

Lenny unhooked his trousers and let them slide down.

"Now turn around!" Lenny felt that he was in the school gym with his bossy PE teacher.

"Now bend down and touch your toes! Touch your toes laddy!"

Lenny stretched to touch his toes. His finger tips hovered an inch above the black lace-up shoes that he'd polished so hard that morning that he could see his face in them. He saw his mouth now. It was grimacing as he tried to touch the point of his shoes. It still grimaced as cold hands landed on his hips. Then he felt a pain around his arsehole and Norris's dick going inside. Lenny wasn't looking at his face in his shoes anymore. He tried to straighten himself up but Captain Hook held him down. In, in, in, in, in, in.

"Get up off the floor lad. You know you've learnt something that'll help you through the rest of your life."

"Now here's a pound note. Don't say anything to the other boys, as I'll have you on report as quick as you can say ice cream. Now, get out and call Martin in."

Lenny went up to his bed. He lay down and cried.

Norris started taking some of the boys on "fishing trips" and sexually abusing them there too. Did he take them one by one into the woods? Did he pick an argument? Did he then order them to drop their pants, bend over and take their punishment? However it occurred, Captain Hook stuck his claw in them, destroyed their Neverneverland and told them: "Don't say a word, or I'll split you up."

Only Dick fought back. Dick was now the eldest boy and a strong boy. He wasn't frightened of Hook and, though Dick took beatings from Hook, he fought back. Dick never went to learn about the facts of life and always refused Norris's invitation to accompany him on night-fishing trips. When Dick caught Norris sexually abusing Carmen they fought. When Dick caught the Captain on Lenny, they fought. When Dick caught the Captain in the playroom on top of a three-year-old girl, they fought.

Norris found a pretext for forbidding Dick's elder brother, Michael, from going near the home and Dick was left to fight along on his own. Hook wanted to banish Dick from Neverneverland but Hook's problem was that Barnardo's closure of their training centre in Stevenage resulted in there being nowhere to send the older boys away to. So Hook told Barnardo's that Dick was causing trouble and being extremely violent. Barnardo's told the police. Dick was 15 when Norris slapped an "unruly" certificate on him.

One afternoon, Dick was playing football on the school playing fields when he saw a Black Maria coming up the school drive. The boys stopped their game and watched inquisitively as three policemen left the van and came walking towards the football pitch.

"Dick Ingham?" shouted one police officer.

"That's me," replied Dick, swaggering towards them, his head held high.

"Come with us."

The Black Maria was there to pick him up. Dick was taken back to the home to pick up a few items of clothing then driven to the assessment centre in which the child killer, Mary Bell, spent many days. The bewildered young man was then sent to an Approved School for corrective treatment – though nobody knew why this boy needed correcting. By the time he was allowed to return to Southport, his childhood was gone.

In Hook's world, what was wrong became what was right. Children lived in fear. They ended up never being sure what was right. It wasn't just what Hook said, it was what he did, what he did to their insides. He was left to torture them at will, to lead them in prayer each teatime:

"For what we are about to receive, may the Lord make us truly thankful."

And the children prayed: "Lighten our darkness, we beseech thee, O Lord. And by thy great mercy defend us from the perils of this night."

But there was no one to protect them from the creaking floorboards of the night.

Some children survived to live with their pain. Carmen didn't. That is to say that the Carmen I had played with in Neverneverland didn't. For Carmen, life's rules, or should I say, society's rules, lost their meaning.

Carmen began to take things, other people's things. You couldn't call it stealing. She wasn't somebody taking from anybody for herself. She was nobody she knew and knew nobody. She got arrested for stealing washing off somebody's clothesline in somebody's garden. Carmen was locked up for committing a crime.

Christ, these words are hard to write.

Eventually a group of children, whom Norris had been sexually abusing, could take no more. They were returning back to the home on a Ribble Bus when Norris appeared at the bus stop in a minibus to pick them up, as had been arranged. But the children had decided that they had had enough of his cruelty. They refused to leave the bus despite his threats and the bus driver's cajoling.

The mystified bus driver said he couldn't wait there all day and drove his bus back to the bus station in the town. When he had parked the bus, the driver once again ordered the children to leave the bus.

"This is the end of the line. It's the terminus and you have to leave now."

The children still refused to leave.

"We want to see someone important and we're not leaving until they come!" they cried.

The police arrived and the children told their story. The police having the story was more than Barnardo's could handle. Within a day Norris was forced to pack his bags and leave. The children never saw Norris again and never will. He was never prosecuted and now he is dead but the evil this man did lives after him. What Norris left behind was a living horror for the rest of many of those children's lives.

To my great regret, I never set foot in the home during the three years after I had left. When I was about to leave Southport for good, I went back to Tudor Bank to see my old friends. None were left. Then I returned some years later and the home had been turned into an institution for mentally impaired children and then a home for the elderly.

Neverneverland was no more. It was as if a great sand dune had swept across from the beach and buried our young lives. Nothing was left but the bricks and mortar. The childish joy had gone, the pranks, the stenches, the loves and the nightmares, the tears and the horror. I had no inkling why. Life had moved on and I moved on with it. I didn't know where the others were and I was left alone with my memories, memories only a child who has been in care can really share.

Denied the chance of living back in the home, Michael Ingham went to live alone in digs. He concluded that he had been abandoned, that nobody cared. He went to drug addiction. After detox, Michael went off to do voluntary work, helping refugees in Afghanistan and Rumania. Michael cared. Then he died young.

His brother, Dick, went abroad to make his fortune. Mary Ingham lasted a year and a half at a foster home before being removed for "Behavioural Difficulties." Like many of the girls, once she had left school and her digs, Mary took a job as a chambermaid in one of the town's hotels. That way she had a roof over her head. Eventually, she went abroad too.

Tom Chorley got a job as a lineman on the railway. He loved trains. He lived alone. He loved children too. One day he was reported for photographing schoolgirls on the station platform. He said that he didn't mean any harm but he lost his job on the railway. He shut himself away. When no more mail could get into Tom's letterbox, workmen broke into his house. They found the rotting corpse of a 35-year-old man. Cause of Death: Loneliness.

Other children joined the Army or the Merchant Navy and most of us drifted around the world. Barnardo's described us as having been "rootless" children but we weren't rootless in Neverneverland where we had each other. We were rootless when they ripped us apart. We search for our roots. But no one can return to Neverneverland.

Many years ago, I learned that Carmen was in a prison somewhere in Nottingham. I assumed that she had been caught stealing. What I didn't know is that Carmen was in Rampton, the Nottingham top security prison for the criminally insane. She is still there.

Norris put Carmen in Rampton. Barnardo's officials gave him assistance. They ignored the cries for help. They could have wiped Captain Hook out of the script because they were the directors of the movie. Instead they left those children to grow up in fear, to hate the night and loathe the day. Wasn't it bad enough to have nobody? But, to be told each day that your words of pain were not worth believing was to be told that you were less than worthless.

Barnardo's officials connived to keep Norris in his position and allow those children who spoke out to be punished. They connived to keep the issue from the courts and Norris was given his freedom to pursue his destruction of children, for another ten years, elsewhere.

Norris's case was neither an isolated case nor the worst case in those days. Nor was the subsequent cover-up. Some say the cover-ups were maintained and abusers tolerated for fear of bad publicity undermining the organisation's fundraising capacity, that the Carmens and Shanias were sacrificed for the benefit of the greater good. But who were Barnardo's to make that choice? Was it done in the name of Christian values? Did Jesus say: "No greater man is there than this, that he lay down his friends for his life"?

It's too late for Norris to be prosecuted but it's not too late for Barnardo's to make amends, to give Carmen some of her life back. Carmen is seven digits, in a top-security prison for the most dangerous people in Britain. That's what happens when you rob clotheslines.

"We don't run children's homes anymore," Barnardo's say. What they don't say is that many of those who were the victims of the homes are still alive and still suffering quietly.

No amount of money will fully compensate for the suffering of Carmen and the Lost Children of Neverneverland. But Barnardo's can go some way by giving assistance to those that have suffered. Barnardo's can help bring relief from some of the pressures of daily life and give money so that the victims can enjoy the years that are left for them.

Barnardo's and those other institutions that presided over child torture can stop wringing their hands then washing them clean and hoping the past will be swept beneath some rolling sand dune. The Prime Minister's wife, Cherie Blair, is now President of Barnardo's and, coincidentally, was studying nearby, at a school in Waterloo, when these events began. If she and Tony have any commitment to human rights, they will make efforts to end the sufferings of tens of thousands of innocents.

As for myself, I am left with the guilt that I had left my friends to Captain Hook's mercy. I ran away. It was many years before I knew what I had run from.

Chapter 14

Taking a Bath

After my first dinner in my new home, my head span and I vomited the whole lot up. It was the first time I had ever eaten an omelette, let alone one fried in butter. At my second dinner I had a goulash put before me. I asked if I could please have some tomato ketchup with my meal. A quite angry, Joan Jameson replied: "Has no one told you that it's rude to ask for ketchup? It's an insult to my cooking." I had no idea why. I did say "please." I liked ketchup. I never got the ketchup anyway.

That was my introduction to well-to-do, middle class life. Living in the Jamesons' four-bedroom, Edwardian, detached house on the other side of town to the home, wasn't quite the dream I had expected. For all my good manners and my grammar school education, I was still a boy from the other side of the tracks. In many ways I still wanted to be.

Keith and Joan Jameson both worked hard at their professions. Keith was a business consultant in some new scientific field and Joan was a lecturer in a college ten miles from the town. They were both in their late thirties and Joan had just given birth to her first child.

Keith was a thin man, about 5ft 2ins tall with a potbelly and a mop of thinning black hair. His head was too small for his body and was dominated by a large hooked nose out of which hairs always protruded no matter how much he picked at them. His confidence came from his achievements in his field of work where he applied his worldly practical outlook with success. Each weekday he'd don his grey suit, pick up his brown leather briefcase and take the train to work in Liverpool. Each evening he'd return to a meal prepared by his wife, play with his baby son, then sit poring over the work he had brought home.

His wife, Joan, was two inches shorter in height than he was and of a slim but fleshy build with a thick mop of fair hair and a rounded fleshy face. Joan was less confident, always feeling the need to stress her achievements to others. Besides, she was struggling to keep her work, her house and her child on track. The house was always tidy and clean and full of the rich aromas of her cooking - aromas that were new and strange to me. The larder was well stocked; the fridge full and their cocktail cabinet never empty of bottles of Martini, Dubonnet, Advocaat, sherries and the like.

A medium-sized porch and vestibule divided the front of the house.

A door on the right led into a large living room stocked with a three-piece suite of garish colours. On the left of the porch was another large room, which I was told was my bedroom. Beside my bedroom was the stairway leading to a landing off which were the bathroom, the Jamesons' bedroom, their son's room, the au pair's bedroom and a large spare room that was full of Keith's tools, decorating implements and junk.

The couple had employed a live-in Danish au pair to care for their son while they were at work. Being a fifteen-year-old boy, I was obviously pleased to have an attractive, long-legged young Danish blonde in my company. But the Danish blonde didn't stay for long after I arrived. I didn't calculate that when the Jamesons took me, Barnardo's gave them not only 56 shillings a week for my upkeep, 10 shillings a week for my pocket money and 15 shillings a week for my clothing allowance. Barnardo's also gave them a babysitter – me.

From the outset I made my own wishes clear.

"IT WAS EVIDENT THAT HE WOULD OPT FOR LODGINGS MAINLY, I THINK, BECAUSE HE SEEMS TO HAVE THE IDEA THAT HE WILL HAVE A GREATER DEGREE OF FREEDOM AND THAT THE PRESSURES WILL NOT BE SO GREAT."

Mr Makin, Child Care Officer, 2nd April, 1968

"I didn't want to be fostered," I said to the Jamesons, "I wanted to go into digs but they said that I couldn't. As far as I'm concerned I don't want another family. I want this to be my lodgings."

Maybe you can imagine how I felt when I said this. I was 15. I didn't want to be with any adults. I wanted, like most 15-year-olds, to be left alone with my friends. What is more, I found my new "foster-parents" manner rather strange, Keith so relaxed and friendly, and Joan so clipped and forced. Why couldn't I have tomato ketchup if it was in the kitchen cupboard? Why couldn't I come and go as I pleased? I was used to operating around clear rules but having the freedom to do as I wished within those rules. I was used to pleasing myself and my friends, not adults.

I know that they were not happy with what I said but Keith at least, made out that he accepted it. They were warned in advance. When the au pair moved out, Keith and Joan asked me to move upstairs into her room. I declined. I didn't want to be part of the family upstairs, just myself downstairs. When they asked for me to travel up north with them for Christmas, I declined. I said that I had been invited to the Granvilles. It wasn't that I felt part of the Granvilles' family, I was stubborn and proud and I didn't want to be drawn in as a Jameson. I was Phillip Roy Frampton and I had nobody and nobody had me and that was how it would stay.

That Christmas that I had said I was going to the Granvilles, I actually stayed in the house. I prepared my own "Christmas dinner" - the type that came in tins and you boiled up. I had friends round and we drank our way through half the Jamesons' cocktail cabinet. Needless to say, the Jamesons weren't too amused.

I was pretty much a brat. But what the Jamesons expected of me, I didn't know. The Barnardo's report of their application to become foster parents reads:

"APPARENT EXPLICIT MOTIVE OF FOSTER PARENT(S) FOR ACTING IN THIS CAPACITY: - A WISH TO HELP DEPRIVED CHILDREN.
"HOW LONG HAD FOSTER PARENTS PREVIOUSLY ACTED IN THIS CAPACITY? - NEVER BEFORE.
"HAD THE FOSTER PARENTS, ON THIS OCCASION MADE STIPULATIONS ABOUT THE SORT OF CHILDREN THEY WANTED? – NONE MADE."

Retrospective Report from Barnardo's Merseyside Division
10th August, 1970

They were kind. We engaged in many interesting conversations about the world we were living through. It was the time of the Paris uprising, the people's heroics against the tanks in Prague's Wenceslas Square, huge protests against Vietnam, hippies, marijuana, LSD, Black Power and the Beatles turning for guidance to a yogi. We discussed it all. Keith was the first person ever to give me assistance with my homework – mainly with maths, for that was his field.

Otherwise, the Jamesons' interests were very different to my own. They were not interested in the slightest in the sports I was involved in or pop music. They didn't have a television and instead listened to the radio and their classical records when they were relaxing in the house. Still, they bought me a transistor radio and I would listen to the pop music on the pirate radio station, *Radio Caroline*, and the plays and short stories on the Home Service whilst I lay on my bed.

I was kept well fed and well clothed. Now that I was with the Jamesons, I could even have three white shirts to wear a week and only had to change my school shirt every other day. They bought me more socks and told me to change them everyday. That was a big change from the once a week routine in the home. My feet stopped smelling. If I requested it they sent me off to school with a packed lunch as well.

At the grammar school I remained happy. I was now in my fifth year. I was still playing football most weekends when I was picked to play for the school rugby under-16 side. I was pretty chuffed. My former detestation of rugby had gone. Being good at rugby was part of being good at school.

Actually, I wasn't much good but I could run and run and I tackled fearlessly, so I got put on the wing or at full-back. Now I was settled in as one of the lads and remained playing in the school rugby team until I broke my finger in the final year. I joined the Rambling Club and went with them on long walks on the peaks of Snowdonia and in the Lake District.

Being the argumentative and mouthy sort, I also joined the senior school Debating Society. I was also a member of the Railway Society. I can't recall having much interest in trains but membership was probably an excuse to get a day off school and travel somewhere. Not that I ever wagged school. In that O level year I was absent for one day and late once. I enjoyed school because I was with my friends. When I went home I was alone. I sat my seven GCE O levels in the summer and passed them with good grades.

My relations with the Jamesons continued at arm's length. That was my doing. When the Jamesons asked me to go on holiday with them to Spain, I declined the offer. I'd never been abroad in my life but I didn't want to be tied up with them. Instead, I hitchhiked up to the Lake District and went climbing with my school friends.

I rebuffed their kindness and it must have hurt them. As far as I was concerned, I owed the world nothing and the Jamesons, nothing. I had been put there by Barnardo's and I wanted to be on my own in lodgings. I didn't want to be beholden to, or the property of, any adults.

You might think that they were very kind and that I was pretty ungrateful. I was pretty confused too as to what this couple wanted.

"Would you like to have a bath with us?" Keith had asked me, very soon after the au pair had moved out.

"No thanks," I replied, "I'll have one later." It was a polite answer to an impolite question. At the time, I just thought: "I don't want to be part of your weird world." I didn't want to play in the bath with any man. I didn't think that I was 15 and that this man was "helping" a "deprived child."

Joan started to walk around the house at night in an unbuttoned pyjama top. Sometimes she would keep it wrapped, sometimes, when her husband wasn't looking and I was present, she would open it wide open displaying her tits and fanny to me. She even did it while they were in bed and Keith was looking the other way engrossed in one of his *Forum* or *Penthouse* magazines. She pretended to be reading and I could see that beneath the sheets she was playing with her vagina. When he was away, however, she took care not to display herself.

I was 15 and didn't know what she wanted of me. She was playing with me. My relationship with her eventually deteriorated as she did. Joan had a breakdown.

When Joan recovered, her teasing displays continued. Otherwise she remained as aloof as before. I hadn't much respect for Keith either. I was now the stronger. He hit me once, punched me hard in the stomach. I had teased him. It didn't hurt. I'd flexed my stomach muscles and grinned at him. But I then knew how far his peace and love would go.

I became estranged from them both to the extent that after an argument, I would stop talking to them for some time. The periods of silence got longer. On the occasions when Mr Makin, the Barnardo's Child Care Officer, visited he had no notion that anything was wrong. I gave him none. I had not an ounce of respect for the goofy, thin and lanky local Child Care Officer. He was approaching retirement age, which probably was why he always appeared in the same tatty, green, tweed suit. His short-back-and-sides haircut emphasised his protruding teeth and the wrinkled skin stretched so tightly over his face that he appeared skeleton-like. He was the skeleton that arrived to remind me that I was still "in" Barnardo's.

I quite despised Makin as a Norris's man. He had been a thorn in my neck since he had started dealing with me in the home. He was someone whose only relationship with me involved giving me regular lectures on my ungratefulness for being Looked After by Norris and being Looked After by Barnardo's. Then he nagged me about my not going to church.

"I HAVE SPOKEN TO HIM A NUMBER OF TIMES ABOUT GOING TO CHURCH, BUT HE IS NON COMMITTAL OVER THIS SUBJECT, SO I DO NOT PRESS HIM."

Mr Makin, Child Care Officer, 2nd February, 1970

My only wish to speak to him was to get him away from my sight as soon as possible. I also didn't know myself quite what was wrong with my relationship with the Jamesons. I wasn't sure quite what was right and what was wrong.

Makin had no idea of what was happening in that house.

"THE RELATIONSHIP BETWEEN THE F.PARENTS AND PHILLIP FRAMPTON IS STILL VERY GOOD. HIS MAIN INTEREST IS IN HIS SCHOOL AND HE SPENDS A LOT OF TIME WHEN HE IS AT HOME READING AND STUDYING."

Mr Makin, Child Care Officer, 6th December, 1969

"PHILIP ENJOYS A GOOD RELATIONSHIP WITH HIS FOSTER PARENTS. HE IS AN ACCEPTED MEMBER OF THE FAMILY AND IS WELL INTEGRATED."

Mr Woods, Executive Officer, 6th May, 1970

Joan continued with her displays while Keith was in the house. It was on one such occasion, on an evening when Joan and I were not talking that I shouted up to her bedroom that I could not find the cough medicine I was taking.

Joan came down to the kitchen dressed solely in her unbuttoned pyjama top. As I stood by the kitchen cupboard she climbed on a wooden stool to reach the medicine shelf. I was stood behind her with my face almost touching her bare buttocks. She placed one foot on a work surface. Dark hair protruded from her fanny. My heart pounded. I wanted to touch her flesh, to kiss it, to feel it.

I didn't. I didn't know what this woman wanted of the deprived child. She handed me the medicine bottle, climbed down from the stool. Opened up her pyjama top to me, glanced down at the obvious erection beneath my pyjamas, then pulled her top shut and said: "You didn't look far enough did you."

It came to the time when Keith was due to go away on a business trip. I had said that I wanted to move out into my own place. Keith said: "If you two don't get on while I am away, then you'll have to."

In his absence, Joan remained aloof. There was only one display. Then nothing. So one night I went up to her bedroom and asked her straight out what she wanted of me: "Why do you keep showing yourself to me? Do you want to sleep with me?"

She said: "No." To my shame I replied: "Well stop showing yourself to me and keep your door shut or I don't know what I might do. I could rape you."

I had no intentions or thoughts of doing any such thing. I was no longer the super righteous young schoolboy of the past but I was still proud. My reply was the response of an immature boy to an ill woman. She had drawn me on to the point where I wanted her to want me. But she didn't seem to want to give herself to me and I hadn't a clue what else to do because I didn't love her one bit. I wanted to express what she was doing to my head but I couldn't find the words to do it. Still, the confrontation was enough to bring the situation to a head.

Being in that house was the nearest that I ever came to being sexually abused. And I felt guilty.

We kept up our clipped conversations until Keith returned. In the next fortnight nothing improved. Keith gave no inkling of what he would do to alter the situation. It was on an evening, one month after Makin had last reported on the "intelligent, studious boy" who was "an accepted member of the family" and "well integrated" that, Mr Makin came and told me the news.

Makin had never liked the "superior," stubborn, young black lad who had given Gilbert Norris so much trouble, never went to church and never gave any thanks to Barnardo's for what they had done for him. He came into my bedroom where I was studying *Antigone* for my Greek and Roman literature Additional O level exam. I was lying on my bed and he lent down, pushing his skeletal head into my face.

"You can pack your things lad. Tomorrow you're off. You've outstayed your welcome here."

I was relieved. I asked: "Where am I going?"

"We've found you some digs in the town," he replied, "You make sure that you behave until tomorrow."

"Free at last," I thought. I had escaped from the madness, which I felt that I had landed in.

Mr Makin acted like I was being punished and sentenced. The next day he arrived in his green Morris Minor and took me and my suitcase and my cardboard box full of books off to my penal colony, a bedsitting room by Southport railway station.

"I WAS ASKED BY MR JAMESON TO REMOVE THIS LAD FROM HIS FOSTER HOME OWING TO HIS ATTITUDE TOWARDS THE FAMILY, AND HIS LACK OF CO-OPERATION WITH THEM.
"WHEN I SPOKE TO PHILLIP ABOUT THE SITUATION, HE COULD NOT GIVE ME A GOOD REASON AS TO HOW THE PROBLEM HAD ARISEN BUT KNOWING THIS LAD AS I DO, I CAME TO THE CONCLUSION THAT THE BEST THING TO DO WAS TO MOVE HIM AS SOON AS POSSIBLE."

Mr Makin, Child Care Officer, 29th June, 1970

If I had told him that I didn't want to co-operate with taking a bath with a man more than twice my age or that I didn't want to play along anymore with a woman's sexual kicks, it would not have made a difference.

"EXPLICIT REASON FOR REMOVAL: FOSTER MOTHER'S ILL HEALTH AND PHILLIP'S BEHAVIOUR PROBLEMS.
"WAS THIS REMOVAL CONSIDERED TO BE A BREAKDOWN: YES.
"WILL CHILD BE LIKELY TO RETAIN ANY SORT OF CONTACT WITH THE FOSTER PARENTS: UNCERTAIN.
"WILL THESE FOSTER PARENTS BE LIKELY TO BE USED FOR OTHER CHILDREN LATER: PERHAPS."

Retrospective Report from Barnardo's Merseyside Division, 10th August, 1970

The reports of Mr Makin, the Norris's man, quickly reverted to a more familiar tune:

"PHILIP HAS BEEN A DIFFICULT BOY FOR A NUMBER OF YEARS, DURING WHICH TIME HE HAS BEEN ANTI BARNARDO, AND DOES NOT KEEP IN TOUCH WITH THE HOME AT BIRKDALE..."

Mr Makin, Child Care Officer, 3rd November, 1970

Still, at 16, I had achieved my goal of living on my own. You might ask why I didn't leave school and find myself a job if I was so anti-Barnardo. I asked that myself. In those days, the government took its duty of care for unwanted children much more seriously. An unwanted child would be cared for by the state until he or she had reached the age of 18. I was aware of this and aware that Barnardo's were fulfilling a duty they had taken on in conjunction with the authorities.

My mother had signed me over to Barnardo's as their property, to do with as they saw fit. I was very, very ungrateful. I wanted nothing from Barnardo's but I knew that if I was to achieve my ambition of getting to university and into a bigger, brighter world, I was stuck with needing their support until I had taken my school GCE A level exams.

I made the Child Care Officer, Makin, aware of my attitude. He knew that Barnardo's still had me by the short and curlies, as they always had. I was their property and at their whim:

"HE IS QUITE FRIENDLY WITH ME BUT I HAVE THE FEELING THAT HE WILL CO-OPERATE WHILST HE IS AT THE GRAMMAR SCHOOL AS HE HAS NO OTHER SOURCE OF INCOME APART FROM OUR HELP, AND HIS ONE DESIRE IS TO GET TO UNIVERSITY."

Mr Makin, Child Care Officer, 15th August, 1970

Makin could have come down harder on me. Why didn't he? It may be because Barnardo's wanted a little feather in their cap from the success of the academically quite bright boy that they once described as "such a poor specimen of humanity" with "doubts about his intelligence."

"PHILLIP IS ACADEMICALLY QUITE BRILLIANT."

Mr Makin, Child Care Officer, 6th July, 1970

It could also have been because Makin wasn't sure how much I was aware of what had been going on at Tudor Bank and acted with caution in case I was angered to stir up trouble for Barnardo's. I would have raised a stink anyway. But I didn't know what Norris was up to because I never bumped into any of the other children from the home and never went back to see the home until it was too late.

On a cold Sunday in June, I arrived at my new home, a bedsit above a newsagent at 75a, London Street, bedsit land, Southport. Mr Makin took me into the shop where a short, plump old lady with dark, brown, greying, permed hair and spectacles hanging from the end of her nose was serving a customer from behind the counter. She was brusque and to the point with her customer, then looked up over her glasses and smiled at the Child Care Officer.

"So this is Phillip," she said, "Well, you'll 'ave a fine 'ome here if you behave yourself."

Mr Makin nodded his skeletal head and I smiled looking round at the shop's counters and shelves cluttered with newspapers, magazines, sweet jars and boxes of chocolates.

"Hello, Mrs Lowe," I said back to her.

"Wait a minute will you?" she said, rushing over to the door which led out to the rest of her house, "I'll just call Arthur to mind the shop while I sort you out."

She vanished behind a faded, red, cotton curtain and her husband Arthur appeared behind the counter. Arthur was the same height as his wife, of wiry build and had a few thin strands of grey hair tossed over the front of his head to convince himself that he still had any hair. He was still in his grubby work clothes. He had just come home from working a night shift on the railway line that ran from the station opposite the shop.

"Yer'll 'ave t'excuse me lad," he said, "I've jus' come in frum work."

Mrs Lowe reappeared. She had no time for any more pleasantries. She was always brusque, always hurried and almost always wore a frown.

"Bring the lad round the back, Mr Makin," she ordered, "and I'll take 'im up to 'is room."

To reach the entry to the bedsits and the Lowes' home, we had to go down a narrow, dark entry to the right of the shop. The same entry also led to the back entry for the second-hand junk shop next door to the Lowes' shop. The entry smelt of piss. It was used by the drunks of the town to relieve themselves as they stumbled home from the pubs after closing time.

Mrs Lowe was already standing with the door open. I noticed her glance at its dark olive paintwork and guessed that she was probably checking how much more of the paintwork had flaked off in the past year. She looked up at me with a quizzical smile as if to say: "I wonder what we have got here."

"Your room's on the first floor at the back, Phillip," Mrs Lowe informed me as she motioned us in to the narrow porch, "Now, mind the stairs. They're pretty steep. And mind that suitcase doesn't scratch the wallpaper."

She was right. The steps were steep. They were very narrow too. I managed to heave my suitcase up the stairs without scratching the wallpaper, though it really didn't seem to matter that much as it sported plenty of mature scratches, tears and grubby fingerprints already. The stairs led to an equally narrow landing where Mrs Lowe briefly showed me the bathroom.

"You'll share it with four other men," she said as she opened the door for me to peek inside, "so don't be taking long in there and don't be reading papers when you're on the toilet."

From what I saw and smelt, she could have no fears on that account. I'd thought the bathrooms in the home were pretty filthy but this one was even grubbier. The lino on the floor appeared to be rotting away and the sink had been left unrinsed after someone had shaved. The toilet bowl was almost green and had a piece of the *Football Pink* floating in it. An empty carton, which would once have been full of those single pieces of rough toilet paper, stood on the window ledge behind the toilet. The window itself was glazed with stains from splashes and dribbles of white toothpaste across it.

I looked in the enamel bath and was counting the tide marks when Mrs Lowe hurried me on:

"Come on. We 'aven't got all day, Phillip."

We moved passed two doors on our right to beside the stairs leading to the second floor on our left.

"This is your room, Phillip," said Mrs Lowe, "It's at the back of the 'ouse so it should be good for yer studyin'."

As she unlocked the door to my new home, I looked around at the wallpaper, patterned with roses. It was so old and faded, that I would never be able to tell whether the red roses sat on a white, a brown or a yellow background. The door to my room had been painted a dull brown colour. Around the doorknob were scratches cut into the paintwork by former tenants on those drunken dark nights when their key couldn't find the keyhole.

Mrs Lowe opened the door and entered the room first. Her eyes darted round to check that all was in order and nothing broken just in case she had to claim for any damage done by her new tenant. She looked at me as if to say: "It's not much lad but you're lucky to have anything for the money they're givin' me."

She was right again. It wasn't much. If this was going to be my Elba, from whence I would plan my assault on the world, I wouldn't be pacing up and down in it. The room was too small to walk more than four paces in any direction. I put my suitcase down and disappeared to fetch my cardboard box full of my books. When I returned Mr skeletal Makin gave me my orders, explaining to me the details of my new situation: "You'll have to behave here lad. Mrs Lowe will give you your Sunday dinner. You get school dinners, so you'll only need a snack at teatime and you've got a cooker as you can see. I know you understand how to use one as you've told me you cooked your own meals quite often in your last place."

"The cooker is electric," Mrs Lowe interrupted, "and I've given you an electric fire." She pointed down to a small two-bar fire, adding: "The meter's outside, by the door. If you don't know 'ow to use it, ask me and I'll show you later."

Makin went on: "We'll send Mrs Lowe a postal order each month for you. That will be your allowance. You get an allowance of 56 shillings a week for your meals and so on. You'll get 25 shillings for your spends and your clothes. Make sure you don't spend it all on silly things. If you run into any special expenditure, like holidays, you can give me a call and we'll see whether or not we will pay it. Otherwise, if you want any more to spend, you'll have to get yourself a part-time job.

"Mrs Lowe has provided you with sheets and blankets for your bed. You'll have to do your own washing in the laundrette down the road but Mrs Lowe says she'll lend you her iron and ironing board to do your ironing. She's put a table in for you so you can do your studying and make sure you do."

Once again he added: "There's to be no trouble here son and I'll visit you once a month to check up on you."

"I'll 'ave to get on, Mr Makin," Mrs Lowe interrupted again, "If you've finished, can we go downstairs and sort out the paperwork about the lad? Phillip, if you've got a radio, you're not to 'ave it on loud and make sure you don't make a noise when you come in at night. There's other people living 'ere and I don't want you disturbing 'em."

My instructions over, the skeleton in the green tweed suit nodded its skull, handed me an envelope with my first month's money and said: "Make sure you don't go mad with it, son."

He then bade me goodbye, leaving me alone in my room. I closed the door and lay face up on the bed.

My single bed with its stained, coarse, woollen blankets stood by the wall so that I could see through the window – not that there was much to see save for the red brick backs of other houses in bedsit land. The window frames of those houses looked as little cared for as the window frame, with its peeling white paint, through which I was peering out.

The wallpaper around my room carried the same faded and stained rose patterns that I'd seen on the stairs and the ceiling was probably once white. Now it was a dirty brown, caked with the deposits from the many previous occupants' cigarette smoke and cooking fumes. Black houseflies cruised above me, some flew around making frenzied circles and others lazed on the dirty cream fabric of the ceiling light's lampshade.

Beside my bed was a small dining room chair painted lime green. On it I could put my clothes. On the other side of the chair was a small wooden cupboard, which Mrs Lowe had told me was the place where I should put my food shopping. Its shelves were speckled with circular grease marks made by the drips from cooking oil bottles and orange circles inscribed by baked bean cans.

On this cupboard stood what my landlady had so grandly described as the cooker. My "cooker" was an electric Baby Belling stove with two rings and a grill beneath them. On one ring I could boil the kettle to make a hot drink. On the other I could heat up some baked beans one day and some spaghetti on the next and I could make toast beneath the grill. There was, of course, no fridge. It was going to be a far cry from the goulash, ratatouille and baked salmon and white wine diet that I had just left.

A large oak wardrobe was jammed between the foot of my bed and the wall. There I could hang my school blazer, my two pairs of black school trousers, my grey gabardine coat and my grey flannels for going out. I could keep my two pairs of black lace-up shoes, my football boots, my size 10 brown FEB climbing boots and my shoe-polishing kit at its base. Beside the wardrobe was a set of drawers for keeping my two grey school jumpers, my six white school shirts, my school tie, my half dozen pairs of grey socks and white Y front underpants, my rugby kit and my mountaineering clothes.

My schoolbooks and the other half a dozen books I had would have to go on the chipped, sky blue Formica table that stood beneath the window. The other wall was taken up by the blocked up fireplace where I would put the rusting, two-bar electric fire. The fireplace mantelpiece would do for keeping my school pens and pencils, rulers, set squares, protractors and my Baby Ben alarm clock. I would have to leave my schoolwork notes in the cardboard box in which I had brought my books.

That was all my possessions and furniture sorted out – in my head, at least. I jumped up from the bed and set to organise myself. As 5pm came round the sounds and odours of teatime in bedsit land drifted in through the window. Windows creaked open, kettles whistled, metal pans clanked, crockery clashed together, toilets flushed and drains rushed as the sweet and savoury scents of boiling beef and carrots then fried fish and vinegar wafted into my garret.

I was almost finished with organising my room when, with barely a tap on the door, in walked Mrs Lowe wearing a green and white chequered cotton pinafore over her navy blue dress. Her greying hair was twisted in rollers beneath a bright yellow cotton scarf.

"You've settled down in your room then, Phillip?" my landlady asked with a smile. I said that I had, then she told me: "Since it's your first day 'ere, I've cooked you your tea and Arthur 'll bring it up."

She added: "You like roast pork, carrots and cabbage, do you? The potatoes are boiled."

"Yes, thank you," I replied as my landlady's eyes darted around inspecting my slight re-arrangement of the room. She turned past me and bent down to look into my tiny larder cupboard. Noticing it empty she stood up and ordered: "You've got no food in at all lad. You better go down to the shop around the corner and get yourself something for your breakfast and tea tomorrow. The shops are all shut tomorrow. I told Mr Makin that I would give you your Sunday dinner but I can't be feeding you all the time. I've got a shop to run and 'e is not paying me for anything else."

"You better 'urry up too," Mrs Lowe hectored as she left the room, "Dinner will be ready in 20 minutes. If you're late I'll keep it warm for you but don't be too long or it'll spoil."

I would have to get used to my landlady's ways, nagging and hectoring and bursting into my room, which had no inside lock on the door. Her main trick was to surprise me at ten o'clock at night, saying: "It's far too late for you to be up, Phillip. It's costing us electricity!" whereupon she would switch off my bedroom light.

I picked up my two keys and my four pound notes and went out to buy a can of beans, a can of spaghetti, some teabags, a bottle of sterilised, long-life milk, some margarine and lard and a loaf of sliced bread. That would keep me for a few days. Once I had bought my provisions, I went to the phone box and called one of my mates and arranged to join them at the social club for Southport Amateurs Football Team. That was where we now spent our Saturday nights drinking beer and hoping that we'd meet a nice girl of our age, or older.

I took the opportunity to take a brief scout around my new area. Across the road were the walls for the yards of the town railway station and nothing else. My side of the street had a few dingy shops run by people living out their days until retirement. Then came the pub where my landlord and landlady would go that night, like every Saturday night, to drink stout and play dominoes.

Closer to the town station entrance, on the busy Chapel Street that marked the centre of the town, stood a second-hand clothes shop followed by two chip shops. I peered at the price list in the Chinese chippy. Two shillings for curried minced meat and chips. That would be my tea on future Saturdays. Indeed I became such a regular that I learnt a few polite words of Cantonese off the young Hong Kong immigrants wearing their nylon blue overalls.

I went around the back of London Street. Many houses posted signs, "Board & Lodgings" and "Rooms to Let." Otherwise the buildings were mainly used for offices. It was one of those seemingly lifeless small districts that sit on the edge of the busy centres of seaside resorts, one of those rundown districts that the day-trippers strolling around the town were not meant to see.

I returned to my room for my tea. As soon as I'd opened the door to the premises, Arthur appeared with a smile on his face and a tray in his hands: "'Ere's yer tea lad. Yer can tek it up yerself."

I came to look forward to my landlady's Sunday dinners, which I ate alone in my room, and, despite Mrs Lowe's nagging and penny-pinching attitude, I became quite fond of the old couple. Not that I spoke to them much. I hardly ever spoke to any of the other tenants either. In fact, were it not for the flushing of the toilet, the clicking of doors and the croaking of smokers' coughs, I would not have known they were there.

The next morning, I woke up alone. I was more alone than at any previous time in my life. But I was at peace. All I had in my life were my Baby Belling, my spitting kettle, the sounds of bedsit land and the hooting of trains. That day I made my breakfast of toast and tea and got out my schoolwork to continue my studies. When I was too tired to study any more, I lay on my bed. When I was too bored to lie on my bed, I went out for a walk hoping to bump into somebody I knew, somebody that I could talk to.

I walked past real couples who had each other, real families with real mothers and fathers and real friends, past pubs full of people laughing and joking, past sports cars and expensive shops, past restaurants serving salmon and avocado, past everything I wanted and didn't have.

It was a lonely walk. I didn't meet anyone to break my loneliness and returned to my little room at 75a, London Street, to an anonymous room in an anonymous house in an anonymous district.

It was a walk I would do many times. Many times I ventured out in the hope of breaking my loneliness. But I walked out alone, stayed alone and returned alone. I turned the key to my prison and my heart sank. I climbed the stairs alone to sit on my bed alone.

That night I picked up H E Bates's *Fair Stood the Wind for France* and joined Franklin, falling in love with Françoise on a river bank, as she assisted his escape from wartime Occupied France. Franklin was my latest hero.

In the absence of anyone I looked up to or any role models in my life, the literary heroes that I came across became of great importance to me. I experienced the adult world around me like a place on Earth experiences the Sun, which sets the rules, tolerates no objectors and is arbitrary in its temper. The Sun holds both the power to provide and to pleasure, and the strength to destroy and punish. Like primitive man with the Sun, I knew something of the adult world around me, and its effect, but understood little of its laws. If primitives worshipped the Sun, so I grudgingly bowed down to the wolves and other adults in my life in order to secure my passage.

None of my heroes were role models per se. They passed by too quickly for that. No single hero emerged, rather there rose up an incessant supply of new heroes. As the waves of a powerful ocean pound the shoreline this way and that, carrying off or depositing the detritus and sculpting the land to bring it to peace with the strength of the sea, so my fictional characters helped mould my value structures.

They demonstrated bravery, determination, strength, romanticism and integrity but sometimes resignation, ruthlessness and weakness.

I picked up on their adulthood and understood that this heroic existence could only await me once I was free. As much as they were heroes past, they were likewise a part of my future. And what a world they offered: galloping across the grey, brown maquis, clambering up jagged rocks and boulders as the sun set over the Sierra Madre, dancing the Tango in Havana, sipping coffee on the Champs Elysees, ambling with a lover over the shadows of oak trees through a bluebell grove, lazing on the sun-drenched white sands beneath the gently wafting palm trees on a paradise beach, crawling over bleak battlefields where the mud stained red and the rattling of machine guns and whistling, passing shells intersperse with the cries of comrades losing limbs, organs or life…

I ached for my heroes' stages but I understood that my only chance of becoming one of the actors was to accept my incarceration and utilise the time for my formal education. My heroes heralded the future and justified my sentence.

Nevertheless, the bright colours of their stage only reinforced the dullness of my existence. Like an inmate in a rural prison who above the walls can see the spring blossom, while he also catches the strains of youthful laughter and lovers' trysts, I was often tempted to break out. For the most part I contained my revolt but only for the most part.

I ached for a release from living on the outside, the penniless summer days, hard, comfortless cold winter nights with my coat draped over my blanket, and the wet windswept days that locked me in my room, forcing me back to my bed and my dreams.

It was a Camus-like introduction to life. It was the freedom I had chosen. No adult had a hold on me. No adult had ever had an emotional grip on me. I carried no scars and bruises from straining the chains of those emotions, no charred skin from scalding words, no severed emotional limbs. Giving up my freedom from adults and going into foster care had been the only means of securing my passage from the outside into the apparent comforts of the wanted world. Now, I was no longer prepared to surrender my freedom, even at the loss of those comforts. I condemned myself to the loneliness of my journey.

I didn't despair. Perhaps I might have done so if I'd sat and pondered on why I had been abandoned by my mother, rejected by the Granvilles, fallen out with Mary Stewart, been branded a troublemaker by Norris, condemned by Makin and thrown out by the Jamesons. But it didn't cross my mind. I was in the right. I was sixteen.

I knew that I had one asset, my ability to perform well at school. I had been put forward by the school to take the Cambridge University entrance examination in Geography and I was determined to work towards it. I started reading CP Snow's novels such as *Strangers and Brothers* and *The Corridors of Power*. That lonely summer I read through all his works that I could get my hands on – *The Affair*, *The Masters*, *The Sleep of Reason*, *The Conscience of The Rich*, *The New Men* and *Last Things*. I read them all and travelled with him and his central character, Lewis Eliot, through the corridors of Cambridge University, Whitehall and Westminster. I was there already. I had hope.

The next day was school and I finished off reading the Antigone. I looked forward to going to school and being with my schoolmates. At school, I was a popular boy with both pupils and staff, and made a Senior Prefect when still 16 and in the Lower Sixth. There I was still different but I was not alone, and consider that I was respected. I participated in everything that interested me, and more. I organised trips for the Rambling Club, including two very welcome jaunts with the girls' high school. The second of these walks took us through three public houses in the rolling hills and shear scarps of the Peak District. On returning to school, I was ordered to the Headmaster's office. Mr Dixon had received a complaint from the high school headmistress, Miss Evans, that the ramble, which was unaccompanied by any of the schools' staff was a "glorified pub crawl." Miss Evans went further, summoning each girl who had attended to her office for a dressing down.

Though Geoffrey Dixon seemed somewhat amused, I was instructed to write a letter of apology to the high school headmistress. I did. It was the letter of a young man of 17, who was beginning to enjoy wielding his pen as sword and shield in his dealings with the adult world. Typically, these early efforts, written from my hovel, were precocious to the point of seeming a little pompous:

"DEAR MISS EVANS
" I AM, AS CHAIRMAN OF KGV RAMBLING CLUB, SORRY TO HAVE CAUSED YOU ANY CONCERN OVER THE TRIP TO GLOSSOP ON WHITSUNDAY. IT IS TO BE HOPED THAT THIS OCCURRENCE WILL NOT IMPAIR ANY SUCH FUTURE EVENTS SINCE IT IS I, THE ORGANISER, WHO MUST BEAR ANY BLAME. IF THERE WERE ANY DECEPTIONS OR MISTAKES, IT IS I WHO COMMITTED THEM... I HAVE HEARD IT WAS DISMISSED AS A 'GLORIFIED PUB CRAWL' BUT THE RAMBLING CLUB OF KGV HAS BEEN THERE MANY A TIME! ...
"MR DIXON WILL TESTIFY THAT MY CHARACTER DEVIATES FROM THE NORM...TO SAY THAT ANY GIRL OR GIRLS AT THE HIGH SCHOOL MUST BEAR THE RESPONSIBILITY WOULD BE AN INJUSTICE, SINCE IT IS I, THE PREFECTS' LUCIFER, WHO HAS LED THEM ASTRAY..."

Phil Frampton, 28th May, 1971

I hitchhiked off on climbing weekends with the climbing club, the Thornleigh Society, and organised the Debating Society – and again joint and very controversial debates with the high school girls.

I was made secretary of my school house. I ended up as captain of the house rugby team and playing in the school's First XV rugby team at full-back. At the end of my last Autumn term in school, my school report read like a list of all the school had to offer:

"SENIOR SCHOOL PREFECT, LIBRARIAN, SENIOR SCHOOL 1ST XV RUGBY TEAM, SCHOOL DEBATING TEAM, HOUSE SECRETARY, DEBATING SOCIETY CHAIRMAN, RAMBLING CLUB CHAIRMAN, THORNLEIGH SOCIETY SECRETARY, ECONOMICS SOCIETY SECRETARY, SENIOR HOUSE RUGBY XV.
"DAYS LATE: 0 DAYS ABSENT: 0
"AN EXCELLENT PREFECT AND AN INFLUENTIAL SENIOR MEMBER OF THE SCHOOL."

Geoffrey Dixon, Headmaster

I had nothing else but my school life that offered me hope and comfort. Makin, the Barnardo's officer, later reported on my school progress:

"PHILLIP IS MAKING EXCELLENT PROGRESS AND THERE ARE NO COMPLAINTS REGARDING HIS GENERAL BEHAVIOUR."
Mr Makin, Child Care Officer, 24th April, 1971

Makin often reported that there were no complaints about my general behaviour at school as if he was surprised.

"I FEEL THAT HE HAS THE CONFIDENCE TO DO WELL IF HE WOULD CHANGE HIS ATTITUDE TOWARDS PEOPLE, ESPECIALLY THOSE WHO TRY TO HELP HIM, BUT THIS WILL TAKE TIME."
Mr Makin, Child Care Officer, 3rd February, 1971

With Makin it would never take place at all. He had only the slightest of ideas of what was going on in this "difficult black lad's" mind.

"PHILIP IS A MOODY ADOLESCENT...A SENSITIVE BOY, FULL OF SELF-ASSURANCE, RESENTFUL OF BEING IN CARE AND HIS SUBSEQUENT DEPENDENCE ON US. HE IS HALF EBO (SIC), AND DESPITE THE ABOVE, HE COPES WITH LIFE. A CLEAN AND TIDY BOY, WHO TAKES A PRIDE IN HIS APPEARANCE...THIS BOY APPEARS TO FUNCTION WELL AND IN ONE POINT OF HIS PERSONALITY (SIC) AND SEEMS DETERMINED TO BECOME INDEPENDENT, PRESUMABLY BECAUSE OF REJECTIONS RIGHT ALONG THE LINE."
Mr Makin, Child Care Officer, 16th December, 1970

"HE HAS NO DESIRE TO KNOW ANYTHING ABOUT ANY FAMILY WHICH HE MAY HAVE, AND WAS VERY STRONG IN HIS REMARKS THAT HE HAS MANAGED QUITE WELL ON HIS OWN."
Mr Makin, Child Care Officer, 3rd February, 1971

In terms of my studying needs, I was a little too active in my school life. I even spent evenings coaching the under 12's rugby team.

At the same time, two girls from the local high school entered my life, one called Christine and the same age as I was, the other called Marolyn and a year younger.

By now I had experienced several teenage crushes on girls or women but each new crush has its own peculiarities. I was 17 and these two almost simultaneous crushes, the one where I was the hunter and the other the hunted, would eventually teach me important lessons.

I first had meaningful contact with Christine when we worked together to organise joint debates between our respective schools. I saw her as a self-assured, relaxed, socially aware, kind-hearted and pretty young woman. Her generous but not thick red lips contrasted with a pallid, white skin, which was sharply bordered by her shoulder-length straight black hair. It was those lips that most beguiled me. When together they cast over her face a look of sadness or, at least, concern. But ripped apart by a smile they revealed all the innocent joy to match the twinkle of her grey green eyes.

This teenage crush on Christine crept up on me, seemingly as randomly as it had in regard to Annabelle, whom you might recall was in the children's home. This new crush proved as maddening, the competition seemed greater, the opportunities for contact and sharing her world more remote. Excuses had to be seized or invented for contact. The more contact was made, the more I cherished her. The more the crush grew, the more I ached to rip it from me and land it on her. Eventually I revealed, but this time not with a clumsy excuse for a kiss, that my crush had landed on her.

At 14 and dealing with my crush, Annabelle had simply seen the option of grasping or totally repelling the hunter. But as I now handled my crush with more caution, so too did Christine handle being my quarry. She let me down with grace, declined my entreaties to let me take her out on all but one occasion, and still allowed me to bask in her company. I snatched at those moments.

I vaguely recall that, at my invitation, she came to a Ralph McTell concert with me. But if I sat there all night radiant at her being by my side, if I ached for a gesture of affection from her during each song, if I slyly leaned over and adored the scent of her hair, it still all ended with a polite, smiling good night and her eyes taking to the pavement then rising to meet mine as she declined to say when she might be able to be in my company again.

Back in my bedsit I envied those school friends who had parents to give them cars to drive and money to impress. I blamed my failure on my poverty. I couldn't pick Christine up in my car and take her on a date. Even if I did I would have to wear my black school blazer or school coat. I could barely buy us both a meal in a restaurant or a ticket for a dance let alone our drinks and a taxi to take her home. So I told myself that I should not have fooled myself and made a fool of myself by supposing that she would be interested in me. I couldn't and shouldn't compete with my peers. This of course was not too charitable on her but it didn't erase my affections. What do we know, at that age, are the keys to unlocking others' love? How we rationalise our failures.

My crush was so great that it would be a long time before the pain and yearning disappeared. Yet, particularly when at her side I relished those sensations nevertheless. Then one day, several years later, I went to meet her in a bar and discovered that the crush, worn out by time and my efforts to cross her border, had slipped away and gone into hiding to recuperate for its next mission. Not only had the passage of time slowly unwrapped my infatuation to reveal more of her true self. I had changed and become a new self with new aspirations. As much as I still cared for her, my new self looked back at his predecessor and patted him affectionately on the head for his naïve folly.

As for Marolyn, I also considered her to be reasonably attractive but where Christine was self-assured and a leader, Marolyn was not. Marolyn went out with some of my school friends. Soon we were studying together in the town library; studies interrupted by whispered conversations across the long wooden tables adorned with reference books and pen cases, or broken off by trips to the local coffee bars to discuss in self-confident ignorance the great issues facing our world.

Then, in one of those late mornings when we would leave our books to slip out and stroll to our favourite coffee bar, Marolyn made me aware that I had become the target of her crush. It was the first time I had known that I was the hunted one. I blushed with discomfort. Her pleas appeared to come out of nowhere, of nothing that I had said or done. But as much as Christine had humbled me by indicating that I was not worthy of her love, so too I felt that Marolyn was not worthy of mine. And how would Christine view me if I was coveted by mere mortals rather than those I had deified? This was a more complex activity, hunting and being hunted at the same time.

But at least I had "experienced" being the hunted one. Often we are totally unaware that we are the target of another's crush. Often the hunter lacks confidence and never picks up Cupid's bow or clumsily misfires so wildly that the arrows fly off to the heavens. Slowly their crush drains away till all that is left is the tidemark of the sensations they once felt for their quarry.

I repelled her crush as well as I could, meeting her pleas with my entreaties. A teardrop appeared as the material reflection of her emotion and her abandonment of the dignity that had restrained her till that morning. I assured her of her value to me as "friend" but in that moment "friend" did not reassure her but hurt her still as it informed her only of the refusal of my love.

In the days that followed I did not run away or avoid her but coped with the irritation of her pleas. Mixed in with the threat to my self-esteem was the flattery to my ego that I had become worthy of another's passion. I did not utilise or even consider this opportunity for sexual gratification. I was too fearful of getting close to her web with its powerful, freedom-draining adhesive of being needed.

Nevertheless I did not flee. We learn that friends are friends because they have a value to us, whether it be for companionship, comradeship or mental or physical stimulation. Ironically, it is because we unconsciously or consciously express to them the value they have for us that we unwittingly, in a look, in a smile, in a word or a gift, set ourselves up as the potential quarry.

As we mature, once aware that the aim of their unwelcome crush has landed upon us, we calculate the value of their friendship and our respect for them against the weight of the crush. If the value of the friendship is the greater, then we reason how to carefully lift that weight, and do all we reasonably can to avoid hurting the hunter.

There are of course times when we can confuse the value of their friendship with the need to satisfy our other desires such as for wealth or status or sex. If then we succumb to the hunter then the relationship can implode, inducing a fireball of hurt, treachery, contempt, mistrust and even revenge.

If the value of their friendship is the lesser then we run a mile, avoid replying to phone calls and letters, and cease to frequent those places where we feel the hunter might discover us.

Even if we have fled, one day, when the crush has abated, we perhaps come across our wearisome hunter and friendship may restart if we still see any value in one another.

Eventually, I managed to successfully lift Marolyn's stifling crush while maintaining her friendship. A new stage in our relationship began of recovered innocence – the love of the childhood sweetheart, platonic, even with desire, but matured and freed by newly discovered borders, yet with tenderness. For she, the hunter had expressed her admiration for me, whilst I had expressed to my hunter, through my caring actions, the value I placed on her friendship.

And so it was also to be with Christine but with I as the hunter accepting my new position as "friend."

In the middle of my new life and loves, you might understand that I left little time for my Cambridge entrance exams and only studied the half of the topics that I thought would come up as questions. I failed to gain entrance to the world of CP Snow and The Masters. None of those topics that I had gambled on coming up appeared on the paper. I was not too concerned. I expected to be able to get into Bristol, which was a university with, I consoled myself, as good a reputation as Cambridge for its geography department.

Besides, despite reading CP Snow and sauntering through the amiable corridors of establishment life, I had, in line with the youth of my era, become quite anti-establishment. Young people were rebelling and joining in protests around the world. The students of the United States, of France, Germany and Britain were storming the campuses and the university senates.

In Brighton, students demonstrated in the nude in front of royalty, in Keele they also took off their clothes. Molotov cocktails seemed to be flying all over the world. The Beatles and Thunderclap Newman were singing about revolution. I read the writings of Che Guevara, Fidel Castro and Jerry Rubin and his Yippies. I looked at the photos of Bobby Seale, Huey Newton and the Black Panthers with their black berets and rifles. They were heroes and I was proud to be black. I wanted to join in the fun and be part of that rebellion against an establishment to which I considered I owed nothing.

But being 17, I was about to come to the end of my time in Barnardo's care. That would mean getting a job while I awaited my expected arrival at university. I would have to pay for my rent and my upkeep. Rather than stay in the town and do so, I applied for and got a job as a live-in porter-cum-waiter in a hotel in Mullion Cove, Cornwall. I sat my A and S level exams and, still 17, I said goodbye to my school chums and went off with my suitcase on a train down to Cornwall.

The day before I took the train south, I lay on my bed when a sudden sobbing burst out from within me. Tears welled up and cascaded down from my eyes, carrying their salts into my mouth and onto my pillow. I was overcome by my perception of the state of my existence. So close to achieving my only real goal of my adolescent years, I finally was able to confront my years of lonely striving and survival. I wept for the loneliness of my journey. But I also now saw that my dream that adulthood would of itself lift this burden of solitude was false. Moving away on my own from the town and my school friends placed on me a new solitude, a new uniqueness. I saw now that my uniqueness would always remain and that my efforts alone would ensure me any happiness. I never wept for me again.

One sunny August day, I sat on the grassy hill overlooking the quay at Mullion Cove and, to the squawks of the soaring seagulls and the crashing of the waves, I opened my letter from the Matriculation Board. I opened it nervously. My eyes first landed on "A, A, A, A." I felt a momentary elation before I realised that those letters only indicated which level of exam I had sat. I actually had achieved two A grades, a B and an E. I was a little disappointed. I wasn't as brilliant as I had hoped. But the results were good enough to get me to Bristol University and my consolation was achieving one S level distinction and one S level merit. Only 30 years later would I learn that my mother had also been on the university's books.

At the end of my time in Cornwall, I hitchhiked to London to see the big city and my godmother, Martha Watson, for the first time. It was an enjoyable first meeting but Martha revealed to me no more about the circumstances of me being placed in Barnardo's than I already knew. I visited the West End where an old man offered me a ticket for a show and invited me to the actors' post-show party. Suspecting his intentions, I declined. After a few days, I hitched up the M1 and M6 back to Southport. The only contact I had with Barnardo's over that summer was to request that a Senior Child Care Officer act as my referee for getting into a hall of residence at Bristol University.

I stayed in the town for a weekend with my former landlady, Mrs Lowe, until I received my full local authority student grant. It was late September 1971 and it was time to go to the Freshers' events at the start of the University term. I left Southport with my suitcase and cardboard box full of books and would not return until a decade later. I was off to a brighter world. Now I had real freedom.

In December 1971, my file was marked closed. I was 18 and had no further contact with Barnardo's. They never did receive my Baptismal Certificate.

"I AM AFRAID WE HAVE NOT HEARD FROM PHILLIP SINCE HE COMMENCED AT BRISTOL UNIVERSITY IN 1971 SO I AM AFRAID THAT I CANNOT HELP WITH YOUR QUERIES."

Mr Woods, Senior Social Worker, Barnardo's,
North West Division, 11th July, 1974

There was to be one further file entry written by an unnamed person. I find it to be strange – like the writer was doodling:

"IS A BOY OF ACTIVE MIND, IN NEED OF A HARD TASK TO TACKLE, AS OBTAINING THE IMPOSSIBLE SEEMS TO GIVE HIM SATISFACTION. ON FIRST MEETING PHILLIP I THOUGHT HE SEEMED AN UNHAPPY BOY, HE WOULD NOT CONVERSE MUCH WITH ANYONE, BUT DURING THE LAST FEW MONTHS, I HAVE SEEN AN IMPROVEMENT IN HIM, HE NOW TALKS MUCH MORE WITH OTHERS, AND HAS QUITE A SENSE OF HUMOUR.

"I HAVE FOUND HIM TO BE AN HONEST BOY, AND PROVIDING PEOPLE ARE FAIR WITH PHILLIP HE IS FAIR WITH THEM. HE IS COLOUR CONSCIOUS, AND I BELIEVE HE IS AFRAID OF BEING HURT, HE SEEMS TO BE WANTED DESPITE HIMSELF. I FEEL HE WILL NEED TO MAKE A SUCCESS OF SOME CAREER BEFORE HE WILL FEEL ACCEPTED BY OTHERS.

"HE HATES TO LOSE IN GAMES, THIS COULD BE HOW HE REACTS TO LIFE IN GENERAL. HE IS INCLINED TO BE PROUD, AND WILL NOT GO BACK ON HIS WORD. ONCE PHILLIP SAYS HE WILL DO A THING HE IS DETERMINED TO CARRY IT OUT. HE DOES OFFER HIS HELP AT TIMES. HIS FAVOURITE GAME IS FOOTBALL, WHICH PROBABLY RELIEVES HIS AGGRESSIVE FEELINGS."

Unattributed, Undated Report

You might ask what the anonymous recorder meant by "obtaining the impossible seems to give him satisfaction." What was impossible? Cambridge? University? A levels? In his mind and many of those in society still, young people in care were and are only fit for fodder for the armed services, the Merchant Navy, the factory floor or domestic service. But some of us emerge strong enough to fight these prejudices that challenge our dreams, and aim for and achieve "the impossible."

Chapter 15

Things We Never Said

Twenty-eight years on, I was travelling on the train to Liverpool. The blue sky was overrun with puffed up columns of anvil-topped white clouds. I was excited and apprehensive, still fearful of going back to the past. On the following day I would return to Southport where the past would rise up higher than those bilious, cotton clouds. But that day was to be a real pleasure, a grand reunion that left me with a huge grin of delight and pride on my face. These were my people.

In 30 years I'd not seen Matron or the other people that I was about to meet. Now I was back to see her and her former charges. I had stepped onto the train with some apprehension. I would have felt awkward in any case. It was 1999. For three decades I had put the home that I'd left, firmly behind me. I feared the smells and sights of hopelessness dragging me back to the yesteryears, pulling me back to that despair of gratuitous poverty, inferiority and yearning. Now I was returning like a prodigal son and feeling some guilt, and feeling some pain.

As to what happened to me after leaving Southport, I could have told them enough tales to fill another two volumes. Suffice to say that when faced with the option of being Dickens's Pip and making my fortune or being Romulus and building Rome, I chose the latter.

The first thing I did in Bristol was to set up Bristol Gypsy Support Group. You might think that strange, as I had never even met a Traveller in my young life. I was actually looking for the excitement of student rebellion that I had heard about, but initially I didn't find the "revolutionaries" impressive. The nearest thing I got to them was a small Young Liberals' student meeting where Peter Hain was spouting revolution through the plum in his mouth. Ruining people's cricket matches didn't impress me either. I needed to do something.

Why Travellers? Perhaps I was still in awe of Hemingway's heroine, Pilar, or expected cosy nights around campfires, surrounded by horse-drawn, gaily painted, wooden wagons. Anyway I needed to feel I could make a difference. So we set about assisting with their children's education and sitting down in the mud in front of the caravans in attempts to prevent the council from towing them away. We lobbied Bristol Council and finally won the Travellers a legal site to stay on in the city.

However, it became apparent to me that the world was on the march. By 1978 I was the national chairperson of the British Labour Party's youth section, sharing platforms at events with the likes of David Owen, then Foreign Secretary in the government, and Tony Benn, Secretary of State for Energy. At the same time, I was a Militant full-time professional organiser. I dedicated 20 years to fighting for a new socialist world for children everywhere.

But Rome was not built in 20 years, let alone one day. The red tide that had engulfed the world in my young days ebbed away. Gone were the days when millions took to the streets demanding social change, when tens of thousands sacrificed their lives in the Third World fighting for socialism. Gone were those times when the people toppled governments across the globe, when Tracey Chapman was, *Talking 'Bout a Revolution.*

In 1993 I left the Militant and started from the bottom in market research. I turned Pip but no Abel Magwitch came along. I wrote the occasional feature article for newspapers and magazines on a variety of issues, making a modest living as a freelance journalist. In time I became a freelance market research consultant and, by chance, a travel writer.

I had little to complain about regarding my personal fortunes. I had done what I had chosen to do. I had had a rich life. I had travelled four continents, met government ministers and murderers, slept in car parks with beggars and in luxury hotels with beauties. I had stared down the barrels of machine guns, hidden from mortal political enemies, fought with and been saluted by police officers, cheated death, had two wonderful daughters, Ellie and Sidonie, got myself a house and enjoyed it all.

During those years, the whys and hows of my childhood gnawed away at me. I wouldn't say that it dominated my thoughts. I was too busy building Rome. But whenever friends asked about my background, I was left to feed them with half a tale and conjecture. I made several attempts to find out exactly who my mother and father were and why I ended up born in care, but succeeded in getting only the faintest of clues. Much of what I was offered was half-truths.

You may recall that when I was 14, I was informed that my mother had died. That was the first thing I had ever known about her. The matron had told me that Martha Watson was my godmother and had informed Barnardo's of my mother's death. The matron could answer none of my questions and advised me to write to my godmother if I wanted to know more.

One year later I received a letter from Martha. With it came another letter, which she explained, would give me more details regarding my mother than she could offer. The letter was from Dollars. At one stroke I had also discovered that I had two godmothers, the latter of which I had never heard of before.

Dollars was anxious to tell me as little as she thought that I could take. She was also adamant that I should not know that I had a half-brother and sister. She was concerned lest I upset their family.

"HE MUST NEVER KNOW THE TRUTH. IT WILL DESTROY ANOTHER FAMILY."

Dollars, 1967

I was to be kept in the dark as much as was possible. She addressed the letter to Martha and sent it first to her to check the storyline. Of my mother and father's relationship all she would write was:

"I BELIEVE THAT SHE WAS VERY MUCH IN LOVE WITH HIM – AM I RIGHT ABOUT THIS? I KNOW THAT SHE WAS VERY UPSET WHEN HE STOPPED WRITING TO HER AND THEN I THINK THAT SHE HEARD OF HIS MARRIAGE."

Dollars, 2nd August, 1968

Dollars added that Mavis was all alone, her mother was dead and was not in contact with her father and therefore had to put me in the home. It wasn't quite true. She went on regarding myself:

"I THINK HE KNOWS THAT SHE FOUND HIM SOME LOVELY HOMES BEFORE HE COULD GO TO BARNARDO'S. SHE SPENT LOTS OF HOLIDAYS AND WEEKENDS WITH HIM, DIDN'T SHE? IT WAS EASIER TRAVELLING AND FINANCIALLY WHEN HE WAS AT SHREWSBURY. SHE COULD MANAGE IT (sic) WHEN HE WAS AT SOUTHPORT FOR THE JOURNEY WAS TOO LONG."

As you will see, the last sentence I have quoted from Dollars was rather a Freudian slip. Besides, it didn't ring true. If my mother could visit me in Devon, Southport being much closer to Birmingham, she could have visited me at least once in those last nine years while she was alive. Neither was it too far to write.

Dollars went on:

"I'M SURE THAT SHE WAS HOPING TO SAVE UP FOR THEIR HOME UNTIL ALL THAT WENT WRONG DIDN'T IT?"

Dollars, 2nd August, 1968

My other godmother alluded in her own letter to the little matter of my christening. She said that Dollars would be sending me my Christening certificate but added:

"I DO NOT KNOW THE NAME OF YOUR GODFATHER. MISS DOLBY AND I WERE BOTH AT YOUR CHRISTENING."

Martha Watson, 19th August, 1968

When my baptismal certificate arrived and said that I was christened in Bristol, I naturally assumed that I must have spent some time there as a child. I hadn't. None of us had been to that christening. I was also puzzled as to why Dollars should have it in her possession.

Of my mother, Martha had concluded:

"I DID NOT SEE YOUR MOTHER MUCH BUT WHEN WE DID MEET SHE ALWAYS SPOKE OF YOU AND I ALWAYS REMEMBER HER SAYING THAT NOT A DAY WENT BY WITHOUT HER THINKING OF YOU."

Martha Watson, 19th August, 1968

Their caution and their little white lies were understandable but they slightly misfired. In truth, Dollars was prepared to sacrifice my comprehension of my past and my self-esteem to protect others. She didn't want me to "destroy another family." It was as if to her I was both the wrecker and the wrecked and, since I had already been damaged, it was preferable to save the ship that was still afloat and leave me adrift.

I was only 16 but to me the pieces didn't quite seem to fit and I wrote Martha back an angry letter. My response also misfired in so much as it made Dollars even more cautious. She wrote an angst-ridden letter to Barnardo's:

"THIS IS ALL A VERY SAD BUSINESS ISN'T IT...I GET THE IMPRESSION THAT HE IS A LITTLE BITTER AT TIMES ABOUT HIS PARENTAGE, AND I DON'T WANT TO ADD TO HIS DIFFICULTIES IF I CAN HELP IT. SOMETIMES I WONDER IF IT WOULD HAVE BEEN WISER NOT TO HAVE WORRIED HIM AT ALL...
"TO MY HORROR I LEARN FROM HIS OTHER GODMOTHER, THAT INADVERTENTLY I MIGHT HAVE DISTURBED HIM CONSIDERABLY IN RELATION TO HIS THOUGHTS ABOUT HIS MOTHER. HE ASKED IF I COULD GIVE HIM HER HUSBAND'S ADDRESS, I SUPPOSE THAT HE WANTED TO KNOW MORE OF HER. UNFORTUNATELY I WAS JUST RECOVERING FROM A VERY BAD ILLNESS AND MY MIND MUST HAVE BEEN FUDDLED WHEN I ANSWERED HIM REPEATING THAT HIS MOTHER WAS NOT MARRIED TO HIS FATHER.
"SHE WAS MARRIED WHILE PHILLIP WAS AT SOUTHPORT OF COURSE BUT I THINK THAT I HAVE GIVEN HIM THE IDEA THAT SHE WAS OF THE PROSTITUTE TYPE WHICH SHE WAS NOT.
"I AM NOT IN CONTACT WITH HER HUSBAND REGULARLY AND QUITE HONESTLY I FEEL HESITANT IN GIVING PHILLIP ANY ADDRESS FOR I AM SO SCARED OF MAKING A HASH OF IT AGAIN."

Dollars, 29th June, 1970

Incidentally, Dollars clearly knew nothing of the reasons for the end of my relationship with the Jamesons. Barnardo's fed her as much as they wished her to hear, just as Dollars tried to do the same to me.

In the same letter, Dollars requested my "birthday particulars" and informed Barnardo's that she had put aside £300 to be given to me when I was eighteen. That, I received very gratefully.

I was grateful too for the moral support and encouragement that both my godmothers gave me in those two years before I went to university. They were my only link with my story. They explained that they had no information about what had happened to my father. I concluded that he had simply been an irresponsible young man and left her in the lurch to return to Nigeria.

Having met Martha Watson in London just before I was due to begin studying at Bristol University. I met my other godmother and her friend, Pixie Johnston, in Birmingham, one or two years later. They were cautious not to shed any more light on what had happened in the past. I kept in touch with them as much as I could whilst I was building Rome. It would be 1980, after Dollars had died, that Martha finally told me that

I did have a half-brother and half-sister. She told me where their father lived and I phoned him up requesting to meet him, not out of anger but out of curiosity.

My first meeting with PK took place in 1981. I have no idea of what he was thinking as he came to our agreed rendezvous at a Chinese restaurant in Bristol. In order that I could meet him I had taken the train from London where I was working for the Militant as a national organiser.

For me, the rendezvous was a success. PK was now a successful architect. My half-brother and sister were at public school and PK filled me in on a few stories about my mother. I requested to meet them but he said he did not wish for me to do so until they were both 21. I thought it a strange request but accepted it and came away with two photographs of my siblings. Later, I discovered that a member of the Labour Party's Young Socialists was rooming opposite my half-sister in a Birmingham college for trainee nurses. Like Balzac's great spy, Vautrin, I made sure that I was kept informed of my sister's movements. I didn't contact her, out of respect for the wishes of her father.

In 1986 and only after my siblings were 21, did Mavis and Dollars's friend, Pixie Johnston, finally put me in touch with them. It turned out that my half-sister was living with her fiancée no more than two miles away from me in the Sale district of Manchester. We met up and I was happy with what I saw. She told me that my half-brother was living in the Forest of Dean where I had spent so much time during my college days in Bristol. I met with him too and was happy. They both attended my wedding in 1986. In turn, I attended my sister's wedding.

An incident occurred at my sister's wedding, which I took to be insulting and racist but do not wish to trouble you with. Sufficient to say that I concluded that I had not found what was left of my family to face racism and ceased contact with them for several years. Blood, it seemed, was not thicker than water.

I restored contact with PK in 1993. The occasion was an announcement in the *Sunday Times* that the Honourable Peter Gilbert Greenall, son and heir of the third Baron of Daresbury and a director of the vast Greenall-Whitley former brewing company, had been declared "Businessman of the Year." The paper also gave his birth date as July 18th 1953. Him, having the same birth date as my own, I had the idea of doing a comparative article on our histories.

However, in researching the article, I also wrote to PK who was helpful and we stayed in touch thereafter. But when I asked PK to tell me more about Mavis's wealthy Uncle Reg, my great-uncle, PK declared that he had not the slightest idea of what I was talking about. You will recall the story earlier in this book of how Uncle Reg, snuck off regularly to make his money on the London Stock Exchange. It was PK who had related it to me. I was certain he had told it to me. There was no one else who could have done so. I thought that maybe it was I who had transferred my imaginings to reality. I let it drop.

Only in 1999 did I contact my half-sister and half-brother again. A snapshot of my story was going to be printed in The Guardian newspaper and I wanted to prepare them.

A few months after the articles appeared, we met up and talked frankly about the past and what had happened to us all. Both my sister and brother were happy to have their older brother around and one who could tell them a little bit more about the mother they had barely known. Both revealed that their childhood without their mother was not so happy. And I can say that I love them both dearly.

One thing that had stuck in my mind was a comment at my sister's wedding from PK. Perhaps he was drunk at the time but at one point in the day he had said to me: "Phillip, I am sorry for all that happened to you and I will make it all up." I was pleased with his noble gesture. But not knowing any of his part in my story, I didn't know what, if anything, he had to make up.

When I received my files and read my mother's words, declaring that she would have to abandon me because PK was "jealous of the child," I was angry. I felt as if his friendship had been a fraud - that I had lived a lie. I wrote to PK declaring that I now realised why he had apologised to me at my sister's wedding and why he had said that he would make it up to me but never did. PK phoned me back equally angry. He denied Mavis's accusation and accused me of being a "gold-digger."

Dollars was obviously right to be anxious about my learning the truth. Since then, I have tried to patch up my relations with him, particularly for the sake of my half-brother and half-sister. Nevertheless, I got round to asking my sister about the story of our great-uncle Reg. The story, which I was sure that I had been given by her father, was she said true. I was relieved to know that my memory had not been playing tricks with me. What she went on to relate also solved a few puzzles as to why PK might have denied knowledge of the Uncle Reg story. I also discovered the tale of Reginald Arthur Cook making a small fortune when I searched on the Internet:

Name *Reginald Arthur COOK*
Birth *8 Sep 1896, Swindon, Wiltshire*
Death *31 May 1972, Swindon, Wiltshire*
Occupation *Clerk, Great Western Railway*
Misc. Notes *Made small fortune on Stock Exchange.*

When he died, our great-uncle had bequeathed a considerable sum of money to Mavis's children. My brother and sister were to receive that when they were 21 years old. True to my sister's nature, later, after her father had informed her of my existence, she declared that I should receive one third of the money. PK said: "No," on the pretext that my being in the Militant would mean that I would have to give all of the money away.

I understood then why PK had not wished me to meet my brother and sister until they had reached 21 and why he had subsequently denied telling me the story of wealthy Uncle Reg.

I wasn't angry this time with PK. I was shocked and saddened. I was also amused. I might have at least been given a chance to get my hands on my Abel Magwitch's money. Perhaps I would have given some of it to the cause I believed in. But a little would have helped when my wife and I were bringing up our own children on a pittance. Instead, I was now not a Pip but a little Oliver Twist, cast into the workhouse and denied his inheritance.

I can honestly say that I did not envy my sister and brother for having that money and am happy that it has contributed to their lives and their children's lives. Instead, I am proud of my sister for thinking of me. I want no more unpleasantness in the lives of the Framptons. Money couldn't buy the richness of my life.

As to finding out about my father and his fate, that has proved much more difficult than finding my mother and her other children. It wasn't till 1978 that I received my first clue. You will know how strange encounters occur in the strangest of places. Well, I was sat in a bar in Montego Bay, Jamaica, when I got talking to a man who declared that he was from Nigeria. In the course of the conversation, I began to relate what I knew of my father's circumstances. I had still not mentioned his name, when the man suddenly slapped the table hard in elation and declared: "It's Isaac Ene! I know Isaac."

The Nigerian businessman went on to relate how my father had a mining transportation business in Enugu and had done very well for himself. The man gave me his own address and before he went suggested that if I had no luck with finding my father, I was to write to him. On my return to England I tried phoning Enugu without success. In those days getting through to a phone in Nigeria seemed almost impossible. I tried to write to Enugu but without success. I wrote to the businessman that I had met but I received no reply. After that flurry of fruitless activity, I let the matter drop.

When the Militant was at its height in the eighties, we had our comrades all over the world. In 1986, I got to know some of our Nigerian comrades when they visited London and they promised to do a little searching around for me. In time, I received a letter from them:

"WE WERE ABLE TO TRACE THE NAME OF 'ISAAC ENEH' TO UDI LOCAL GOVERNMENT AREA (LGA) IN THE NORTHERN PART OF ANAMBRA STATE IN EASTERN NIGERIA...WE ARE SURE THAT THE NAME IS FROM UDI. UDI LGA IS FAMOUS FOR COAL MINING AND WE THINK IT IS NOT AN ACCIDENT THAT THE 'NAME' HOLDS A MINING TRANSPORTATION FIRM. MOREOVER UDI LGA IS IN THE SUBURBS OF ENUGU, THE ANAMBRA STATE CAPITAL..."

Comrade Iyo, 1987

Once again however, my attempts to contact the Isaac Ene concerned were thwarted. I let the matter drop until I heard that I could access my Barnardo files and felt that they would give me a better clue. When I received my files, I contacted the Nigerian Embassy and International Services. No joy. I also wrote to all the Ene names that I could find who were reported in the Nigerian telephone book as resident in Lagos or Enugu but at the time of meeting my former childhood friends from Barnardo's in 1999, I was none the wiser.

As to the Granvilles, the couple that had fostered me at four and put me back into the home when I was four, I kept in touch with them. I met up with them occasionally until one day in 1996, when I received a phone call from their son, Paul, to inform me that they were both very ill and in different hospitals. Apart from the serious illnesses of my younger daughter, Sidonie, I had not experienced much personal angst in my life. I was little prepared for what was to come.

George Granville had retired from his job as a minister of religion. He had already suffered for a long time with leukaemia but was still active for the church and assisting in raising funds for a local hospice when first his wife Florence was taken ill and had to spend most of her time in hospital. While George was on his own in their house and suffering from a virus, he slipped and fell. He lay unconscious for some time and the virus developed into a very serious pneumonia.

Let me take you with me, in confidence, into his hospital room for one of the salutary experiences of my life.

My first reaction as I stood by "Uncle" George's hospital bed was a stunning guilt. This pristine room with its two hopeful bursting flower vases and comforting chair would become the Guilt Room. He would lie almost motionless driving on my guilt with that supreme questioning silence that the dying command. I, in turn, would wriggle and twist with my answers until I threw my guilt back at him with a cruel: "Why?"

Guilt had lurked all the way down the A56 as the Manchester to Chester road glistened in the heavy rain thrown down by a dark grey heaven. Should I have seen the ageing minister and his wife more often? Should I have shown them more gratitude for their affections? Should I have got down to see them at a sprint when I had learned that they were both seriously ill and being cared for in two separate hospitals? Was I uncaring? Unloving?

Isn't it so when we are about to confront the dying voices, hands and faces of those we have held, at least for a while, in our affections?

As I donned a mask and white coat to protect the retired, fragile Reverend from infection, the thought passed through my mind that it was my unholiness, my sinfulness, which was being kept at bay. Opening the door I for a moment felt that Guilt was at bay until my eyes met the shrunken, emaciated frame lying between its white sheets.

In those seconds I did not recognise him. Before me was not the bold, upright giant of a worldly-wise man that my images commanded. Here were a face and hands shrunken and shrivelled, a bald head with wisps of grey hair and a mouth so contorted that I had a split second of doubt as to whether I was before my "Uncle" at all. Guilt. How little could I have known him in recent years that I couldn't recognise him? Little wonder he didn't greet me. Only the realisation that his mouth was devoid of the dentures he had worn for years offered me an excuse for my shocking failure to identify him.

I tried to throw out words to him, swearing my love and my hopeless hope for his recovery. I stammered my apologies for not seeing him more often. Not a word changed the grimace on his face. Why was he not welcoming me? Why did he not respond to my words? Was he condemned to silence or I condemned for sinfulness? The uncertainties sent Guilt searching for answers but none would come. Was he aware of my presence? No answer. Was he unhappy at my presence? No answer. Silence. A numbing breathtaking omniscient condemning silence.

As the void threw questions at me so I began to search through the past.

"Yes, I did care for you. Yes, I didn't always show it. Did I love you? I don't know. Did you love me? I don't know. I never knew.

"Why did you do that?

"Why? If you loved me, why did you take me in then throw me out? How was I supposed to feel at four years old, thrown back to being alone with nothing? With Nobody. Yes, I know that you and 'Aunt' Florence still had me during the school holidays for a few days and always sent me presents for my birthday and Christmas and I was happy that you did. Don't think that I'm not grateful.

"But why should I come to a conclusion that you loved me when you were in your house and I was in the institution where nobody had mums and dads, just 'aunts' and 'uncles' who took you for holidays and sent you presents and 'aunts' who ran the home and washed your clothes and told you what to do and when to do it and punished you when you had been naughty and when you had not?

"This horrible silence, a grave silence, the silence that beckons the grave. Accusatory. Just whose judgement day is it?

"Maybe you don't want me here because I have sinned so badly. You such a saint. Always even-tempered, always thoughtful, always kind. So kind. So what did I do wrong that you let that car come and take me away? Here you greet me like the arrival of the devil's priest come to say the last rites. In your eyes I have sinned so badly but I still want you to know I care for you.

"Yes I stole, picked pockets, shoplifted, lied, uttered profanities (unwittingly) at your table, embraced atheism, fought for the champions of Godlessness, had a child born out of wedlock, broke nine of the Ten Commandments and abandoned my marriage. And yes, I joked with my children that God was only Dog spelt backwards.

"I suppose you're right to not to want to see me. We're a million deeds apart. I always respected you. I respected your attempt to help others. I couldn't respect the creed you fought for. I hope you respected my attempt to help others if not the ideas I fought for.

"Well, OK I did a lot of bad things but did you really expect me to end up a saint when you threw me amongst the unwanted? What a world you must have dreamed in? A few years ago someone told me that my mother had hoped that I would go to university. Did she know how many kids went from orphanages to university? Did she really think that I would, untutored and unaided, surrounded by petty crime and hopelessness, lovelessness and indifference join the then cream of society's youth? We were the scum, the rotting detritus of societal inadequacy that collected in the silent waters where human indifference met society's net protecting itself with Wel-fare. We were neither meant nor expected to Fare Well.

"Did she know how many children came out of orphanages in a living hell, buggered to bits by Father This and Uncle That? Did society care? In Rio, They shoot their street children. In Britain, They housed them for paedophiles to sodomise. Too late the investigations in the children's homes of North Wales, South Wales, Manchester, Merseyside, London, West Midlands. All is revealed now. Who cared then?

"You hooked me in then cast me back, like a legless doll left to cry beneath the wheel-less trains, toeless socks and spine-crushed books. But all those years I cared for you."

"We cared for you!" he hissed through my thoughts.

"I didn't mean to hurt. I want you to recover. What will Florence do without you? What will your children, Paul and Chris do? I care for them too. I'm sorry. It's not the time to argue. It's just the Guilt and Things We Never Said. Things we'll never know."

It was the first and last argument that we ever had. It was all in my head, with not a word spoken. We never had another conversation.

The fury of my feelings shocked me. Where had they come from? Had I unknowingly held them through three decades and suppressed them? No. I had suppressed the questions. The magnificence of my unconscious strategy filled me with awe. I had brushed my queries aside in order to strengthen my chances of survival.

I understood then how I had forced myself, like a trapped animal, to accept each situation and change of fortune that befell me as a child. As far as possible I had thus been able to avoid rage and risk, my subconscious constantly repeating that the balance of forces was not in my favour.

Just as I had retreated from explosive questioning, so I retreated from all but the pettiest crimes, retreated from abusive situations, retreated from ever returning to the home and retreated from adults into my lonely bedsitting room in Southport. I had accepted hurt and accepted rejection then picked myself up like a young cub expelled by the pack to wander in the wilderness and survive with whatever herd I might come across.

George and Florence died within six months of each other. Only when I read my files did I really understand them. Each year I take my daughters up to see their son, Paul, and his wife in the Lake District and am also in touch with the Granville's daughter.

To complete my story, let me tell you that in the course of my efforts to secure my Barnardo file, Barnardo's sent me their magazine, the *Guild Messenger*. It was part of their defence of the fact that I couldn't have my file for another two years.

I didn't even glance at the magazine for several months. I did eventually because I was due to tell the story of accessing Barnardo's files on my childhood to the press. Maybe it was subliminal; but I had always been unclear as to how to spell Barnardo's. I say, Barnardo's, you say Barnardoes. Thesaurus gave me no help. I pulled out the Barnardo's magazine and peered inside.

I glanced at the obituary column. In it the death and funeral of Michael Ingham in Southport was reported. I recalled that he had been a childhood friend; probably the best friend I'd ever had in the home. At the funeral was another woman, Emily Brotherton, who the magazine reported had been in the home with Michael. I knew then that I must have known Emily as well. I wanted to make contact and see how she was and if she knew what had happened to everybody. I wrote to Emily, courtesy of Barnardo's and she replied. After 30 years we would meet up again.

Accessing my files had taken me on a trip into my past. I never thought that it would take me back to Southport, let alone to the little family I would find sat around Matron. Emily set it all up with her friend Barbara who had also been in the home. I went to meet Emily in Birkenhead and we spent a whole night in reminiscence before travelling to the reunion next day.

Barbara was off getting in the shopping for our gathering. I was sat out on her patio looking at Matron. She was buried in blankets protecting her from the "cold" in the blazing sun. Her 96 years were clearly playing on her as she struggled for words and memories. I struggled for memories too as I tried to draw a response from her that was more than an empty smile.

I'd not seen Matron in 30 years or Barbara or the other people that I was about to meet. Our common bond was that we had all spent our formative childhood years in Matron's care in a Doctor Barnardo's Home. Matron had been the superintendent of the two homes which most of us had passed through in Southport. Now I was back to see her and her former charges.

"I'm cold. Fetch me a hot water bottle!" cried Matron clutching her blankets.

"You can't have any more heat," replied Barbara, "It's hot out here and you'll kill yourself."

"Let me then," retorted Matron. After such an active life, looking after others, she now had to suffer being "in care" herself.

There was Matron reminding me again of those deaths where Things Never Said torture one's mind, where the dying are, though breathing, lost to the world. Things Never Said, a collection of whys, hows, hopes, loves, fears that can entangle the living with remorse. Her sporadic and brief moments of lucidity teased. Was she playing hide and seek, peek-a-boo, with our feelings or was she snatching at those fast disappearing windows of clarity? I asked myself whether she could remember me, whether she could hear me, whether her four-word responses were because of her annoyance with me, her disapproval or the hurt I might have caused her? I watched her shrinking eyes. They betrayed her smile with a dim sparkle like that of a sickly child brought sweets.

We would never again approach Things Never Said. They would be left to hover in the air forever. Otherwise she might have asked why I was so ungrateful, why I spurned her, never returned to see her after she had retired? Even the "naughty" ones, like Mark Lancaster whom she sent to a remand home, had been to see Matron.

But at the home I'd been pleased to see her leave. By then I'd become an angry young man and, if she still loved me now, she couldn't show it and I wouldn't reciprocate. If I had felt that she could understand my words I would have been impelled to say sorry. But if she could hear sorry then she could say sorry, for I had discovered that she had played a much more decisive role in my life than she had ever admitted.

You might conclude that what Matron had done was, part of the cruelty common to the middle class matriarchs and patriarchs of her age - Victorian. On the other hand, you might have concluded that her actions were dictated by love, misguided or otherwise. Seated next to her, I wanted to ask why. Was her silence a fear of having to answer? Was that vacuity hiding embarrassing truths, words that once uttered might crack her frail body? I let the matter rest.

Besides, she was just another player in the drama that had shaped our childhood. What Matron had done had not ruined my life and I was thankful for that. In vain, I ached to clarify then penetrate those motives that had dictated her actions. Nothing could be said. Nothing was said. Things Never Said would have to hang around forever.

Barbara returned with her shopping and set about preparing food for her guests. She had spent many years caring for Matron. In the past seven years she had taken over fully by inviting Nana, as Barbara called her, to live in her house in a tranquil working class district of Southport. Barbara had long been the point of contact for many of the "kids" who had left the Barnardo's home in Beach Road and, Matron being there, Barbara's house was the focus of many gatherings of the Beach Road clan.

Today the gathering was to meet Phillip; the bright, coloured boy who wore tortoiseshell, wire-rimmed, National Health specs and disappeared from everybody's sight back in 1968. 1968, when Paris and Prague were consumed in revolution, when Johnson was bombing Vietnam and the Black Panthers were on the march and hippies swarmed the parks. Phillip had returned six US Presidents, six British Prime Ministers and many revolutions later. The shilling had fallen to the five pence, the gallon to the litre, plimsolls to trainers, beer to wine, fish and chips to Balti chicken and the royal family to disrespect.

What had become of us all? In ones and twos, some with partners or children, some without, the "kids" took their seats around the table on the sun-drenched patio. David Jones, a lithe and cheerful fifty-year-old gas fitter, his brother Jimmy, Shania with her sons, Sheryll, Susan, Joe with his daughter, Emily Brotherton with her husband and one of her sons, Martin Williams and Dick Ingham straight from work. Black, White, Asian, we had been golliwogs all.

The beer and wine flowed and we talked, and talked and talked. Matron sat amongst us holding up her vacant smile. There she was, the background to all our childhoods, occasionally responding to an approach with a syllable or two.

We talked of those not present: David Bryant who'd gone to sea then settled in New Zealand before returning to Manchester and Pat Bryant living in the States and still married to Peter Donaldson who'd taken her out when she lived in Beach Road. Mark Lancaster, last heard of in the States. Mary Ingham who'd married and gone off to live in Canada and was now in New Zealand and Carmen Smith, last heard of in Rampton prison. Emily Brotherton's siblings Don, John, Jimmy, Donna and Pamela all living somewhere in or around Yorkshire.

Then there was the list of missing "kids" of whom not a word had been heard. Until this moment this is where I would have featured in these gatherings with: Mickey and Jenny Thompson, Kenny Hutchings, Colin Smith.

And finally there were those for whom only hushed words and lowered eyes in remembrance would suffice. Brian Reynolds, Michael Ingham and Tom Chorley who all died before their 50s.

I respect them all; the unwanted and unsung heroes and heroines of British society, who suffered at the hands of "care" and "don't care" with thousands of other "unwanted" children. That these children grew up to make something of their lives from the chronic neglect that was the "care" system is a tribute to their own courage and fortitude. We were not children who'd spent a few years in the homes. We had spent almost all our childhood there. We were what we call "Lifers." Yet from our ranks came skilled workers, office workers, businessmen, policewomen, writers, mothers and fathers.

Spare me a moment to ask you to reflect on whether it is not time that society stopped looking on children in care and care leavers as damaged goods? Time to marvel at how, out of so little, so many children rejected and incarcerated by society were able to shape reasonable lives as adults within society? Time to say sorry and pay tribute?

And I thought back to the street kids I'd met in India and the six-year-old rag pickers in Bangalore. They'd slept in the streets and rose at five in the darkness of morning to pick up garbage from the roads and sell it on. They saved up some of their earnings and each week tripped off to the cinema with a packet of bidis to smoke. A hard life but they lived and would become adults. If they became thieves then it would be because there was no other way to survive. If we were kept in homes was it because this society didn't want more thieves or was it out of altruism?

There were undoubtedly kind-hearted individuals who gave so much in the belief that they were improving the lot of unfortunate children. Today, if society can give so much as a thought to those "unwanted" children becoming adults then it will provide bountiful resources and a truly caring upbringing in "care." With all the wealth and knowledge in our society, such children should be looked on as an opportunity to develop fine adults fully contributing to this world rather than future prison fodder.

Society pays for its neglect.

Children become Adults.

I looked on with pride at the "kids" I had been separated from for years. We talked like long-lost cousins – or maybe inmates at a Dartmoor reunion. Of course there were many scars, scars of physical abuse, sexual abuse, psychological abuse, rejection, nervous breakdowns and death. But these were largely hidden today. This was a happy day when we laughed at our fortunes and even some of our misfortunes.

"I still remember when I was three crying out for my mother in the home," said Dick Ingham, "A nurse came and shouted at me: 'Shut up! You haven't got a mother.'"

The scars were there just beneath the surface and ready to rise once alcohol and recollections loosened the mind. Other tensions also lay hidden but these were the tensions of a family nature, of personal hurts and misgivings held by some of others sat around the table. For this was truly a family miraculously kept together around the figure of Matron, the ghost of Captain Hook, shared childhoods and the efforts of Barbara who had placed herself at the centre of the Lost children of Neverneverland. I left that gathering with tears of joy in my eyes.

Chapter 16

Prince 2Ls

One month after the gathering in Southport, I at last received a call from Nigeria. It seemed that my enquiries regarding my father were about to bear fruit. The caller telephoned during the middle of the night and left me a message requesting for me to phone him back. I did so with excitement the following day. The caller said that he knew my father but the news was not good. Apparently my father was ageing, very unwell and living in a tiny village in the wilds of Cross River State.

"Could I write to him?" I asked.

"There is no point," the man's voice said, "He has severe diabetes and his eyesight is very, very bad."

"Could I write to his children?"

"He is living with his grandchildren and they cannot read."

"Could I have his phone number?"

"He is not on the telephone."

So the conversation went on regarding my father. Finally the man said: "However, there is one way in which you can help us and help yourself. We are five government accountants working for the Central Bank of Nigeria. There has been a Japanese company's overspend on a government contract and we have $35 million that we wish to get out of the country fast. If you can help us, we will give you 20 per cent of the money. All we need is an offshore account. You can send us your details and we will put the money into your account."

I knew then that the information about my father was bogus. Behind the voice was a simple fraud waiting to empty my bank account – not that they knew my account was empty. They were trying a 419, as the Nigerians call it – a con trick, not on the government but me. I faxed a message back later saying that I would have to set up an account in Jersey but I was a poor student and would need them to send me £1,000 before I could do what they wished. My fax was never replied to.

A week later I received another midnight call. This time it was a faxed message but my fax was off and the sender spent the night waking me up in an attempt to get the fax through. I fixed my fax in the morning and it finally came through. I still have it. It came from a purported Professor Uba Ahmed who claimed to work as the computer scientist for the Foreign Transfer & Telex department of the Nigerian Central Bank.

The professor assured me that I had a large amount of funds waiting for me in the bank and he was defending it for me by keeping away all manner of hawks. He could get it to me but I had to act quickly because the government was due to confiscate all unclaimed debts very soon. The condition was that I should maintain complete silence of his plan. In return all he said he required was:

"1. YOU WILL GUARANTEE TO GIVE ME 10% OF YOUR MONEY PAYABLE IMMEDIATELY THE MONEY IS CREDITED TO YOUR ACCOUNT.
2. YOU MUST PROMISE TO RE-TRANSFER THE FUND INTO ANOTHER ACCOUNT WITHIN FIVE WORKING DAYS...THIS IS A SECURITY MEASURE.
3. YOU WILL PAY FOR MY WIFE AND SON AIR TICKET OUT OF NIGERIA TO YOUR COUNTRY, RECEIVE AND ENSURE THEY ARE COMFORTABLY SETTLED TO SECURE MY OWN PERCENTAGE BEFORE I START..."

Prof. Uba Ahmed, Director Foreign Transfer Dept., 24th August, 1999

Having been almost bitten once, I let my supposed chance of wealth go. I suffered another attempt to 419 me before a Chief Enemour contacted me from Enugu. I had met him briefly in London a few years ago and had written to him. He faxed back promising to assist me by putting his niece, a Victoria Adiobi, onto tracking down my father.

Within a short while Victoria felt able to inform me that my father had died two years previously. He had become a "big man," a chieftain. He had died leaving many sons and daughters but the family would welcome me, as it was a great pride to have even his illegitimate child as first son. So I was indeed a prince all along.

I was Prince Phillip, the one with two L's. I was the Prince formerly known as comrade. Whether I can confirm Victoria's story and claim or disclaim my crown, time alone will tell. I am apprehensive of delving my hands into the murky waters in my father's country where twelve letters appealing for assistance in finding my father only released a swarm of crocodiles. But Victoria's story did cheer me up. I had no wish or reason to disbelieve her. For some unknown reason, my contact with Chief Enemour came to an end and he ceased to reply to my calls or faxes.

Later, I found the following on the Internet. It seems that at the very time that I had become the Chair of Labour's Young Socialists in the UK, my father, then Prince Isaac Ene, was among other things lording it as Deputy Master of a Masonic Lodge.

"DIARY OF GRAND MASTER MASON'S TOUR OF NIGERIA, GHANA, TOGO, SIERRA LEONE AND THE GAMBIA
18th May to 4th June, 1978

by BROTHER CAPTAIN ROBERT WOLRIGE GORDON OF ESSLEMONT,
Grand Master Mason

"22nd May. We took off for Enugu to visit the Lodges in the three Masonic areas in Eastern Nigeria. On our arrival we were met by Brother Chief Etim Ekpenyong, Brother Prince Isaac Ene, Brother Chief W. Pepple, Brother S.O.Williams, and a considerable number of other Brethren. After lunch and a rest we went to the grounds of the Enugu Masonic Temple where we were treated to a very fine display of African dancing. ... The Brethren assembled in the Lodge Room, with Brother Ekpenyong acting as Master, Brother Ene as Depute Master and Brother Williams as Substitute Master. 23rd May I rose early and was ready to leave at 8 a.m., but we did not get away until after 10. Out first stop was at the home of Brother Prince Ene where we were entertained to refreshments..."

Another surprise came when I contacted the Archive Department of the Royal Academy of Music in London to seek confirmation of my mother's LRAM qualification in the early fifties. They kindly agreed to conduct a search of their files for Mavis's qualification. So you can imagine my surprise when I received a letter from the Academy:

"THIS IS TO CERTIFY THAT MURIEL FRAMPTON GAINED THE LRAM TEACHING DIPLOMA ON PIANOFORTE IN JANUARY 1955...HER MARKS FOR EACH EXAM WERE AS FOLLOWS: PRACTICAL 75, AURAL 82 AND RUDIMENTS, HARMONY, MUSICAL FORM & ANALYSIS, 86"
Assistant Registrar, Royal Academy of Music, 24th May, 2000

I wondered whether it was they or I who had made a mistake with regard to her name. I called them back and explained that there had been a mistake. The young woman at the end of the line informed me to the contrary: "That is the only M Frampton who we have a record of gaining an LRAM between 1929 and 1960."

I was left to consider whether, Mavis had used an assumed name, but there was no sense in that because what was the point of showing people a certificate with the incorrect name. Perhaps the Academy had got her name wrong but surely then it would have been in Mavis's interest to correct it. The only options that I had left were, that either the Academy had lost her file or that my mother had not secured an LRAM after all and that her claim was a fabrication.

I hated to think that she had lied to even her friends but it made me wonder whether I would ever truly know my mother at all. Eventually, this riddle, at least, was partially solved. My half-sister sent me a copy of Mavis's Royal College of Music certificate. It declares that in April 1952, Mavis:

"SATISFIED THE EXAMINERS IN PIANOFORTE (TEACHING) AND IS HEREBY DECLARED TO BE AN ASSOCIATE OF THE ROYAL COLLEGE OF MUSIC."

At the same time, Mavis was also declared a Licentiate of Trinity College of Music in London. So perhaps the muddle was in Barnardo's heads.

I went over my files again. Then I saw the reports that my godmother, Martha, had kept sending me "Dear Pip" gifts all the way through my childhood even though my other godmother had reported that their lack of contact with me was at the matron's insistence. Yet Martha remained in contact. Was it Mary Stewart who had stopped my mother from contacting me after Mavis had said she would rather forget about me or was it Mavis who fed Dollars with those words?

Perhaps the scars of abuse and her torrid childhood had brought Mavis so low in her self-esteem that she had come to believe that no one took her words seriously; that, forced into a corner, she would say whatever was required to get out of it; that she faced this way and that, fearing society's scorn. Indeed, in my search for my heritage, I at last came across Donald Frampton CBE who was now running Donaldson's Nurseries in Worthing. All of 81 years of age, he had spent years visiting registry offices, churches, cemeteries and the like to compile his Frampton family tree. You may recall that my grandfather, Clyde Frampton, had been a cousin and acquaintance of Donald. Donald sent me a copy of the tree. There on the Frampton branches were Clyde and Winifred, Mavis and Arne and the latter couple's two children. There was no Phillip. Phillip was a Mavis secret, a deception, which was to die with those who owned it.

It may be true that the lies people tell live after them but the truth is oft interred with their bones. Yes, I believe that I will never really know who my mother and father were. But there again, I might have more surprises to come. For whilst we have a precarious existence as "thought" well before we emerge from the womb, so too do we continue, as "thought," on our uncertain road, long after our heart ceases to beat.

Meanwhile, there remain those stark words spoken by Mavis: "I'd rather forget about him altogether" – thin traces of black ink that I cannot forget. How often I return in my thoughts to those words and the moment that I came across them. At that moment my mother was suddenly no longer a fallen gracious princess but a cold, callous woman deserving of every punishment. At that moment she was hurtling me, her own child, over a cliff into a deathly chasm empty of past and present. I was to disappear at her pleasure. She was to survive on my misfortune.

We hurtled, mother and child, over the cliff's edge. The image of my princess lay broken below with myself beside. But I was young and my bones supple. I survived. I clambered back out of the chasm.

I tried to forgive. I found myself summoning all I could of my compassion and understanding of her circumstance. I needed to rescue her from my condemnation. I tied a rope to us both and climbed back up the cliff face. I dragged her up in my esteem. How hard I struggled.

I must confess to you that we have not yet reached the cliff top. There are days when storms rage. On those days, I weaken. I recall that she never reached out a hand to me. We slip back down the face. On other days I rest until the sun shines and gives me the strength to pull her back up. I warm to my task, have pity for her weakness and am grateful for my strength.

Perhaps I will never get her back to the top.

Finally, what of my former childhood sweetheart, Mary Ingham? Well, she got to hear of my articles in The Guardian and very soon I had a call from The Guardian informing me that Mary had e-mailed the newspaper asking them to pass on a request for me to get in touch. I was overjoyed. I hadn't expected to ever see her again. I phoned her and then e-mailed her eagerly. She informed me that she would return to England for a short while in the month of October and that hopefully we could meet up.

We did so. I wasn't sure that we would get on but from our correspondence I felt that we still had a great affinity. I met Mary and her daughter on a sunny but cold, autumn day at Southport's Chapel Street Station. Mary was wearing a denim suit and now a Canadian accent full of "Gees" and "My, oh Mys." We had both clearly aged. I had lost a lot of hair and Mary had a few grey streaks but remained as pretty and as slim as I had once known her.

We all three linked arms and strolled around the town with smiles and confidence. "It's our town now," I declared. It was a far cry from the days when we lurked round as seemingly illegal outcasts, the kids from "that place." The seagulls hovered overhead. They could see that we weren't ugly ducklings anymore. "Very fine swans indeed!" they squawked, as they followed us down Lord Street.

We had both, by and large, been lucky. We had jumped the hoops and missed the ditches. Pip had met his Estella and we talked and talked of our pasts, both shared and otherwise. We decided to return to our house of Miss Havisham, Tudor Bank, and see the old place once more. Off we went into Birkdale, down Westcliffe Road, past the dentists where the girls were sexually abused and the road where my life almost came to an end as a young boy.

When we turned into Beach Road, the leaves were scattered across the pavement in reds and browns, in golds and yellows as they had always been at that time of the year. We passed through the main gate of Tudor Bank and there we were back in our childhood. Unlike Dickens's house of Miss Havisham, the home was not a ruin. But Mac's Garden – our forbidden garden, had been built upon. So too had the Sandpit where we made sandcastles and much of the Pitch where we played Dare, Force, Truth and Promise. Only the old house was still standing. It was now an old people's home. I wondered if they ever heard the floorboards creaking.

With our child eye we could each still see little Shania and Carmen playing in the Sandpit, their hand-me-down purple dresses dirtied by mud, their yellow ribbons hanging loose in their hair. I could still see Dick Ingham in his hand-me-down short, grey pants jumping off the top of the slide and Mickey running at me making a fearsome noise and holding a stick as if it was a rifle. There was Michael sitting on the ground with flowers in his long black hair and making a daisy chain for his neck. Emily ran out of the garage door, chasing her sister and Brian Reynolds was bowling a tennis ball at Tom on the Pitch. Matron was stood at the window in her yellow bonnet, calling us in to get ready for church.

Then I heard a voice interrupting my dreams. It was that of the proprietor's son, asking us very politely what we were doing standing and gazing around.

"We used to live here," I said smiling at the man who was in his thirties, "This was ours once."

We didn't stay much longer as wizened, wrinkled faces appeared at the windows of what had been the downstairs playroom. Instead, we went off for a walk down Rotten Row and peered up at the fence to the home from which we once peered down. On that day and in the days to come, it dawned on me just how much we had shared between the two of us. Not only was there a return to the tenderness of childhood but also that comfort and ease in each other's presence. They were feelings that I had never experienced with another woman before because there was no mystery in our backgrounds, no black hole of comprehension.

I could not say that I had thought of her a great deal over the intervening 30 years. I could not say whether those feelings of tenderness had disappeared or remained in the turmoil of my life. But now it seemed that they had risen from a hidden storage depot in my consciousness, sensations once hidden away for my own protection but now flooding each nerve in my body, sensations, which I fear will be unique to my thoughts of Mary forever. And so too, I accepted that the sensations of childhood would be with me till I have lost the capacity to draw on my senses.

Eventually, Mary and I were ready to say farewell. I'd like for the sake of our story, to be able, as did Dickens's Pip, to end by saying: "I saw no shadow of a future parting." Instead, Mary, with her daughter, boarded the plane that would take her back over two continents and oceans to return to her husband and home. In her suitcase were her brother, Michael's, ashes.

As for myself, I took the opportunity to return to that lonely beach and its empty sands. I put my face into the sea breeze and strolled towards the lapping waves. Up above the seagulls soared. The rushing wind prevented me from hearing all their boisterous chatter. I left them to it. I thought of my search through my records and others' stories for my identity, and the more that I have delved and deduced, the more I understood where my identity lay. My real identity lay not in their stories and the circumstances that they imposed on me but in how I reacted to those circumstances. Most importantly, my essence was moulded by the results of those reactions. My search led me to consider "how and why?" I had reacted to each situation. I concluded that whatever else I might discover of each individual in this story and their actions, I foremost remained what I had created out of circumstance and not what circumstance had created out of me.

I thought of that part of my search that had taken me through fallen angels, irresponsible young men, scheming spinsters and well-meaning ministers - people crushed by the social prejudices of their time. Behind me was the weakness of the human condition. It was not all one way. Love, courage and fortitude had battled with prejudice, rejection, deception and cruelty.

In all this, my heroes were we, the urchins, hidden in Britain's underbelly. We were the characters required to show fortitude in the midst of rejection and cruelty. You might ask yourself why so many authors contrived with the establishment to paint a picture of the rescued unwanted given a life of bliss by a caring society. The establishment perpetuated a myth. They drew a veil across the suffering of the unwanted in their care.

I understand my personal fortune. I never had any adult there to love me but equally, I had no one pecking at my head, threatening to take that love away. Most children are taught to see the world partly through the eye of their parents. Ungifted with this parent eye, I was left with only my child eye, and just as deprived of one sense our other senses grow stronger, so too my child eye developed and learned to see the world through its own dimensions. Hard as it was, I had to learn to love myself and nobody took that love away.

Besides, though the characters in my story were masters of my childhood, I have since had 30 years of being in control of my own fate. I was one of the lucky ones. If I had been five years younger, I could have ended up in Rampton, like Carmen. I do not complain for myself. Forgive me for concluding that many children's lives could have been very different had a few honest words been spoken, had some ears cared to listen.

I catch your thoughts that many of you who were wanted didn't have an easy time as children either. True. But ask yourself another question. Why is it that when a wanted child disappears, a whole nation stirs but missing children "in care" are more often than not simply a note on a police file? For the sake of children today, do not underestimate what it means to be a teenager, walking those streets alone – with nobody, with no one.

The End

Postscript

“The origins of this inspiring book stem from two powerful long articles Phil Frampton wrote for The Guardian in 1999 - on his campaign as an adult for access to his file that Barnardo’s had kept on him while he was a boy in care and the effects that reading it had on him. It led to important changes to Barnardo’s after care policy.

“This is an important and moving book not just about child care policy, but the uplifting story of a man with an indomitable spirit. He went on to serve as national chair of the Care Leavers Association for three years, 2000-03.”

Malcolm Dean, Assistant Editor and Social Affairs Leaderwriter of The Guardian

In 2002, Phil Frampton appeared as a witness before the House of Commons Home Affairs Select Committee regarding Police investigations into abuse in care.

If you wish to discuss any of the care issues raised in this book or to assist or make a contribution to care leavers and young people in care, please contact:

Care Leavers Association (CLA)

Run by and for care leavers of all ages from 18 upwards, CLA promotes and campaigns for positive change for all care leavers in the UK.

CLA, PO Box 179, Shipley, BD18 3WX   www.careleavers.com

A National Voice for Young People in Care and Leaving Care

A young person-led organisation run by and for young people from care. ANV creates campaigns, puts on events and lobbies government to make positive changes for the 60,000 children and young people currently Looked After in England.

A National Voice, National Co-ordinator, Central Hall,
Oldham St, Manchester M1 1JQ   Tel 0161 237 5577
www.anationalvoice.org